DATABASE

DATABASE

Step-by-Step

Mark L. Gillenson
IBM Systems Research Institute

A Wiley-Interscience Publication
John Wiley & Sons
New York / Chichester / Brisbane / Toronto / Singapore

Library of Congress Cataloging in Publication Data:

Gillenson, Mark L.
  DATABASE: step-by-step.

  "A Wiley-Interscience publication."
  Includes bibliographies and index.
  1. Data base management.   I. Title.
QA76.9.D3G523 1985   001.64'4   85-6525
ISBN 0-471-80702-8

Printed in the United States of America

10 9 8 7 6 5 4 3 2 1

To My Parents:

Sam and Sarah Margolis

Preface

Database, the study of data storage and management, is a burgeoning discipline in the rapidly expanding fields of computer science and data processing. As in the evolution of any discipline, it began as the study of a relatively small body of knowledge, by a limited group of practitioners in industry, and by faculty and graduate students in universities. Today, we find that both the number and depth of database subtopics have grown dramatically. A wide variety of data processing and nondata processing personnel, across the gamut of industrial and nonindustrial organizations, are exposed to the topic. As a university subject, it is increasingly migrating to the undergraduate computer science and business administration curriculums.

An unfortunate, if not surprising, characteristic of the database field, is that to have a thorough understanding of it, to eliminate the mysteries of how so significant an accomplishment can actually be made to work in the cold silicon and metals of the machines, a large amount of interconnected information must be assimilated. It is difficult to understand why a hierarchical data structure might be used without understanding the problems of data redundancy and multiple relationships. It is difficult to understand how to gain access to the records in a network structure without understanding the fundamentals of access methods. It is difficult to understand the need for a data administration function without understanding the principles behind the database approach. Such a list of interconnected concepts could go on indefinitely in this field.

The purpose of this book is to explain the PRINCIPLES behind database and the broad range of database subtopics IN A MANNER THAT LEAVES NOTHING TO THE IMAGINATION. On the other hand, it does not attempt to exhaustively cover every detail of the field. It does not require a substantial data processing background as a prerequisite, but assumes only that the reader understands elementary computer principles and elementary concepts of computer programming. It approaches the subject in a methodical progressive manner, which will insure a *confident understanding* of the subject of database.

This book is intended to be used as the text for a first course in database, or as an introduction to the field for data processing professionals or others whose work exposes them to the database environment. Included is material on basic data definitions and structures, access methods, database management systems characteristics and approaches, database design, management aspects of the environment, and other assorted topics in the field.

Finally, I would like to leave the following thought with my fellow computer scientists, lest I offend their collective sense of precision. In its attempt to cut through the maze of database detail and yet hit hard at the basic concepts while surveying the entire field, this book may generalize or oversimplify a few points. I simply suggest that the trade-off is well worth it. The readers of this book who need only a basic understanding of database will benefit from that tradeoff, while those who expect to go on in database will, after building a solid foundation here, have plenty of opportunity to go into more detail and be more precise in further courses, work experiences, and books. This book is intended to be a "user-friendly" introduction to the entire field of database—period.

The views expressed in this book are those of the author and do not necessarily reflect those of the IBM Corporation

Mark L. Gillenson

New York, New York
July 1985

Acknowledgments

A number of my database colleagues reviewed chapters of this book, making invaluable comments and suggestions in the process. Chief among them were Charley Bontempo and Judy King, both of whom read large sections of the book and were always available to discuss ideas about its construction. Additionally, I would like to acknowledge Art Amman, Jake Ever, Chuck Haspel, Alice Jones, Jack Lebow, Mike McGuire, Fred Page, Dick Schlough, John Sears, and Moshe Zloof. My thanks also to those students of the IBM Systems Research Institute and of Pace University in New York City who read and commented on the manuscript and tested the exercises at the ends of the chapters.

I would also like to thank the management of the IBM Systems Research Institute, specifically Allen L. Morton, Jr., Program Director, Alfred M. Pietrasanta, Director, and Robert W. DeSio, Director of the Corporate Technical Institutes, for providing a stimulating and supportive atmosphere for the writing of this book.

To Jim Gaughan and the crew at John Wiley and Sons, my thanks for their support of this project and their professionalism in publishing.

Lastly, I am grateful to Irene Gillenson, Edith and Marty Sherr, and Marion and Jack Zack, for a very special kind of help given to me while I was writing this book.

M.L.G.

Contents

CHAPTER 9: THE PSEUDO-RELATIONAL APPROACH TO DATABASE

CHAPTER 10: DATABASE DESIGN

CHAPTER 15:   THE FUTURE   373

INDEX   381

DATABASE

1

Introduction

Introduction

This book is about data. Facts. Pieces of information which we need to manage our businesses, governments, banks, universities, and every other kind of human endeavor. It's about ways of managing the data itself, so that the exact data that we need will be there when we need it. It's about computers and the way that a computing environment known as "database" is the solution to the problems caused by the huge amounts of data that we are increasingly storing in them. It's about a key part, maybe the most important part, of today's data processing technology, about which everyone associated with data processing must have a fundamental understanding.

Let's begin by tracing man's concern with data from its beginnings to the current day.

Data and Computers

The Origins of Record Keeping

Mankind has been interested in data for at least the past 12,000 years. While today we often associate the concept of data with the computer, there have, historically, been many more primitive methods of data handling. In fact, some of them are still in use today.

In present day Iraq, one can find shepherds who keep track of their flocks with pebbles, Figure 1.1. As each sheep leaves its pen to graze, the

Figure 1.1. Shepherd using pebbles to keep track of sheep.

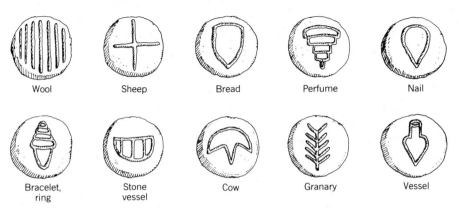

Figure 1.2.   Ancient clay tokens used to record merchandise in transit.

shepherd places one pebble in a small sack. When the sheep return, the shepherd discards one pebble for each animal, and thus has a way of knowing whether he has lost any of his flock. In fact, that method of record keeping is a variation of the most ancient method known.

Excavations in the Zagros region of Iran, dated to 8500 B.C., have unearthed clay "tokens" or "counters" which, it is theorized, were used for record keeping in primitive forms of accounting. Such tokens have been found in sites from present day Turkey to Pakistan and as far afield as Khartoum. They date from as long ago as 7000 B.C.

By 3000 B.C., at the present day city of Susa in Iran, the use of such tokens had reached a greater level of sophistication. Tokens, with special markings on them, Figure 1.2, were sealed in hollow clay vessels, which apparently represented bills of lading, accompanying commercial goods in transit. The tokens represented the quantity of goods being shipped and, obviously, could not be tampered with without the clay vessel being broken open. Inscriptions on the outside of the vessels, and the seals of the parties involved, provided a further record. The external inscriptions included words or concepts such as "deposited," "transferred," and "removed."

At about the same time that the Susa culture existed, people in the city-state of Uruk in Sumeria kept records in clay texts. With pictographs, numerals, and ideographs, they described land sales and business transactions involving bread, beer, sheep, cattle, and clothing.

Other neolithic means of record keeping included storing tallies as cuts and notches in wooden sticks and as knots in rope. The former continued in use in England as late as the medieval period, the latter was used by South American Indians.

Data Through the Ages

In retrospect, the primary origins of the interest in data can be traced to the rise of cities. Simple subsistence hunting, gathering, and, later, agrarian cultures, had little use for the concept of data. But as we have seen with the cities of Susa and Uruk, cities, and the attendant culture that began with the Bronze age forever changed the way we live. The beginnings of mass production, the specialization of labor, the use of money, and the bartering of ones services and products for the necessities of life all required the keeping of data in records.

As time went on, more and different kinds of data and records were kept. These included calendars, census data, surveys, land ownership records, marriage records, data on temple contributions, and family trees, Figure 1.3. Merchants had to keep track of inventories, shipments, and wage payments in addition to the production itself. As farming went beyond the subsistence level and progressed to the feudal manor stage, there was a need to keep data on the amount of produce to consume, to barter with, and to keep as seed for the following year.

The Crusades took place from the late eleventh to the late thirteenth centuries. One side effect of the the Crusades was a broader view of the world from the perspective of the Europeans, with an accompanying increase in interest in trade. A common method of trade in that era was the establishment of partnerships among merchants, ships captains, and owners to facilitate commercial voyages. That increased level of commercial sophistication brought with it another round of increasingly complex record keeping: specifically, double-entry bookkeeping.

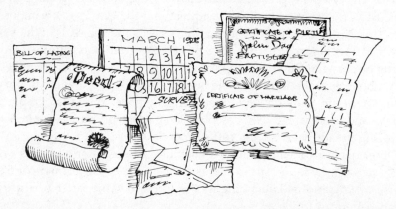

Figure 1.3.   Increasing number of kinds of data with the advance of civilization.

Double-entry bookkeeping originated in the trading centers of fourteenth century Italy. The earliest known example is from a merchant in Genoa and dates to the year 1340. Its use gradually spread, but it was not until 1494, in Venice (about 25 years after the first movable type printing press in Venice came into use), that a Franciscan Monk named Luca Pacioli published his "Summa de Arithmetica, Geometrica, Proportioni et Proportionalita." That work had an important effect in spreading the use of double-entry bookkeeping. Of course, as a separate issue, the increasing use of paper and the printing press furthered the advance of record keeping as well.

As the dominance of the Italian merchants declined, other countries became more active in trade and concomitantly with data and record keeping. Furthermore, as the use of temporary trading partnerships declined, and more stable long term mercantile organizations were established, other types of data became necessary. For example, annual as opposed to venture-by-venture statements of profit and loss were needed. In 1673 the "Code of Commerce" in France required that a balance sheet be drawn up every two years by every businessman.

Early Calculating Devices

It was also in the seventeenth century that people began to take an interest in devices which could "automatically" *process their data*, if only in a rudimentary way. One of the earliest and best known was produced in France in the 1640s by Blaise Pascal, reportedly to help his father perform his job as a tax commissioner, Figure 1.4. It was a small box which contained interlocking gears and was capable of doing addition and subtraction. In fact, it was the forerunner of today's automobile odometers.

In about 1694, Gottfried Wilhelm von Leibniz built a more sophisticated device, consisting of cylinders and wheels with interlocking teeth, Figure 1.5. It was capable of multiplying and dividing, with one multidigit number entered initially, and the other represented by turning a gear that number of times. Leibniz's device suffered, in practical use, from the same poor machining skills of the day as Pascal's, but its principles were to be used in fairly contemporary mechanical calculating devices.

In 1805, Joseph Marie Jacquard of France invented a device which automatically created patterns during the textile weaving process. The heart of the device was a series of cards with holes punched in them; the holes allowed strands of material to be interwoven in a sequence which produced the desired pattern, Figure 1.6. While Jacquard's loom wasn't a calculating device as such, his method of storing fabric patterns as holes in punched

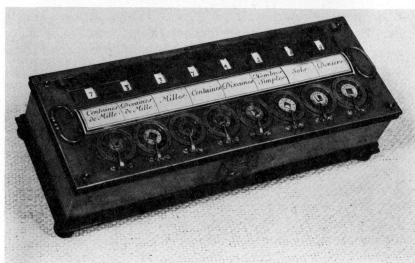

Figure 1.4. Pascal and his adding machine. (Courtesy IBM Archives).

Figure 1.5. Leibniz and his mechanical multiplier. (Courtesy IBM Archives).

7

Figure 1.6. The Jacquard loom. (Courtesy IBM Archives).

Figure 1.7. Babbage and his Difference Engine. (Courtesy IBM Archives).

cards was a very clever means of *data storage,* which would have great importance for computing devices to follow.

The last of the early computing geniuses was truly a man ahead of his time. Charles Babbage was a nineteenth century English mathematician. During the 1820s and 1830s he developed and built a machine which he called the "Difference Engine," Figure 1.7. Sophisticated for its time, it was capable of tabulating series of numbers derived from complicated polynomials. Such tables were needed in navigation and astronomy. Beginning in 1833, Babbage began to think about another invention which he called the "Analytical Engine." He never completed it (again, the state of the art of machinery lagged the creativity of the mind) but included in its design were many of the principles of modern computers. The Analytical Engine was to consist of a "store" for holding data items and a "mill" for operating upon them. Babbage was very impressed by Jacquard's work with punched cards. In fact, the Analytical Engine was to be able to store calculation instructions in punched cards, which would be fed into the machine together with punched cards containing data, to operate on that data and produce the desired result.

Practical Large-Scale Calculating

The development of practical computing and tabulating devices required two things: (1) a large scale data storage and processing requirement and (2) a certain base level of manufacturing skills and mechanical and electrical devices. By the late nineteenth century, machining skills had reached a sufficiently advanced level, and a need involving a massive amount of data occurred as well: the U.S. Census.

The 1880 U.S. census took about seven years to compile by hand. It was estimated that using the same manual techniques, the compilation of the 1890 census would not be completed until after the 1900 census data had begun to be collected. The solution to processing the census data was provided by a government engineer named Herman Hollerith. Basing his work on Jacquard's punched card concept (as had Babbage), he arranged to have the census data stored in punched cards. He built devices to punch the holes into cards and devices to sort the cards, Figure 1.8. Wire brushes touching the cards completed circuits when they came across the holes, and advanced electromechanical counters. Using Hollerith's equipment, the total population count of the 1890 census was completed one month after all of the data was in. The complete set of tabulations, including data on questions which had never before been practical to ask, took two years.

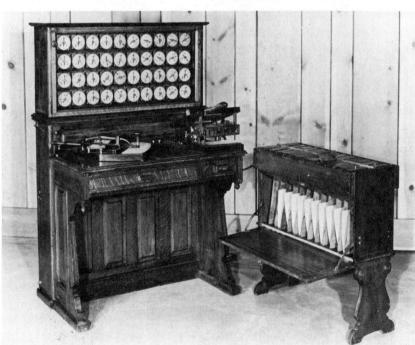

Figure 1.8. Hollerith and some of his early punched card equipment. (Courtesy IBM Archives).

Figure 1.9.   An early NCR cash register. (Courtesy NCR Corp.).

In 1896, Hollerith formed the Tabulating Machine Company to produce and commercially market his devices. That company, combined with several others, eventually formed what is today the International Business Machines Corporation (IBM).

The census bureau, while using Hollerith's equipment, continued experimenting on its own. One of its engineers, James Powers, developed devices to automatically feed cards into the equipment and to automatically print results. In 1911 he formed the Powers Tabulating Machine Company, which eventually formed the basis for the UNIVAC division of the Sperry Corporation.

It was also during this time period that another major advance in mechanized data tracking was made. The cash register, invented in 1879, was aggressively marketed by the National Cash Register Company, and progressively gained acceptance in retail businesses of every description, Figure 1.9.

As society increased in sophistication, so did the volume of its data and the complexity of the ways in which it had to be processed. Inventors made further advances in response. During the 1920s and 1930s, Vannevar Bush at the Massachusetts Institute of Technology (MIT), and others at such institutions as the Moore School of Engineering of the University of Pennsylvania developed important "analog" computers (based on continuous

Figure 1.10.   Electro-mechanical punched card based data processing equipment, circa 1940. (Courtesy IBM Archives).

measuring devices as opposed to discrete items, such as holes in cards), primarily for military ballistics calculations.

During that same period, and continuing into the early 1960s, commercial data processing was performed on a variety of electro-mechanical punched card based devices. They included calculators, punches, sorters, collators, and printers, Figure 1.10. The data was stored in punched cards, while the processing instructions were implemented as collections of wires plugged into specially designed boards which in turn were inserted into slots in the electro-mechanical devices.

As World War II approached, the pace of development quickened. George R. Stibitz at Bell Laboratories, and Howard H. Aiken at Harvard produced sophisticated electro-mechanical digital computers. Aiken's Mark I, completed in 1944, had 72 numerical "counters" or storage positions and took five seconds to do a multiplication operation.

The first large, viable, fully electronic computer was also hastened by the ballistics needs of the military during the war. Called the Electronic Numerical Integrator and Calculator (ENIAC) it was begun in 1943 at the Moore School by John W. Mauchly and J. Presper Eckert, and was completed in 1946, Figure 1.11. It had 18,000 vacuum tubes and could perform 5000 additions per second. It was about 1000 times faster than the Mark I.

Figure 1.11.   The ENIAC. (Courtesy Sperry Corp.).

With the advance into fully electronic computers having been made, other developments followed rapidly. In 1945 John von Neumann, working from his and others' ideas, proposed a stored program computer. The first such machine, called the Electronic Delay Storage Automatic Computer (EDSAC), was completed in 1949 at Cambridge University in England by Maurice Wilkes. In 1952 the MIT Whirlwind I, introduced in the late 1940s, was the first to incorporate core memory.

Commercial Computers

After WWII, scientific advances and increasing business needs brought on by new societal expectations caused still further increases in the kinds and volumes of data to be processed. This brought renewed pressure on data processing capabilities. In 1947, Eckert and Mauchly formed the Eckert-Mauchly Computer Corporation, and in 1951 delivered the UNIVAC I (Universal Automatic Computer), Figure 1.12, to the census bureau. That company was eventually absorbed by Remington Rand (later Sperry Cor-

Figure 1.12. The UNIVAC I. (Courtesy Sperry Corp.).

poration), which continued to produce computers with the UNIVAC name. In 1953 IBM, which had a very strong presence with electro-mechanical calculating equipment and some early vacuum tube-based devices, produced its first electronic computer. The IBM 701 was a scientifically oriented machine with a vacuum tube memory. It was followed by the business oriented 702 and then in 1955 by the 705, which had a core memory, Figure 1.13. Those machines and others of their ilk came to be known as "first generation" computers.

The late 1950s and early 1960s saw the advent of transistor, as opposed to vacuum tube, based computers, Figure 1.14. These machines, which became the "second generation" computers, were much more reliable, smaller, and faster, than those of the the first generation. In addition to being incorporated into large computers, this new technology, combined with improvements in core memory technology, created the first viable smaller scale computers, which became highly successful and proliferated at a rapid rate. Such machines were the first computers for many thousands of corporations. The mid- and late 1960s saw the rise of the "third generation" of computers. Based on integrated circuits, third generation computers were another major step forward, Figure 1.15.

Figure 1.13. The IBM 705. (Courtesy IBM Archives).

Figure 1.14. A second generation computer: The NCR 304. (Courtesy NCR Corp.).

16

Figure 1.15. A third generation computer: The UNIVAC 1108. (Courtesy Sperry Corp.).

Modern Data Storage Media

Paralleling the growth of equipment to process data was the development of new media to store the data on. The earliest form of modern data storage was punched holes in some appropriate paper medium. In the 1870s and 1880s punched paper tape was introduced in conjunction with early teletype equipment. Of course we've already mentioned that Hollerith in the 1890s and Powers in the early 1900s used punched cards as a storage medium. In fact, punched cards were the only data storage medium used in the increasingly sophisticated automated accounting machines of the 1920s, 1930s, and 1940s. They were used extensively in the early computers of the 1950s and 1960s and could still be found well into the 1970s, in smaller data processing installations, in a progressively reduced capacity.

By 1936 both Eastman Kodak and Bush, with his "Rapid Selector," were recording digital data photographically. While the data could be read back with photoelectric cell technology, this was a nonerasable medium. While nonerasability in a data storage medium can be an advantage for some data processing applications, it is too limiting for most and thus photographic storage has always had only limited use.

The middle to late 1930s saw the beginning of the era of magnetic storage media, with Bell Laboratories experimenting with magnetic tape for sound storage. In 1937 there was early work in Germany on oxides for use in magnetic storage. In 1937 and 1938 Bush expressed some early ideas on magnetic storage on plate-like objects. In 1939 at MIT, magnetic strips on

Figure 1.16.   An early ERA magnetic drum unit, circa 1948. (Courtesy Contral Data Corp.).

the backs of accounting cards were wound around a drum for reading. With the advent of World War II, these efforts slowed or stopped.

In 1942 at MIT, Perry Crawford wrote a thesis describing the idea of magnetic drum storage. Beginning in 1943, and continuing into the early 1950s, Engineering Research Associates (ERA) conducted experiments with and developed such devices, Figure 1.16.

In the late 1940s there was early work on the use of magnetic tape for recording data and further thought on flat plate magnetic storage. Specifically in 1947, Eckert and Mauchly developed a magnetic tape unit. In 1948 and 1949 IBM furthered magnetic tape development. Also in 1947, ideas on flat plates and flat donut-shaped plates for large scale random access data storage were expressed at the Aberdeen Proving Grounds and at the National Bureau of Standards, respectively. In 1948 and 1949, Potter Instrument experimented with strips of magnetic tape stretched on a flat frame.

By 1950, others, including RCA and Raytheon, were developing the magnetic tape concept too. Also in the early 1950s, Aiken developed tape units with vacuum columns. In 1952, both UNIVAC and Raytheon offered commercially available magnetic tape units. In 1953 IBM offered tape units, Figure 1.17. From the mid-1950s to the mid-1960s, magnetic tape gradually became the dominant data storage medium in computers. Magnetic tape

Figure 1.17.   An early IBM magnetic tape drive. (Courtesy IBM Archives).

technology has been continually improved since then, and is still in broad use today, particularly for archived data, Figure 1.18.

In 1952 and 1953, ERA, followed by UNIVAC offered the first commercially available magnetic drums, Figure 1.19. In 1953 and 1954 IBM offered drums in some of its early computers. They were joined in 1955 by Control Data. Also in 1955, UNIVAC "File Computers" contained the first large capacity drum storage.

In 1956 and 1957, IBM developed magnetic cards as a memory device for typewriters.

In 1953, IBM began work on its 305 RAMAC (Random Access Memory Accounting Machine) fixed disk storage device. By 1954 there was a multiplatter version, which became commercially available in 1956, Figure 1.20. In 1957 the first shipment of devices with movable-head disk drives was made. At about that time, experiments began with removable disk packs which were introduced commercially in 1963, Figure 1.21. During the mid-1960s a massive conversion from tape to disk as the preeminent secondary storage medium began to take place. At first, the disk storage environment

Figure 1.18. A later magnetic tape drive. (Courtesy IBM Corp.).

Figure 1.19. A later ERA magnetic drum unit, circa 1950. Courtesy Control Data Corp.).

Figure 1.20. The IBM RAMAC disk device. (Courtesy IBM Archives).

was geared towards the removable pack philosophy, with a dozen or more packs being juggled on and off a single drive as a common ratio. As data recording densities increased, the pack to drive ratio decreased to the point that in 1976 IBM marketed a disk drive with a nonremovable pack. Continual improvements in disk technology have led it to become the standard data storage medium in use today, Figure 1.22.

Among the newest data storage media are "mass storage" devices and the diskette. In 1974 IBM introduced the "Mass Storage System." It consisted of a "honeycomb" of small cylinders with magnetic tape wrapped around them, Figure 1.23. On command, the device would select a cylinder, wrap its tape around a reading device, and transfer the data. While slow compared to disk storage, this technique is capable of storing huge amounts

Figure 1.21. A disk drive unit of the mid-1960s. (Courtesy Control Data Corp.).

Figure 1.22. A modern sealed disk drive unit. (Courtesy IBM Corp.).

22

Figure 1.23.   Tape cylinders of the IBM Mass Storage System. (Courtesy IBM Corp.).

of data. At the other end of the spectrum, the diskette is a small, flexible, inexpensive, coated plastic disk which was introduced in different forms in 1971 and 1973, Figure 1.24. Diskette drives are the principal secondary storage devices used in today's microcomputers.

Today's Data Processing Environment

Eventually, the boundaries between computer generations became indistinct. We speak of today's fourth generation of computers as being based on very large scale integrated (VLSI) circuits. This technology and countless other improvements have continued the simultaneous trend of decreasing price and increasing performance.

Figure 1.24.   A diskette. (Courtesy IBM Corp.).

Computers now range from desktop "home" or "micro" computers, Figure 1.25, to incredibly powerful large machines, Figure 1.26. Storage facilities have become faster, more reliable, and capable of packing data in an increasingly dense fashion. Networks of far flung computers, tied together by a variety of communications media, have flourished.

Software, the various kinds of instructions that make the machines run, has also continuously advanced. Highly sophisticated operating systems allow many people to use the machines simultaneously. Database management systems permit nonredundant data storage and complex data access. Special development systems permit certain application programs to be quickly created subverting the slow traditional programming process.

In short, the computer has become a part of virtually every business process. This is a trend which is sure to continue.

Figure 1.25. A microcomputer: The IBM Personal Computer. (Courtesy IBM Corp.).

Figure 1.26. A modern large scale computer: The IBM 3084. (Courtesy of IBM Corp.).

The Information Age

Which brings us back to the starting point for all of that activity: data. It took thousands of years for people to cultivate an interest in the simplest kinds of data. It took a few hundred years to develop basic calculating methods and devices to the point that an interest in more sophisticated uses of data became practical. And it has taken only about the last 30 years for data processing to reach a point at which people are speaking of the decline of the "industrial age" and the birth of the "information age."

One crucial aspect of the information age, and one that we have already had to begin dealing with, is managing the huge volumes of data involved. Walk into a large company's data processing installation today and you're likely to find shelves of tape reels and stacks of disk packs, together with rows of devices to read from them and write onto them. Of course, new developments in hardware are continually producing devices that can cram more data in the same amount of space. But in a way that adds to the problem rather than solving it, because it just encourages people to capture and store more and more data without having sufficient means to manage it properly.

The amount of data that large and even not so large firms have today is almost unbelievable. We're talking about billions, trillions, and more individual pieces of data. And more often than not, the way that they manage—or, more accurately, mismanage—it is horrendous, if somewhat understandable. It's not as if we're talking about managing a company's employees. Even the largest companies have only a few hundred thousand of them, and they don't change all that frequently. Or the money that a company has: sure, there is a lot of it, but it's all the same in the sense that a dollar that goes to payroll is the same kind of dollar that goes to paying a supplier for raw materials.

In data, we have a commodity of tremendous volume, each piece of which is different from the next. And it has the characteristic that much of it is in a state of change at any one time. And nowadays it seems that everyone in the company wants access (usually instant access) to it for one purpose or another. Furthermore, with so much data processing development taking place, it's difficult to keep track of what data already exists. For this and other reasons the same data tends to be stored several (or many) times over for different applications.

Is there no hope? Are we to be buried in a seemingly endless mass of unmanageable data forever?

Fortunately, there is a class of methodologies—really more of an environment—for storing, accessing, and in general, managing data which can form the foundation for survival in a world which is going to become ever more data oriented as time goes on. That class of methodologies or environment has come to be known as *database*.

This Book

Database emerged as a recognizable subject and discipline in the mid-1960s, but for some time was limited in concern to a relatively small portion of the data processing population. Through the 1970s it grew to be a major focus of data processing activity for many organizations. But with more and more data processing people exposed to it and expected to understand and use it, it became clear that there was a tremendous lack of understanding of the fundamental concepts of the subject. The advent of the 1980s made that situation even more acute.

Database is a very powerful concept. It forms an ingenious solution to some vexing problems. As a result, it unfortunately tends to be a multifaceted and complex subject, which appears difficult when one attempts to swallow it in one gulp. But database is approachable and understandable if one proceeds carefully, cautiously, and progressively step-by-step.

This book is a straightforward introduction to database. It takes a step-by-step approach which leaves no gaps in its explanation. Each chapter progressively adds more to an understanding of the fundamentals of database. It is an understanding that no one in data processing can any longer afford to be without.

References

Crawford, P., conversation on February 3, 1984.

Gleiser, M., "Men and Machines Before Babbage," *DATAMATION*, vol. 24, no. 10, October, 1978, pp. 125–130.

Goldstine, H. H., *The Computer from Pascal to von Neumann*, Princeton University Press, Princeton, NJ, 1972.

Gordon, M. J., and Shillinglaw, G., *Accounting: A Management Approach*, 4th ed., Richard D. Irwin, Homewood, IL, 1969.

Hendriksen, E. S., *Accounting Theory*, revised ed., Richard D. Irwin, Homewood, IL, 1970.

Littleton, A. C., and Yamey, B. S., *Studies in the History of Accounting*, Richard D. Irwin, Homewood, IL, 1956.

Rosen, S., "Electronic Computers: A Historical Survey," *Computing Surveys*, vol. 1, no. 1, March, 1969, pp. 7–36.

Schmandt-Besserat, D., "The Earliest Precursor of Writing," *Scientific American*, vol. 238, no. 6, June, 1978, pp. 50–59.

Shurkin, J., *Engines of the Mind*, W. W. Norton, New York, 1984.

Stevens, L. D., "The Evolution of Magnetic Storage," *IBM Journal of Research and Development*, vol. 25, no. 5, September, 1981, pp. 663–675.

Tropp, H., "The Effervescent Years: A Retrospective," *IEEE Spectrum*, vol. 11, no. 2, February, 1974, pp. 70–79.

Questions and Exercises

1.1. Draw a time line for the last two hundred years comparing the development of data processing devices to the development of data storage media.

1.2. Do you think that the comparative development of data processing devices and data storage media was uneven? Did the speed of growth of one inhibit the growth of the other?

2

Simple Files and Storage Media

What is Data?

Records and Entities

Let's begin by thinking about a single piece of data. A single piece of data represents a single fact about something that we are interested in. In our company, it may be the fact that employee John Smith's employee number is 31719; or it may be the fact that our largest supplier of bolts is located in Chicago; or it may be the fact that the telephone number for one of our customers, the Acme Company, is 555-8003. A *piece of data* is a single *fact* about something that we care about in our surroundings.

Usually we have many facts to describe something of interest to us in our environment. For example, let's consider the facts that we might be interested in about that employee of ours, John Smith. We want to remember that his employee number is 31719, his salary rate is $5.50 per hour, his homecity is Detroit, his homestate is Michigan, and so forth. We need to know these things in order to process Smith's payroll check every week, to notify his family in case he will be home late, to send him a company greeting card at New Years, and so forth. It certainly seems reasonable to collect together all of the facts about Smith that we need for those purposes and to hold all of them together. Figure 2.1 shows all of the facts about John Smith that concern payroll and related applications.

Since we have to generate a paycheck each week for every employee in our company, not just for Smith, we are obviously going to need a collection of facts like those in Figure 2.1 for every one of our employees. Figure 2.2 shows a portion of that collection.

It will simplify matters later if at this point we can relate some of the items that we have come across thus far to some of the many terms that are a part of file and database terminology. The collection of facts about a particular employee (one line or row of the table in Figure 2.2) is called a *record*. Each kind of fact (e.g., employee number or homecity) is called a *field*. The collection of payroll facts for all of the employees, that is, the entire table in Figure 2.2, is called a *file*. The file in Figure 2.2, which is about the most basic kind of file imaginable, is often called a *simple or linear file* (linear since it is a collection of records listed one after the other in a

Employee Number	Employee Last Name	Employee First Name	Salary Rate	Home city	Home state	Home Telephone
31719	Smith	John	5.50	Detroit	MI	313-555-5186

Figure 2.1. John Smith's payroll facts.

Employee Number	Employee Last Name	Employee First Name	Salary Rate	Home city	Home state	Home Telephone
06337	Jones	Fred	4.30	New York	NY	212-555-9207
09155	Smith	Susan	5.90	Atlanta	GA	404-555-2287
16840	Adams	John	10.00	Atlanta	GA	404-555-4301
31719	Smith	John	5.50	Detroit	MI	313-555-5186
38102	Baker	George	7.00	Atlanta	GA	404-555-7739
. . .						

Figure 2.2. Payroll file.

long "line"). We will speak of the layout of each record of a file (the column headings in Figure 2.2) as the *record type,* and each individual record (each row in Figure 2.2) as an *occurrence* of that record (or of that record type).

Put in a slightly different, but closely related way, each thing that we are interested in keeping track of (the real physical object or event, not the facts about it) is called an *entity.* John Smith, the real, living, breathing person who you can go over to and touch, is an entity. A collection of entities of the same type (e.g., all of the company's employees) is called an *entity set.* An *attribute* is a property or characteristic of an entity. Smith's telephone number, employee number, homecity, and so forth, are all attributes of his. Relating these terms back to files, we can see that a record *describes* a particular entity (at least in terms of one or several applications). A file describes an entire entity set. A given attribute is represented as a field value.

Another handy feature of the file in Figure 2.2 has to do with the employee numbers field: its values are unique. Since each employee has a unique employee number, we can use that field to distinguish between the different employee records. Such a field (or combination of fields) is called a *key* field of the file.

Relationships

So far we've been concerned with maintaining facts about a particular entity. Another very important kind of information is the collection of ways that different entities *relate to each other.* Such interactions are described as *associations* and *relationships.*

Suppose that in addition to the employee, there is a need to store data

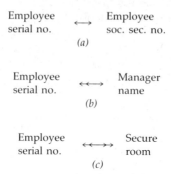

Figure 2.3. Relationships: *(a)* one-to one, *(b)* one-to-many, and *(c)* many-to-many.

about each nonmanagement employees' social security number, manager, and the rooms which the employee is authorized to be in. There is exactly one social security number and one manager associated with each employee, facts which are called *unary associations*. In addition to there being one social security number associated with a given employee, looking at it the other way, for a given social security number there is exactly one employee associated with it. In this case there is a unary association in each direction, and this is called a *one-to-one relationship*, Figure 2.3a.

Returning once again to employees and managers, while for a given employee there is only one manager, for a given manager there may be many employees working for him or her. Thus there is a unary association in one direction and a *multiple association* in the other direction, and the combination is called a *one-to-many relationship*, Figure 2.3b. (Note that the single arrowhead denotes the unary association, while the double arrowhead denotes the multiple association.)

Finally consider the situation of employees and secure rooms. An employee may be authorized to be in several rooms, while a room will have several employees authorized to be in it. That's a *many-to-many relationship*, Figure 2.3c.

Simple Files

Let's review what we've established thus far. It may all seem rather simple, but it forms a solid foundation for what lies ahead.

The basic notion of data is establishing a collection of needed facts about things (entities) in our environment that we care about. In concept at least, we can envision each such collection to form a row of a table (record of a file) which brings together the data of each "occurrence" of that type of entity. Again, the table or file in Figure 2.2 contains a row's worth of data about each of our employees.

This brings us to the first of several times in this book that we shall face the following question:

"That last paragraph sounds perfectly logical to me, as a human being, but how can a "nuts and bolts" (or more accurately, a "circuits and chips") computer be made to make sense out of it?"

At each such juncture, this book will answer such questions at an appropriate level for a practitioner or student of data processing or a user or manager of it. It will not get into the electrical or mechanical engineering details.

In order to approach this first question at hand, it will be necessary to take a look at the appropriate kinds of data representations and data storage devices available, information which will actually be quite useful throughout the book. The characteristics of those devices will be important considerations both in the ways that we can access data and in the performance that we can expect to achieve in doing so.

Data Storage Concepts

Data Representations

You're probably familiar with the concepts of bits and bytes and the basic ways of forming data with them, but in the spirit of completeness let's begin with a review of that material.

A *bit* or binary digit is simply a two-way switch, which at any moment is set either one way or the other way. Over the years, this idea has been physically embodied in little metal rings (or "cores") being magnetized in one direction or the other, spots on punched cards either being left alone or being punched out, spots on metal oxide coated plastic or aluminum being magnetized in one direction or the other, and so on.

Since there is not much in the way of data that can be recorded in a single bit, groups of bits are combined together to form a medium for data storage. In many of today's computers, eight bits are grouped together to form a *byte*. Groups of bytes, or in some computers other groups of bits, are combined to form *words*. The two main kinds of data that we are interested in storing are numeric data and alphabetic data.

There are three common ways of storing numeric data, usually called binary, decimal, and floating point. A "binary number" is simply a number represented in the binary, or base two, number system, in a string of bits, each of which has the value zero or the value one, as the binary system requires. For example, the string of bits

0111001

represents the number 57.

A "decimal number" is formed by assigning a particular bit sequence in a byte to have the value 0, another sequence the value 1, and so on through 9. For example, if 11110101 represents the decimal digit 5 (note that the last four bits form the number 5 in binary), and if 11110111 represents the decimal number 7, then

11110101 11110111

represents 57 in this system. Since only four bits are needed to represent the 10 different decimal digits, this representation can be compressed so that two decimal digits appear in a single byte

01010111

in this example. This system is known as "packed decimal," and is quite straightforward, except that an additional byte may be required to represent the sign of the number. The decimal system was devised for business applications with high data input and output requirements, because of its relative ease in transferring data to and from input and output devices.

Floating point numbers are intended for scientific applications which often require very large or very small numbers. While there are some variations on the theme, a floating point number consists of three parts: the sign, the characteristic, and the fraction. In general the characteristic is an exponent which raises the base of the number system to some power. The result is then multiplied by the fraction to obtain the result. For example,

5E243

might be a notation for 10 (the base of the number system) raised to the power 5, times .243, or 24,300. If the amount of storage allotted to the fraction is small, and the range of the exponent, allows very large or very small numbers, some precision may be lost, but with the numbers and applications being dealt with, that usually doesn't matter.

Characters are represented as assigned bit sequences in a particular "code" that the computer operates with. Two of the most common such codes are the Extended Binary Coded Decimal Interchange Code (EBCDIC), which represents each character as an eight bit sequence (one character per byte), and the American Standard Code for Information Interchange (ASCII) which is a seven bit code. For example, in EBCDIC the bit sequence 11000001 represents the character A, 11000010 represents the character B, and so on. To form the word SMITH in a computer's memory would require five bytes of storage, the first containing the bit pattern for S, the second the pattern for M, and so on.

So storing a record in a computer's memory is a matter of a program causing the correct bit patterns for the alphabetic fields of the record and the correct representations for the numeric fields of the record, to be stored in consecutive storage positions. The record in Figure 2.1 would be stored as several bytes to represent the employee number 31719 in, say, packed decimal format, followed by a byte with the bit pattern for a character S, followed by a byte with the bit pattern for a character M, and so on. For an entire file, the records might simply follow each other in memory. Which brings us to the point of discussing the different kinds of memory and some of the various types of storage devices that are available today.

Basically there are two levels of storage or memory in a computer system: primary memory and secondary memory.

Primary Memory

Primary memory is the place that data being processed, programs in the process of executing, and portions of the system coordinating and control programs (operating system, database management system, network control program) must be. At the byte or at the word level, each storage location can be singled out and directly reached by the computer's central processing unit. Because it is so critical to the overall operation of the system, primary memory must be extremely fast in terms of the storage and retrieval of its contents. In theory, it might be nice if primary memory was unlimited in size and all of the programs and data files associated with a system could be stored in it. But because of the speed and other requirements placed upon it, primary memory requires comparatively expensive technologies. That, and the fact that primary memory is limited in size by the system's addressing schemes used to access its contents, allows it to be only large enough to store a very small fraction of a systems programs and data files at any one moment.

Primary memory used to be made of little doughnut shaped pieces of iron called "cores" (the term "core memory" used to be synonymous with the term "primary memory") which were strung together with wires running through them. Each core represented a single bit, and the wires running through them could both set the two directions of magnetism on the cores, which represented the zero and the one values, and could sense them to determine their current values at any later time. Today primary memories are made with newer integrated circuit technologies. The concept of the bit remains the same, but the speeds involved have increased tremendously.

In any case, primary memory can be thought of as a vast array of bits, arranged into bytes and/or words. Each byte or word has an address and can be accessed by the central processing unit, to store new data or retrieve existing data, very rapidly.

Secondary Memory

The Need for Secondary Memory.   Because of the scarcity of primary memory, the vast volumes of data and the programs that process them are held on secondary memory devices. Individual records or groups of records of a file are loaded from secondary memory into primary memory when required for processing (as are programs when they are to be executed). A loose analogy can be drawn between primary and secondary memory in a computer system and a person's brain and a library (Figure 2.4). The brain cannot possibly hold all of the information that a person might need, but let's say, a large library can. So when a person needs some particular information that's not in his or her brain at the moment, he or she finds a book in the library that has the information and, by reading it, transfers the information from the book into his or her brain.

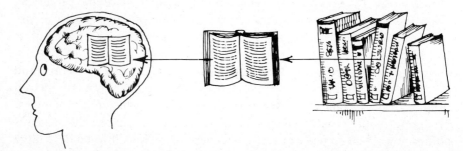

Figure 2.4.   Primary and secondary memory are like a brain and a library.

Sequential and Direct Access.   While data processing applications come in a countless number of variations, there are fundamentally only two kinds of access to stored data that any of them require. In this book we shall refer to these two kinds of access as sequential access and direct access.

The term *sequential access* means that the application must retrieve and process all or a portion of the records of a file one after another until all of the required records have been processed. The records in the file may be ordered by the values of some key field, they may be in chronological order with the most recently inserted record placed at the end of the file, or they may be in no particular order at all. A common example of sequential processing is producing a company's payroll checks every week. Since all of the company's employees must be paid, it might as well plow through all of the employee payroll records, which will probably be ordered by the employee number field, one after the other until a paycheck has been generated for each employee. Ordering the file by employee number will facilitate control and update of the file and will probably simplify distribution of the paychecks.

The other mode of access will be referred to in this book as *direct access*. It is described as the need to find one specific record in a file and retrieve it with the usual, but not strict, assumption that it must be retrieved very quickly. The record is retrieved either to simply present it to someone for their perusal, to process or modify it in some way, or both. An example of this type of data access requirement is an airlines reservation system. When a customer telephones an airline to make a reservation or simply to get information about a flight on a certain date, the reservations clerk, usually sitting in front of a video display terminal, must be able to quickly retrieve the data on the requested flight. We might also pursue the employee payroll file example a bit further in this direction by suggesting that there will be times when an employee payroll record must be retrieved directly. For example, if one specific employee gets a salary raise and we want to record that new data, then we want to find and process just his or her employee payroll record and no other.

The two predominant forms of secondary memory in use today are magnetic tape and magnetic disk. Magnetic tape is a sequential storage medium and thus supports sequential access. Data is stored one character after another down the length of the tape, and there is no direct access to it. Most database applications today require direct access, and so tape is not much of a factor in the realm of database.

Disk Storage Devices.   Databases require storage devices that are very large in storage capacity, are very fast in terms of storage and access times

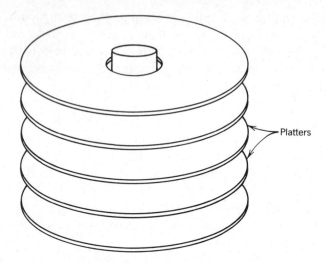

Figure 2.5.   A disk pack.

(although not as fast as primary memory), provide a direct access capability to the data, and are less expensive than primary memory units of comparable capacity. By far the most common such device in use today is the *magnetic disk* unit.

A single magnetic disk is a hard, round, aluminum platter with an iron oxide coating on its two surfaces. Usually several disks are stacked together, mounted on a central rod, with some space between them, into a *disk pack,* Figure 2.5. The disk pack arrangement is a permanent one; the disks are not interchangeable or removeable. The disk pack is placed in a device known as a *disk drive* which has read/write heads capable of storing data on and retrieving data from the disks surfaces, Figure 2.6. The disk pack spins on the disk drive at a high velocity (e.g. 2400 rpm), causing any given piece of data to be potentially accessible many times each second.

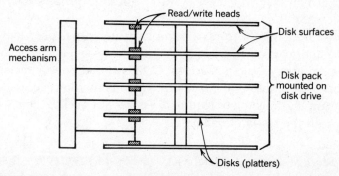

Figure 2.6.   A mounted disk pack showing the access arm mechanism with its read/write heads.

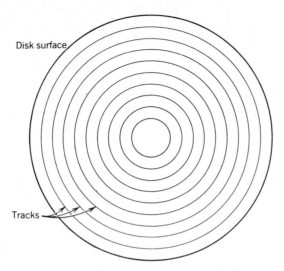

Figure 2.7. Tracks on the surface of a disk.

It is important to understand how data is arranged on the disks and the related performance factors in retrieval operations. Data is stored, serially by bit, on concentric circles on the disk known as *tracks,* Figure 2.7. There may be fewer than one hundred or several hundred tracks on each disk surface, depending on the particular device. Let's number the outermost track, track 0, the next track 1, and so on. You might assume that the way a file is loaded onto a disk pack would be by filling up all of the tracks of one disk surface, then all of tracks on the next surface, and so on. In fact, that is not the way that it is done.

Track 0 on surface 0, track 0 on surface 1, and each of the other "track 0's" on the pack, (one per surface) are logically combined into *cylinder* 0. The same logical cylinder arrangement is made for every such set of tracks with the same index number on their respective surfaces. It's as if you looked at the disk pack from the top and could select a set of the concentric circle tracks, one per surface, and each right over the other forming a "cylinder." Thus the total number of cylinders in a disk pack is equal to the number of tracks on any one disk surface.

The reason for the emphasis on the cylinder concept has to do with the read/write hardware in the disk drive. It would be too expensive and cumbersome to have a read/write head for every track of every surface. So the read/write heads are designed to move from track to track as required. The arrangement shown in Figure 2.6 is one of the earliest and simplest of that sort. There is a movable access mechanism that consists of a set of arms with read/write heads. Each arm has two read/write heads on its far end, and fits into the space in between two of the disks. In that design, one of the read/write heads on an arm is capable of accessing the disk surface above the arm, and the other head is capable of accessing the surface below the arm. Thus as can be seen in Figure 2.6, there is one read/write head per surface. Furthermore this entire, comb-like, access arm assembly is designed to move as one solid object. You can't have the head for surface 0 positioned at track 10 of that surface and at the same time have the head for surface 3 positioned at track 35 of that surface. If one head is at track 10 of its surface, then they are all at track 10 of their respective surfaces. This arrangement has two consequences. One is that it holds down the cost and the complexity of the disk drives. The other is that it creates the concept of the logical cylinder for the following performance oriented reasons.

There are four major steps or timing considerations in the transfer of data from the disk pack to primary memory:

1. Seek Time: Moving the access arm assembly to the correct cylinder from whatever cylinder it's currently positioned at.
2. Head Switching: Selecting the read/write head that accesses the particular track (surface) of that cylinder which the required data is on.
3. Rotational Delay: Waiting for the desired data to arrive under the read/write head as the disk pack is spinning on the drive.
4. Transfer Time: The time to actually move the data from the disk to primary memory once steps 1–3 have been completed.

Head switching takes virtually no time, since it is simply a matter of throwing an electrical switch. On the average, rotational delay takes half the time of one full rotation of the disk, and of course is unavoidable anyway. Transfer times are rather fast, and, again, are necessary in any case. The slowest part of the process, and the one that there's not much that can be done about, is the seek time: the movement of the access arm assembly. But there is a way to turn the situation to advantage, and that's where the concept of the cylinder comes in.

If the records of a simple file are in order by some (key) field, it is a good assumption that for at least some of the applications which use the file, the records will be accessed, one after the other, in the same key order. Furthermore for reasons which we will delve into later in this book, there are many database situations in which closely related pieces of data stored in different record formats will be accessed together. In both of these cases, if we store the data initially by filling all of the tracks on one cylinder, then all of that data can be retrieved *without having to move the access arm assembly.*

We position the assembly to the correct cylinder, start reading from the first required track of that cylinder, and then just flip an electronic switch to activate a different read/write head and read another track of that same cylinder. The alternative, filling all of the tracks of one disk surface, then moving on to the tracks of another surface, would always require access arm assembly movement to go from the data on one track to related data on a nearby track (on the same disk surface).

Over the years there have been tremendous improvements and a wide range of variations in disk technology. These include:

- A range of from 1 to as many as 16 disks in a disk pack. (This amounts to from 2 to 30 tracks or surfaces per cylinder, since in multidisk disk packs the top surface of the top disk and the bottom surface of the bottom disk are normally not used.)
- Some disk drives are designed so that disk packs can be removed and replaced with other packs as frequently as desired. Others have permanently mounted, nonremovable disk packs. An advantage of nonremovable packs is that engineering tolerances can be finer, allowing for a higher data recording density.
- In some cases the access arm assembly with its read/write heads is part of the disk drive unit, in others it is actually part of the disk pack and connects to the drive when the pack is mounted in it.
- As opposed to the original design of one access arm assembly reaching all of the data on the disk pack, there are more recent designs with more than one such assemblies. In some cases different assemblies access different disk surfaces, in others they access different cylinders of the same set of surfaces. Obviously these variations open the way for multiple, parallel accesses of a given disk pack.
- Recently particularly in the field of microcomputers, there has been the advent of the diskette. This is a variation that has a single disk (two surfaces), is only a few inches in diameter, and is made of a thin, pliable, iron oxide coated plastic base. When spun in a disk drive, it flattens and so can be used as a disk normally would be.
- A related kind of device is called a *magnetic drum*. It is a cylindrical unit with circular tracks wrapped around it. A drum is permanently mounted in a device that spins it and which provides *one read/write head per track*. The consequences of that arrangement are that access to data is extremely fast but because of limited storage capacity and high cost, drums are normally used to hold systems programs and associated data, as opposed to application data files.

Data and Disk Formats. There are two other issues, both concerning aspects of the ways that data can be arranged, which we will take up now. The first involves variations in the way that records can be structured. The second involves issues of data placement on the disk.

Record Formats. The records in the file in Figure 2.2 are called *fixed length* records. Every record in the file is of the same length, with the same field types in the same order as every other record in the file. Alternatively there are files that consist of *variable length* records, each of which may consist of different fields and vary in length within a specified range.

Each record in the file in Figure 2.2 is called a *logical record.* Since the rate of processing data in the central processing unit is much faster than the rate at which data can be brought in from secondary memory, it is advisable to transfer several, consecutively stored, records at a time. Again as mentioned previously, this has implications both for simple sequential files and for database structures as well. Once a *physical record or block* of several logical records has been brought into primary memory from secondary memory, each logical record can be examined and processed as necessary by the executing program.

Track Formats. Finally there is the question of how to place the data records on the disk tracks, so that they can be found once the system has determined that they are on a particular track.

Typical of track formats are the "count-data" format and the "count-key-data" format used in the IBM 3330, 2305 (with some modifications), 3340, 3344, 3350, 3375, and 3380 disk devices. Figure 2.8a illustrates the count-data format. The beginning of the track is denoted by a marker known as the "index point." Following that is a small gap. Gaps of varying lengths separate all of the different items on the track and give the disk drives time to perform certain functions. Next is the "home address" which includes such information as the cylinder number, track number, and a flag indicating whether the track is defective. Next is a special record called the "track descriptor record" which contains such information as the number of bytes left on the track after the last data record and if this track has a defect in it, the address of the alternate track that contains the data which should have been on this one. Finally we reach the data records, which consist of three parts: an "address marker," a "count area," and a "data area." The address marker is a special indicator that will allow the drive to determine where the beginning of the record is on subsequent retrievals. The count area repeats the cylinder and track numbers and the indication of whether or not the track is defective, and contains such additional in-

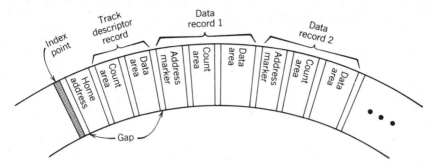

Figure 2.8a. IBM disk track format: count-data format.

formation as the record number (of the records on that track), the length of the data area to follow, and the fact that this file is in count-data, as opposed to count-key-data format. The data area contains all of the actual data of a physical record or block.

The count-key-data format, Figure 2.8b, is the same as the count-data format, except that there is a "key" area in between the count and data areas of each data record, and an indication in the count area of the length of the key. The key area usually contains the value of the highest key among the key values of the logical records in that block. Because of these key areas, the count-key-data format can be used by the system to more quickly locate records on the basis of key value.

A more recent development is the "fixed-block architecture" used in the IBM 3310 and 3370 disk devices. While in the other devices previously discussed, the user sets the length of a block (the "blocking factor" is the number of logical records in a physical record) for a particular data file, the FBA devices have fixed, 512 byte blocks for all data files. Special hardware and software features juggle the data in ways unique to the FBA based devices.

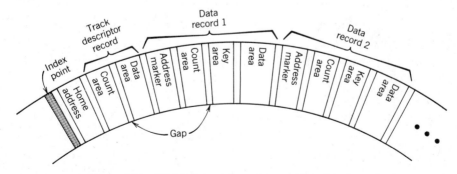

Figure 2.8b. IBM disk track formats: count-key-data format.

Storing Simple Files

Now, let's return to our earlier question of how to take the concept of the simple file and convert it into a form suitable for computer storage and use.

As we've seen in this chapter, both numeric and alphabetic data can be represented as series of bits. A given record is simply a composite string of all of the bits needed to represent each of its fields. And a file is a composite string of all of the bits needed to represent each of its records.

A decision is made as to how many logical records should go into making up one physical record. Then using say, the count-key-day format, the file is loaded, one physical record at a time, onto a disk pack. The data is loaded, serially by bit, on one track of a cylinder, then the next track of the cylinder, and so on until the cylinder is full. Then the process continues with the next cylinder, and the next, until the entire file has been loaded.

References

Bohl, M. *Introduction to IBM Direct Access Storage Devices*, Science Research Associates, Chicago, IL, 1981.

Martin, J., *Computer Data-Base Organization*, 2nd Edition, Prentice-Hall, Englewood Cliffs, NJ, 1977.

Questions and Exercises

2.1.   What is data? Do you think the word "data" should be treated as a singular or plural word? Why?

2.2.   Name some entities and attributes in a university environment.

2.3.   Name some entities and attributes an insurance company would be concerned with.

2.4.   Name some entities and attributes a furniture store would be concerned with.

2.5.   What is the difference between a record type and an occurrence of that record. Give some examples.

2.6.   This file is used in the data processing system of an automobile manufacturer.

Vehicle Number	Vehicle Model	Color	Date of Manufacture
. . .			
527360	Sedan	Blue	9-12-84
527482	Coupe	Red	9-23-84
630975	Sedan	Red	9-27-84
644182	Sedan	Brown	9-27-84
. . .			

a. Name one of the entities described in the file. How would you describe the entity set?

b. What are the attributes of the entities? Choose one of the entities and describe it.

c. Choose one of the attributes and discuss the nature of the set of values that it can take.

2.7. Consider the entities you found in question 2.2, 2.3, or 2.4 and describe some relationships among them.

2.8. Why are relationships between entities important?

2.9. Write the number 84 in the binary, decimal, and floating point representations.

2.10. Discuss the reasons for having both primary and secondary memories in a computer system.

2.11. Describe an application which would require sequential access and an application which would require direct access to the automobile file in question 2.6.

2.12. What is a cylinder in a disk pack? Why is it important to data processing applications?

2.13. In your own words, describe how data moves from a disk pack to main memory.

2.14. Why is it necessary to have special formats for data on disks? Describe one such arrangement.

3

File Organizations and Access Methods

Accessing Data

In the last chapter we established the concept of the simple file, using a payroll file as an example. Now let's talk about the ways we can use it in the payroll and other related applications.

There are four actions that we can take with a file:

1. Simply look at a record without changing it
2. Modify a record (e.g., an employee's salary rate changes)
3. Insert a new record (e.g., a new employee is hired by the company)
4. Delete an existing record (e.g., an employee leaves the company)

Depending on the nature of a particular application, a given program might perform all or only some of those four functions on a file that it accesses. But in addition, there is the question of *which* record or records we want to operate on at a given time.

It's easy enough to visualize the data in a payroll file, and to understand the concepts of sequential and direct retrieval. And we've talked about the general principles behind actually putting data on a disk. But arranging data on a disk so that it will be available for sequential retrieval or for direct retrieval or both, in an efficient manner, is another level of detail which we must pursue before we can go any farther. It is a somewhat complex matter, but certainly understandable, if we take it gradually, step-by-step.

We refer to the way that we store the data for subsequent retrieval as the *file organization*. The way that we retrieve the data, based on it being stored in a particular file organization, is called the *access method*. (Note in passing that the terms "file organization" and "access method" are often used synonymously but this is technically incorrect.)

File Organizations and Access Methods

Introduction

Let's pursue the question of file organizations and access methods with the same example data that we've been using. Remember that, as Figure 3.1 demonstrates, each record consists of the same set of fields as every other record in the collection. For every employee we want to maintain the person's employee number, last name, first name, salary rate, and so forth. Again, we will refer to that general outline or structure of the record as

Employee Number	Employee Last Name	Employee First Name	Salary Rate	Home City	Home State	Home Telephone
06337	Jones	Fred	4.30	New York	NY	212-555-9207
09155	Smith	Susan	5.90	Atlanta	GA	404-555-2287
16840	Adams	John	10.00	Atlanta	GA	404-555-4301
31719	Smith	John	5.50	Detroit	MI	313-555-5186
38102	Baker	George	7.00	Atlanta	GA	404-555-7739
.						
.						
.						

Figure 3.1. Payroll file.

the "record type" and the data for a specific employee (31719, Smith, John, 5.50, . . .) as an "occurrence" of that record, or simply a "record". We will take a look at the major file organization and access method possibilities that exist for such simple collections of records, all of the same type.

Simple, Linear Files

Sequential Files. The simplest way to store a collection of records is in one long list. If the records are in sequence, in terms of one or more of the fields, then we call the arrangement a *sequential* (or "key-sequential") file. Thus, the payroll file in Figure 3.1 is really a sequential file. The field(s) that the file is sequenced on is called the *sequence field.* A field with unique values that identify the records of the file is called a *key* field. In the payroll file the records are sequenced by that key field, which is often but not always the case.

In a simple sequential file, the only way to retrieve the data is to start at the beginning of the file and read one record after the other, in sequence, until you reach the record you are searching for. That sounds terrible if you are only looking for one specific record and it is. Sequential files, without additional devices that we will discuss shortly, were never meant for direct access applications. But they do have the beauty of simplicity, and there are many applications for which they are very well suited. Back to payroll: Every Friday we want to write a payroll check for every employee in the company. In order to do so, we need each employee's record in the payroll file. We might as well read them, one after the other, from the payroll file shown in Figure 3.1. If we are interested in writing the checks

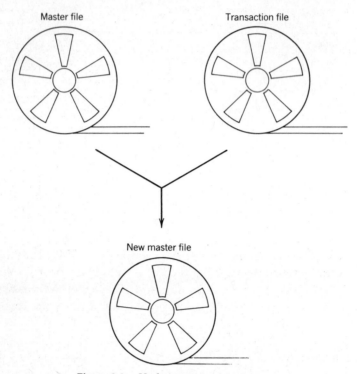

Figure 3.2. Updating a sequential tape file.

in an order other than Employee Number order, then perhaps that file should be stored in that other order.

Sequential files have been around for a long time and the peculiar ways that they have to be processed are classic parts of computer lore. In addition to the problem of simple access discussed previously, are the problems of insertion and deletion of records. After all, you can't insert a new record in between two records that are physically nudged up against each other on the storage device, and you can't delete a record unless you can find it first, which brings us right back to the direct access problem again. The way that it's done is illustrated in Figure 3.2, for updating a sequential file (called the "master file") on a tape. A "transaction file" is set up on another tape. It includes the new records to be inserted, the key field values of the records to be deleted (with an appropriate delete code appended), and the key field values of the records to be updated plus the new data that constitutes the update. All of these are sorted together in the same key field sequence that the master file is in. A program starts reading through the two tapes in tandem, looking for matches of the key fields for the delete and update operations, and for the proper spot to place the new records for the insert operations. While it's reading through the master and transaction tapes, it's also creating a new tape, called the "new master", which will contain all of the data from the master tape, subject to the changes dictated by the transaction tape. Unaffected records are simply copied onto the new master tape. Records to be deleted are simply not copied onto the new tape. Records to be inserted are placed onto the new tape, merged into the correct location to maintain the key sequence. Updates are performed and the updated records are copied over to the new tape in sequence. At the end of the entire operation, the new master tape and file become the master tape and file. The original tape is often kept around as backup in case something goes wrong with the new tape.

Non-Sequential Files. There are circumstances in which it makes sense to have a simple linear file which is not sequenced by any field. One example of the use of such an arrangement is the chronological "pile" in which every time some new data, or record, is received, it is plunked down at the end of the file. The data is said to be stored in "arrival sequence".

But it may also make sense to maintain such nonsequential files for a broader class of application situations. Nonsequential files, assuming that they serve some useful purpose in the first place, have the following clear advantage. No time or effort have to be spent to maintain the file in physical sequence by merging, sorting, or any other manipulation, either when the file is first created, or later on when new records are added to the end of the file. But what about their serving a useful purpose? And if they're not in any sequence, how can you find a particular record you are looking for? Clearly for this to make any sense out of nonsequential files, there must be a way to find particular records in them directly. Another intriguing thought is that although such files are not maintained in any *physical* sequence, it might be useful to be able to, at some time, for some application, read the file in sequence based on the values of one or more fields. That may sound contradictory, but it's not, as we shall soon see. In fact, such files are quite common today and will be discussed many times in this book. The mechanism for providing direct access to, and externally maintaining the sequence of, such files is described in the next section.

Indexed Files

As we have said, there are legitimate reasons for wanting to store records in simple linear files, which are not in physical sequence by any field while at the same time:

1. Expecting to be able to access those records directly, and
2. Expecting to be able to retrieve those records in sequence by some field, whether or not the file is stored in physical sequence by that or any other field.

All of this sounds *so good* that we are at once tempted to expand on it and say that it might also be desirable to have *sequential files* whose records can be accessed directly and whose data can be retrieved in sequence based on a field *other than* the key field on which the file is physically sequenced. While all of this may sound like it's counter to what we've already said about linear files, there is a device that can be added to the picture to accomplish just these goals. That device is called an *index*.

The interesting thing about it is that, while we will, of course, explain it here in terms of computers, the principle involved is exactly the same as for the index in the back of a book. After all, a book is a storage medium for information about some subject. Think of the page numbers as addresses of "chunks" of information, namely whatever words are on those particular pages. The table of contents in the front of the book merely summarizes what is in the book by major topics, and is written in the same order as the material in the book. But what do you do if you want to find some specific piece of material, too minor to be mentioned in the table of contents, without having to laboriously page through the whole book? What you do is turn to the very end of the book and look up the item in the index. The index is arranged alphabetically by item, without regard to where a given item appears in the book. As humans we have the ability to efficiently do a quick alphabetic search through the index to find the topic of interest. Then what? Next to the item that you find in the index appears a page number. In fact, it is a "direct pointer" to the page in the book where the material appears. You go directly to that page and find the material there, Figure 3.3.

The simplest kind of index for a data file, the *simple linear index*, will be discussed and illustrated in this section. Of course this term should sound familiar, since we have been talking about simple linear files, and in fact such an index is merely a usage variation of that kind of file.

Based on the foregoing discussion, there are four distinct cases to discuss in the usage of an index (simple linear or otherwise) with a simple linear file. The four cases are distinguished by whether or not the file is stored in sequence by some field, and whether the desired operation involves the direct retrieval of a single record or the retrieval of all of the records of the file in order by some set of field values. The following chart and text explain the four cases.

	The file is in physical sequence by some field	The file is not in physical sequence by any field
The concern is direct retrieval of a single record	Case 1	Case 3
The concern is retrieval of all of the records in order based on the values in some field.	Case 2	Case 4

1.   The file is stored in physical sequence by some field and in addition direct access is needed via one of the fields (which may or may not be the sequence field).

When the *search field*—a specific value of which will be used to identify the record sought in a direct access—is the *same* field as the "sequence field" (the field used to physically sequence the file), then this case is a classic in the area of file organizations and access methods called *indexed-sequential organization*. Because of its historic importance and interesting implementations, it will be treated separately in the next section of this chapter. In the other case, the file is stored in physical sequence by some field, and direct access is required, but the search field is *different* than

Figure 3.3.   The index in a book.

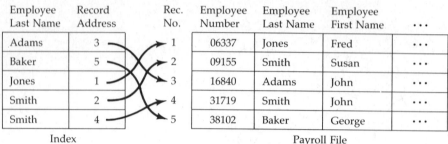

Employee Last Name	Record Address		Rec. No.	Employee Number	Employee Last Name	Employee First Name	...
Adams	3		1	06337	Jones	Fred	...
Baker	5		2	09155	Smith	Susan	...
Jones	1		3	16840	Adams	John	...
Smith	2		4	31719	Smith	John	...
Smith	4		5	38102	Baker	George	...

Index

Payroll File
(Sequenced on Employee Number)

Figure 3.4.   Sequential file indexed on a different field.

the sequence field. In that case, the fact that the file is in sequence (by that other field) is irrelevant. The file might as well not be stored in any physical sequence at all. Thus in essence, the situation is really the same as that of case 3, and will be discussed there.

2.   The file is stored in physical sequence by some field and there is a requirement to be able to retrieve the records in sequence by some field.

Obviously, if the field on which the retrieval is to be based is the field that the file is physically sequenced on, then this requirement just amounts to reading the records in their physical sequence. The other, somewhat more interesting, case, is when the requirement is to retrieve the records in sequence based on the values in a field *other* than the one on which the file is physically sequenced. The right-hand side of Figure 3.4 shows the Employee Number, Employee Last Name, and Employee First Name fields of the Payroll File of Figure 3.1 (the rest of the fields are assumed to be there too). Notice also that the records of the file are numbered, 1,2, ... These numbers, known as "relative record numbers," are clearly a form of addressing individual records. It is the case that given a relative record number, the systems software is capable of making some address calculations and directly finding the record associated with it. Remember that the Payroll File is in sequence by Employee Number. The left-hand side of Figure 3.4 shows a simple linear index, designed to provide sequential access to the Payroll File by Employee Last Name. The left-hand column of the index is identical to the Employee Last Name column of the Payroll File, except that it has been sorted so that the values are in alphabetic order. The right-hand entry of each row of the index is intended to provide the address of the record in the Payroll File which contains the value of the Last Name Field in that index row. The address can take the form of an absolute or actual disk address, or the form of a relative record number, which is the case

Employee Last Name	Record Address		Rec. No.	Employee Number	Employee Last Name	Employee First Name	...
Adams	5		1	31719	Smith	John	...
Baker	4		2	06337	Jones	Fred	...
Jones	2		3	09155	Smith	Susan	...
Smith	1		4	38102	Baker	George	...
Smith	3		5	16840	Adams	John	...

Index   Payroll File
(In No Particular Sequence)

Figure 3.5. Non-sequential indexed file.

in Figure 3.4. Thus if we wish to retrieve the records of the file alphabetically by Employee Last Name, we simply read the index, line by line, and pick up record number 3 (the one for Adams) in the Payroll File, followed by record number 5 (the one for Baker), and so forth. Notice that there are two employees whose last names are Smith. That's why there are two lines in the index for the name Smith (in no particular order), each pointing to a different "Smith record" in the Payroll File.

3. The file is not stored in any physical sequence, but direct access is needed via one of the fields.

Figure 3.5 shows the sample payroll records of Figure 3.1, physically stored so that they are not in sequence by any field. It also shows an index into that new file based on the Employee Last Name field. This index is and must be in sequence by Employee Last Name. Suppose that there is a need to directly find the payroll record for Jones. First, a program known as a "search" program or routine would find Jones in the third line of the index. We won't stop here to discuss search routines, but they work, in concept, much the same way that a person would search for an item in the index at the back of a book, quickly "homing in" on the desired item. Once Jones is found in the index, the associated index entry indicates that the record in the main file with an Employee Last Name field value of Jones is relative record number 2. The system can then go directly to record number 2 in the main file and pick up the record for Jones.

4. The file is not stored in any physical sequence, but there is a requirement to be able to retrieve the records in sequence by one of the fields.

Let's revisit the unordered file in Figure 3.5. In case 3, we showed how to use the index in that figure to find a record in the file directly. But that same index can also be used to retrieve the records of the file in the sequence of the field that the index is based on (Employee Last Name in this case), even though the file is not stored in physical sequence based on any field. As in case 2, this is accomplished by starting with the first line of the index (which is in order by that field) and reading down it line by line, each time retrieving the record in the main file indicated by the address in the index line. In this case, we would retrieve record number 5 first (the one for Adams), followed by record number 4 (the one for Baker), and so on.

Let's review a few of the points about indexes and notice a few others. By the way, these characteristics are conceptual in nature at this point and may vary in actual implementations that exist today.

- An index can be built based on any field of a file, whether or not the file is in physical sequence based on that or any other field.
- An index can be built based on a combination of fields. For example, in the Payroll File example, we might want to be able to directly find a record based on Employee Last Name *and* Employee First Name. The index in that case would include both an Employee Last Name column and an Employee First Name column, as well as the required column with the corresponding address into the main file.
- Any index can be used both for direct access based on the indexed field and for sequential retrieval of the records according to the sequence of that field.
- Many separate indexes into a file can exist simultaneously, each based on a different field or combination of fields of that file. The indexes are quite independent of each other.
- When certain changes are made to the file, the indexes must be updated. For example, if the value of one of the fields in one of the records in the file changes, and if there is an index built for that file based on that field, then that index must be updated. For example, in Figure 3.5, if Susan Smith marries and adopts her husband's last name (Eller), then not only does record number 3 in the Payroll File have to be updated, but the fifth row of the index must be changed as well. Eller must replace Smith in that row of the index and the entire index must be resorted into alphabetic order again. Obviously the field values in the index must at all times match the corresponding field values in the main file for the concept of the index to make any sense. This is also true if a new record is inserted into the file, or an existing one is deleted. The index must actually be resorted with the new data, either on the spot, or at some later time. If it is to be done at a later time,

which, as we shall see is usually advantageous in terms of performance, then the updates must be kept in a list which can somehow be accessed in case a retrieval must be done based on one of the new entries before the index is resorted.

Indexed-Sequential Files

Introduction. As we said in the last section, when a file is sequenced on a particular field, and an index for that file is built based on that *same* field, then the arrangement is known as an *indexed-sequential file.* The benefits of such a structure are clear for certain applications. For example, consider the Payroll File constructed in an indexed-sequential fashion, with the Employee Number field used both as the sequence field and as the field on which the index is based. Using that one file, we can generate payroll checks in sequential, employee number order every Friday, and using the index, we can directly find individual records for updates (e.g., if employee 31719's salary increases).

Indexed-sequential files have a long history in data processing, emerging as a natural extension of simple sequential files. Two aspects of indexed-sequential files have been studied in depth over the years and a number of variations of them have emerged. These two aspects are the structure of the index, and the way that new records are added to the file so that both the sequential and direct access nature are maintained. We will take a look at three ways of structuring indexed-sequential files, paying particular attention to the index structure and the insertion method for new records. The three variations are the simple index, the multilevel hardware oriented index, and the B-tree oriented index.

Simple Index. Figure 3.4 showed the Payroll File sequenced on the Employee Number field, together with an index based on a different field of that file. Figure 3.6 shows the same file, still sequenced on the Employee Number field, but with a simple linear index based on the *same* field. Such an arrangement, using a simple linear index, is perhaps the simplest kind of indexed-sequential file. It should be clear at this point that the records in the file in Figure 3.4 can be accessed sequentially by employee number since they are stored one after the other on the disk pack in that order. They can also be retrieved directly by employee number using the index with an appropriate search routine.

You may well wonder what the point is of creating a separate index which repeats one of the fields of the original file in the same order. If you can apply a search routine to such an index to find a record on a direct

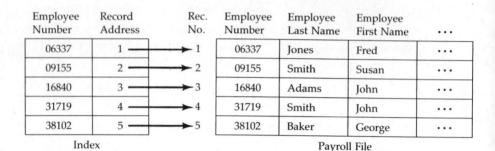

Figure 3.6. Sequential file indexed on the sequence field.

basis, why not apply the same search routine to the main file and save all of the bother of having a separate index? The answer lies in the fact that whatever is being searched has to be dragged into main memory for the actual search work. The larger the file gets, the larger the index becomes, and the larger the index becomes, the bigger a job it becomes to search through the index for the particular key value sought. If it is too large for all of it to be in primary memory at one time, then a scheme has to be developed to shuffle parts of it into and out of primary memory from secondary memory during the search. This can quickly become an unacceptable bottleneck. And if the entire records, rather than just the search fields, have to be brought into primary memory for the search, then the problem is compounded to a much worse degree. (Of course, for a large file so many index records would have to be brought into primary memory that it wouldn't matter how small they are and this organization would be impractical.)

As for the question of how to insert new records into the file, the situation is the same as for the sequential files that we discussed earlier. The file has to be rewritten, with the new record(s) inserted in the correct sequence, or it has to be resorted in place. Entries for the new record(s) must, of course, also be placed in the correct sequence in the index, necessitating a sorting operation there too.

Multilevel Hardware-Dictated Index. To introduce another type of index, consider the following situation. Let's say that you go to a large, eight story department store to buy a copy of a particular book, Figure 3.7. You could wander down every aisle of every floor until you find it, but even the most compulsive shopper would find that unacceptably tedious. More likely the first thing that you would do upon entering the store is to look for the store directory. It alphabetically lists all of the different departments

Figure 3.7. The levels of search in a department store.

in the store and indicates which floor each is on. You find the entry for "Books" and note that it is on the fifth floor. So you take the escalators up to the fifth floor. There are a number of different departments on that floor and so rather than wander around the floor looking for the books department, you ask a store employee where it is. He or she points you to it, and you walk over. You could look through every shelf in every bookcase in the books department until you find the one that you want, but the different bookcases have signs on them indicating topical categories (fiction, cookbooks, etc.). So you scan the signs and find the bookcase with the category of books that the one you're looking for fits in. The books in each bookcase are organized alphabetically by author, so you scan the shelves of that bookcase until you find the book that you want.

Think about that series of actions. You successively narrowed the search, based on physical characteristics of the environment (first floors, then departments on a floor, then display cases—bookcases in this example) until you had it down to a small enough number of pieces of merchandise to scan for the one that you wanted. It sure beat an exhaustive search of every item in the store from the ground floor up!

An example of an analogous search procedure for a record in a computer file is IBM's Indexed Sequential Access Method (ISAM). It too successively narrows the search for the sought after item (record) based on physical characteristics of the environment (the disk packs).

Figure 3.8 shows a personnel file and its associated three level index organized in the ISAM style. (The third index level is stored in the combination of the "track 0's" of all of the cylinders.) Each record consists of a number of fields: the five digit employee number, which will serve as the key field, the employee's last name, and so on. Employees were assigned employee numbers on a random basis when they joined the company, so their names are in no particular sequence relative to the employee

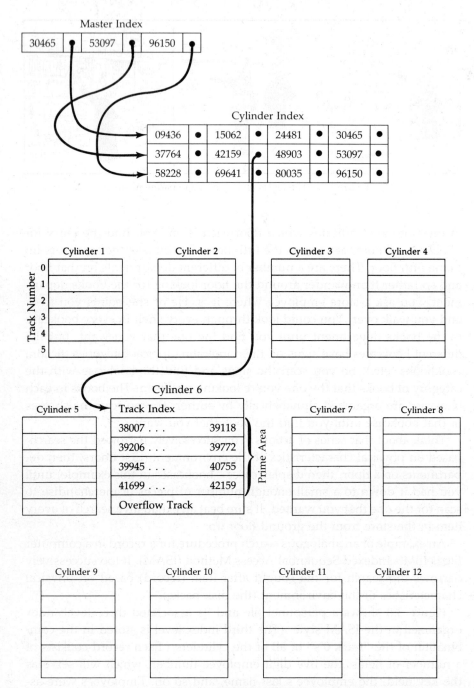

Figure 3.8. IBM ISAM file: Index and data.

	Normal Entry for Track 1	Overflow Entry for Track 1		
Track Index	39118 T1 39118 XX	39772 T2 39772 XX	40755 T3 40755 XX	42159 T4 42159 XX
Prime Area	38007 Jones . . .	38642 Adams . . .	38750 Taylor . . .	39118 Hall . . .
	39206 Carter . . .	39353 Newton . . .	39541 Jones . . .	39772 Allen . . .
	39945 Smith . . .	40230 James . .	40617 Sloan . . .	40755 Potter . . .
	41699 Baker . . .	41837 Dodd . . .	41922 Logan . . .	42159 Smith . . .
Overflow Track				

Figure 3.9. IBM ISAM file: Cylinder 6 in detail.

numbers. Let's assume that we are dealing with disk packs which have six recording surfaces, meaning that there are six tracks per cylinder (numbered 0-5). Initially the records are stored sequentially, based on the key field, in the "prime area," which in Figure 3.8, is tracks 1–4 of each of the twelve cylinders. Figure 3.9 shows cylinder 6 in more detail. There are 16 records in our personnel file with key values from 38007 to 42159 and they happened to fall into the prime area of cylinder 6 when the file was loaded. Before going into the matter of the index, note and remember that whatever else can be said about the ISAM organization, the data is laid out sequentially in the prime area. By reading each prime area track of each cylinder in sequence, the file can easily be retrieved, record by record, in order by the employee number (key) field.

Now let's see how the multilevel (also called "nonlinear") index provides for direct retrieval of the records based on the employee number field. As Figure 3.8 illustrates, there are basically three levels of index, each of which contains a subset of the keys of the file. Each index level maintains its keys in sequence. The first level is called the "master index" and can be assumed to be in primary memory. The pointers from the master index lead to groups of cylinder pointers in the "cylinder index." In Figure 3.8, the cylinder index has three such groups (each row is a group). Each pointer in the cylinder index points, uniquely, to a particular cylinder. The first track (track 0) of each cylinder is called a "track index" and leads to a given track on that cylinder, where the record with a particular key value will be found.

Let's take an example and see how that process works with the file shown in Figure 3.8. Suppose that the record sought is the one for employee 40230. The access method scans the master index from left to right looking for the first key value *higher* than 40230. That's 53097. It then follows the pointer associated with value 53097 to the second row, or group of key values, in the cylinder index. It repeats the process, scanning that group of keys from left to right, looking for the first value higher than 40230. That's 42159. Now it follows the pointer attached to that value to the beginning of cylinder 6, as shown in the figure. The first track of that cylinder (track 0) contains the track index for that track. Switching to Figure 3.9, we see that the track index consists of a "normal entry" and an "overflow entry" for each track in the prime area of that cylinder. A normal entry contains the highest key value on the track and the track number (or address). An overflow entry, initially, also contains the highest key value on the track and a dummy entry (shown as XX in Figure 3.9). The system scans the normal entry values, again looking for the first value higher than 40230. That's 40755. The pointer associated with 40755 indicates that the record with key value 40230 will be found on track 3 of that cylinder. The system then scans track 3 until it finds the record with key value 40230. As in the department store example, that may sound complicated at first, but it's incomparably more efficient than conducting a sequential search for the same record.

As you look at Figure 3.9, a problem may occur to you. It looks like the data, as initially loaded, fills each of the prime area tracks, and that's true! When new records are added to the file where do they go, how does the file remain in sequence and how is the direct access to all records preserved? Good question!

The answer begins with the overflow tracks at the end of each cylinder (and other so called "independent overflow areas") and includes the overflow entries in each track index. Suppose that we want to add a new record, with key value 38693, to the file. The system will proceed through the three index levels, as if it were trying to find the record with that key value. Following the same search reasoning described earlier, it would decide to place the record on track 1 of cylinder 6 (see Figure 3.9). But of course, it finds that track to be full. It then proceeds to insert the new record in its rightful place on the track, slides all of the other records down one position to the right, and bumps the last record on that track off to the overflow track, as shown in Figure 3.10. The track index values for track 1 are changed so that:

1. The normal entry shows the new highest key value of all of the records on the track proper (which is now 38750).

2. The overflow entry shows:

    a. The *last* overflow record for that track by *key value* (which is 39118), and

    b. The *first* overflow record for that track by *address (which is track 5, record 1).*

38750 T1 39118 T5 Rec 1	39772 T2 39772 XX	40755 T3 40755 XX	42159 T4 42159 XX
38007 Jones . . .	38642 Adams . . .	38693 Hughes . . .	38750 Taylor . . .
39206 Carter . . .	39353 Newton . . .	39541 Jones . . .	39772 Allen . . .
39945 Smith . . .	40230 James . . .	40617 Sloan . . .	40755 Potter . . .
41699 Baker . . .	41837 Dodd . . .	41922 Logan . . .	42159 Smith . . .
39118 Hall . . . T1			

Figure 3.10. IBM ISAM file: Cylinder 6 with record 38693 added.

Figure 3.11 continues the illustration with the addition of the record with key value 38444. It gets placed in that same track 1, and the record with key value 38750 gets bumped into the overflow track. Maintaining the sequence, the track index now shows 38693 as the highest key value on track 1 proper, 39118 as the key value of the last record of that track that was placed on the overflow track, and track 5, record 2 as the address of the first overflow record for that track. Notice also that all of the overflow records for a given track are "chained" together in a linked list. As shown in Figure 3.11, if a record that should be on track 1 of that cylinder isn't there (and has a value higher than 38693) the track index points first to the record with key value 38750. Then if that's not the desired record, it has a pointer associated with it that points to the next record, in sequence, that would have been on track 1 had there been enough room there, and so on. The logic of the overflow entries in the track index sounds more complicated than it is. In effect it tells you *where* the first overflow record for the track is, and *what* the last overflow record for the track is.

The system must obviously use the overflow arrangement both in conducting subsequent sequential retrievals and direct searches. As more records are added to the file, more prime area tracks will have one or more

38693 T1 39118 T5 Rec 2	39772 T2 39772 XX	40755 T3 40755 XX	42159 T4 42159 XX
38007 Jones . . .	38444 Evans . . .	38642 Adams . . .	38693 Hughes . . .
39206 Carter . . .	39353 Newton . . .	39541 Jones . . .	39772 Allen . . .
39945 Smith . . .	40230 James . . .	40617 Sloan . . .	40755 Potter . . .
41699 Baker . . .	41837 Dodd . . .	41922 Logan . . .	42159 Smith . . .
39118 Hall . . . T1	38750 Taylor . . . T5 Rec 1		

Figure 3.11. IBM ISAM file: Cylinder 6 with record 38444 added.

of their records bumped to overflow. First the overflow track on the same cylinder will be used, then, when that fills up, independent overflow tracks on other cylinders will be used. Retrieval and search operations will get progressively slower as two tracks have to be read, in the case where the regular overflow track is used, and the disk access arm mechanism has to jump around among the different cylinders, in the case where the independent overflow tracks must be used. To help fix that problem, the file must be occasionally reorganized. In that operation the entire file, overflowed records and all, are read in key sequence and written onto *the prime areas* of another set of cylinders, while the system builds a new set of appropriate indexes.

B-Tree Oriented Index. While the ISAM multilevel index concept was an important step forward in the history of data processing, it does have its shortcomings. For one thing, its being inherently dependent on the physical attributes of the storage devices limits its flexibility. The way that overflow records are handled makes retrieval cumbersome as the number of overflow records builds up. And in the same vein, it requires comparatively frequent reorganizations to move the overflow records back into the prime areas.

A newer kind of multilevel indexed sequential file has been developed which is hardware independent, and is capable of absorbing new records in a much less traumatic way than in ISAM. It is based on a structure known as a "B-Tree." An example of this newer organization is the Key Sequenced Data Set (KSDS) of IBM's Virtual Storage Access Method (VSAM). The term Virtual Storage Access Method (singular) is really something of a misnomer, as VSAM is actually a collection of three different access methods, one of which is KSDS. The other two are Entry Sequenced Data Set (ESDS) which is designed for sequential files, and Relative Record Data Set (RRDS) which is used for hashed (see the next section) files.

Figure 3.12 illustrates the KSDS arrangement. The storage space in KSDS is divided into *control intervals* and *control areas*. A control interval is the unit of transfer of data between primary and secondary memory. It may be, but need not be, a disk track. A control area is made up of a number of control intervals. It may be, but need not be, a disk cylinder. The multilevel index, like that of ISAM, is hierarchical in nature, and may increase in depth as the file grows. There is one index record at the topmost level, and the index fans out downwards from there. The number of levels in the index is dependent on the size of the file, and the size of the index records. All of the index records of the lowest level of the index are collectively known as the *sequence set*. There is a single sequence set record for each control area of the data file and there is the option for each sequence

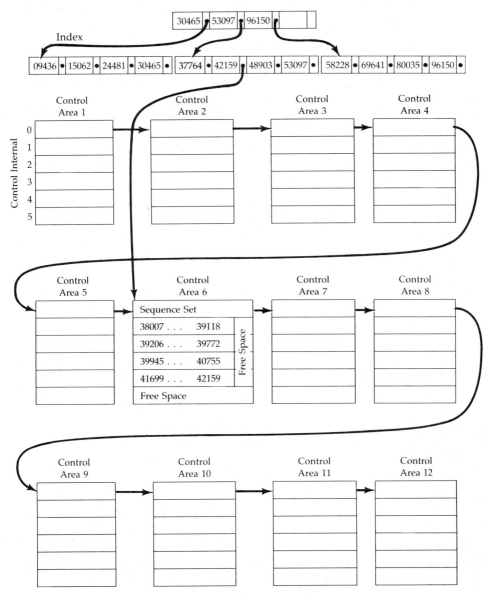

Figure 3.12.   IBM KSDS file: Index and data.

set record to be stored with the control area that it indexes. This is for performance reasons and is illustrated in Figure 3.12.

    The entries in the index are constructed in much the same way that they were in ISAM. An index entry at a given level of the index represents the highest index entry of one of the index records at the next lower level of the index, and points to that index record. For example, in Figure 3.12,

Entry for
Track 1

Sequence Set	39118 T1		39772 T2		40755 T3		42159 T4		free T5	
	38007 Jones . . .	38642 Adams		38750 Taylor		39118 Hall		free space		
	39206 Carter	39353 Newton		39541 Jones		39772 Allen		free space		
	39945 Smith	40230 James		40617 Sloan		40755 Potter		free space		
	41699 Baker	41837 Dodd		41922 Logan		42159 Smith		free space		
	free control interval									

Figure 3.13.   IBM KSDS file: Control Area 6 in detail.

entry 30465 in the top level index record points to the index record in the next level down which ends with (its own copy of) entry 30465. Each entry of a sequence set record points to a single control interval of the data file control area that it indexes, and, consistently with the indexing scheme, contains the highest key value of the data records in that control interval. This is illustrated, for control area 6, in Figure 3.13.

It will turn out, as we shall soon see, that while the data in a given control interval will always be in sequence, the control intervals may, as time goes on, get out of sequence because of insertions. The question then becomes: How can the file be retrieved in key sequence? The answer is that the sequence set records always keep track of the correct sequence, and the sequence set records are all linked together by a set of "horizontal pointers," as shown in Figure 3.12. By following the chain of sequence set records, and ignoring the higher levels of the index, the file can be retrieved in key sequence.

Again as in ISAM, to find a record on a direct basis, the system starts at the left of the single index record at the top of the index hierarchy, and scans to the right looking for the first value higher than the key value of the record being sought. It then follows that pointer down to an index record at the next level of the index, and continues this process until it reaches the correct data file control interval which it scans for the target data record.

The real beauty of KSDS lies in the way that new records are inserted into the file. In ISAM, insertions caused increasingly long access paths to some records as the overflow chains grew. In KSDS, all records have the same access path length regardless of how many new records have been inserted. The frequent reorganizations needed in volatile ISAM files are reduced. One of the things that makes this possible is the way that free

39118 T1	39772 T2	40755 T3	42159 T4	free T5
38007 Jones . . .	38642 Adams	38693 Hughes	38750 Taylor	39118 Hall . . .
39206 Carter	39353 Newton	39541 Jones	39772 Allen	free space
39945 Smith	40230 James	40617 Sloan	40755 Potter	free space
41699 Baker	41837 Dodd	41922 Logan	42159 Smith	free space
free control interval				

Figure 3.14. IBM KSDS file: Control Area 6 with record 38693 added.

space is deliberately left in the file as it is loaded. Figure 3.13 shows free space left in each control interval containing data records and one control interval left entirely free. Additional free control areas are also provided. This free space, used as described in the following, forms the basis for the KSDS insertion technique.

Figure 3.14 shows control area 6 with the addition of the record with key value 38693. Based on key sequence, this record should be placed in control interval 1, and, in fact, it can be, because there is sufficient free space in that control interval to accommodate it. The new record is inserted in between the records with key values 38642 and 38750; the records with key values 38750 and 39118 are shifted to the right so that the insertion does not disturb the file sequence.

Figure 3.15 shows control area 6 with the addition of the record with key value 38444. As in the last case, that record should go into control interval 1. But this time there is no room for it, all of the free space in the control interval having been used up already. So the system goes through an exercise known as "splitting." It begins by looking for a completely free control interval in the control area. If it finds one it divides all of the data on the full control interval plus the new record being inserted, leaving about half the data on the original control interval, and putting the other half on what was the completely free control interval. Thus in Figure 3.15,

38642 T1	39118 T5	39772 T2	40755 T3	42159 T4
38007 Jones	38444 Evans	38642 Adams	free space	
39206 Carter	39353 Newton	39541 Jones	39772 Allen . . .	free space
39945 Smith	40230 James	40617 Sloan	40755 Potter . . .	free space
41699 Baker	41837 Dodd	41922 Logan	42159 Smith . . .	free space
38693 Hughes	38750 Taylor	39118 Hall	free space	

Figure 3.15. IBM KSDS file: Control Area 6 with record 38444 added.

the records with keys 38007, 38444 (the new record), and 38642 remain on control interval 1, while 38693, 38750, and 39118 are all moved to control interval 5. The sequence set is changed, as shown in that figure, so that the keys in it, representing the highest key on each control interval, remain in sequence, even though the control intervals no longer are.

What would happen if this process continued to the point that a new record had to be inserted into a full control interval and there were no more free control intervals left in its control area with which to perform a control interval split? Then a new, completely free control area would be obtained and the entire control area would split. About half of the control area's data would remain on it, and the other half would be moved to the new control area. But, as you will remember from Figure 3.12, every control area must be pointed to from the next to the lowest level of the index (the level just above the sequence set). So the addition of a new control area to the file means that a new entry must be added to that level of the index. That's fine, as long as there is room in the appropriate index record. If not then it splits, causing another entry to be added to the index level above it. The highest index level may only consist of one index record. So if this process ever backs all the way up to the top index level, and finds the index record there to be full, the system must split that index record and add another index record at a new higher level (what will be the new top level) of the index.

Hashed Files

There are many applications in which all file accesses are to be done on a direct basis and speed is of the essence. For such situations, the best approach is the *hashed file*. Let's assume, just to be consistent, that we're still working with our payroll records, but that now we are only concerned with fast direct access. Let's also assume, just for the sake of argument, that each of the records is 100 bytes or characters long.

So we have some unspecified number of records, each 100 bytes long, each with a 5 digit unique numeric key field. If there were no restrictions at all on how to store the file on a disk pack, how might we go about storing the records for the fastest possible access? Figure 3.16 shows a view of one way to store the data. Suppose that we choose an arbitrary starting point, or address, on the disk, and place the record (if it exists) with key field value (Employee Number) 00000 there. Then we place the record with key value 00001 at the point 100 bytes beyond the arbitrary starting point. The record with key value 00002 starts 200 bytes beyond that point, and so on for every record (or, really, the ones that exist) through the record with key value 99999.

Address	Employee Number	Employee Last Name	. . .
0	00000	Dobbs	. . .
100	00001	Taylor	. . .
200	00002	Miller	. . .
. . .	. . .	. . .	
50,000	00500	Garner	. . .
. . .	. . .	. . .	
9,999,900	99999	Monroe	. . .

◄——————— 100 bytes ———————►

Figure 3.16. Generalized direct file.

If we want to find the record with key value 00500, then after multiplying that number by the record length 100, we look at the position on the disk 50,000 bytes forward from the arbitrary starting point of the file, and there we find the record we're looking for. What could be simpler? Or faster?

But as so often is the case when something seems so simple, there is a fly in the ointment (or, since we're dealing with computers, maybe we should say a bug in the ointment). Although we can accommodate 100,000 different records with a 5 digit decimal key, we probably don't have 100,000 records to store. Perhaps there are only 200 employees in the company. The point is, that in order to use the simple method of storage and retrieval previously suggested, we would have to reserve 10 million bytes on the disk, enough for the full potential of 100,000 records, even though we know that we only have 200 records to store, which only require 20,000 bytes of storage. The difference between 10,000,000 bytes and 20,000 bytes represents a huge and unacceptable amount of wasted space on the disk. That's the catch. But still, being able to "associate" a key value with a storage location, is a very tempting thought.

What about the following variation? Can we work on the premise of having only a limited amount of storage space set aside for the file, and converting the key field value into one of those available storage addresses? For example, can we take a five digit key field with value 52866 and convert it to relative storage location 116 (out of, say, 250)?

Figure 3.17 shows a schematic of a disk storage area, in which we can store 250 records (numbered 0 to 249), each 100 bytes long. Perhaps we have 200 records to store and, in addition, want to leave room for further expansion. Try the following method as a straightforward way of converting from the key value to a storage location. Divide the key value (52866) by the number of storage locations (250). The result, with a handy pocket calculator, is 211.464. But remember back to grammar school and "long division"; another way of expressing that result is a quotient of 211, and a remainder of 116. The remainder, in that division, will *always* be an integer from 0 to one less than the divisor (250), or 249 in this case. But that is the same number of storage slots (each 100 bytes long) that we allocated in the area shown in Figure 3.17. What if we simply store the record with a particular key value at the storage location indicated by the remainder of the division of the key value by the number of storage locations, as demonstrated above? In order to retrieve the same record at a later time, we would go through the same procedure and look for the record at the location indicated by the division operation. The technique we have been talking about is called the *division-remainder method*, and is one of many so-called *hashing methods* that can be used for key conversion in hashed file storage.

There is one problem that may have occurred to you. Surely continuing with the previous example, there may be many five digit numbers, which when divided by 250, have 116 as the remainder. But only one of them (the first one that came along) can be stored at that location. This problem is known as the *collision* problem, and the two (or more) key values which "hash" to the same storage location are called *synonyms*. But all is not lost; there are several ways to deal with that situation. Figure 3.18 shows the same diagram as in Figure 3.17, but with some extra storage space added beyond the original 250 slots, and a new pointer or address field added to each record. As an example, assume that we stored three records, with key values 52866, 37616, and 25116. These three key values happened to

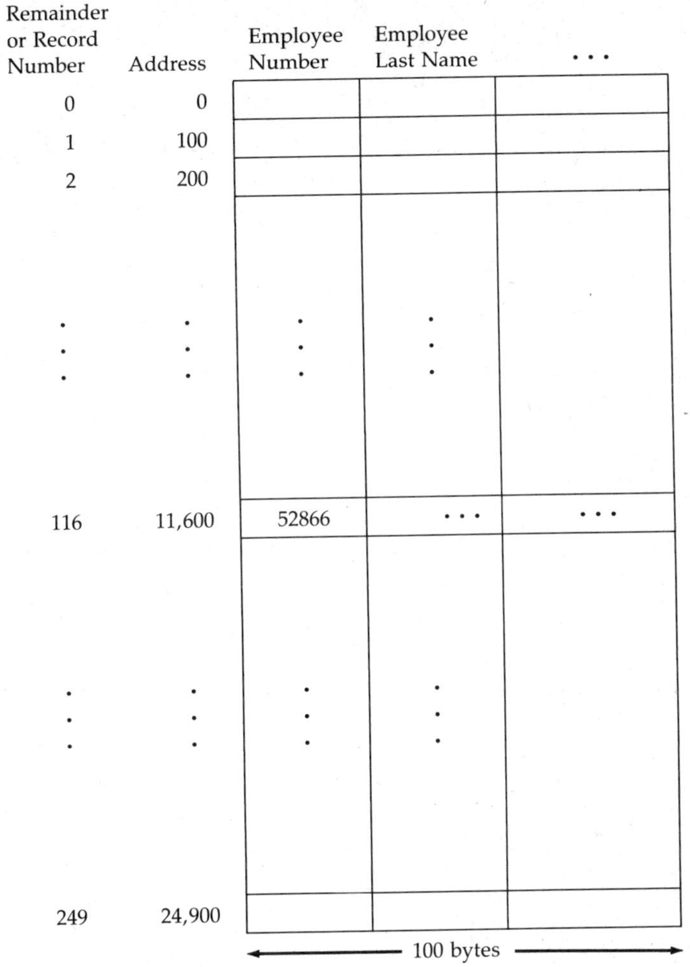

Remainder or Record Number	Address	Employee Number	Employee Last Name	. . .
0	0			
1	100			
2	200			
. . .	. . .	. . .	. . .	
116	11,600	52866	. . .	. . .
. . .	. . .	. . .	. . .	
249	24,900			

◄─────── 100 bytes ───────►

Figure 3.17. Direct file, Division-Remainder method.

hash to the same storage location, 116. One is stored at location 116, another is at 250, and the third at 251. Notice how the new pointer field forms a "chain" connecting the three together. If you try to find the record with key value 25116 at location 116, you find the record with key value 52866 there instead. Then you follow the pointer at the end of that record to location 250 (27,500 bytes into the file), and there you find the record with key value 37616. This record in turn points to location 252 where you finally find the record you were looking for, the one with key value 25116.

There are several other things to point out about hashed access methods.

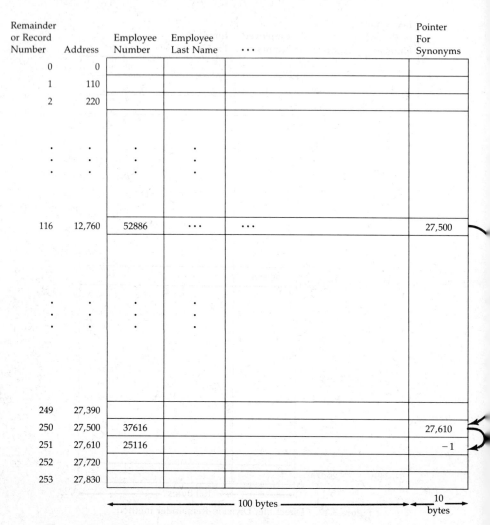

Figure 3.18. Direct file, Division-Remainder method (with chained synonyms).

- There is no physical sequence of the stored data. The nature of the hashing methods is to scatter the records in the allocated storage area in a way that makes direct access as efficient as possible, without regard to anything else, including sequence.
- Over the years, many different hashing methods have been developed, the division-remainder method being but one.
- The most important measure of the goodness of a hashing method is how well it minimizes the number of collisions. The only way to find that out is to actually try to store a given set of records with a given

hashing method. Sometimes changes can be made in the parameters of a method. For example, in the division-remainder method, it's known that, in general, if the number of storage locations, and thus the divisor, is a prime number, or is odd and can't be evenly divided by any number less than 20, then there is a better chance of having fewer collisions. So in the example that we were looking at, instead of allocating 250 storage locations, we would allocate a number equal to the next prime number above 250.

Conclusion

It's still early in the book, but we've already made tremendous progress in developing data storage concepts. In Chapter 2 we saw how bits and bytes can be arranged to represent data, and how that data can be organized into simple files. We also discussed the manner in which these bits and bytes representing the data can be placed on disk media.

In this chapter, we developed another critical data storage idea: that there are some applications that require records of a file to be available in sequence by some field value and some applications that require records of a file to be available on a direct basis. Based on the types of applications that access them, some files must be set up for sequential retrieval, some for direct retrieval, and some for both. We proceded, in this, chapter, to discuss different schemes for organizing data records for those three categories of retrieval requirements.

But while we've built a strong base to work from, the simplicity of (independent) simple files, unfortunately, leaves much to be desired in efficiency in some common data storage situations. We will take a look at these problems in Chapter 4.

References

Bohl, M., *Introduction to IBM Direct Access Storage Devices*, Science Research Associates, Chicago, IL, 1981.

Kroenke, D., *Database Processing*, 2nd ed., Science Research Associates, Chicago, IL, 1983.

Lewis, T. G., and Smith, M. Z., *Applying Data Structures*, 2nd ed., Houghton Mifflin, Boston, MA, 1982.

.Tremblay, J. - P., and Sorenson, P. G., *An Introduction to Data Structures with Applications*, 2nd ed.- McGraw-Hill, New York, 1983.

Questions and Exercises

3.1.   What is a file organization? What is an access method? What do they accomplish?

3.2.   What is a sequential file? What are some advantages and disadvantages of their use?

3.3.   Describe the procedure for adding records to a sequential file.

3.4.   Do you think that records in a sequential file can be updated without generating a new master file? Why or why not?

3.5.   In your own words, describe what an index is.

3.6.   Since using an index to find a record in a file entails some work, that is, executing the index search algorithm, why is such a retrieval considered to be "direct"?

3.7.   Describe the use of a simple linear index for direct retrieval of a single record. Does it matter whether or not the file is in physical sequence by the field that is indexed?

3.8.   Describe the use of a simple linear index for sequential retrieval of all of the records in a file. Does it matter whether or not the file is in physical sequence by the field that is indexed?

3.9.   Create a simple linear index for the file in Figure 3.1 based on the Salary Rate field.

3.10.   What are the implications for index based direct retrieval and for index based sequential retrieval if the indexed field is not unique?

3.11.   What is an indexed-sequential file organization? Describe a set of applications that requires a file to be organized that way.

3.12.   What is the advantage of a multilevel index over a simple linear index?

3.13.   Consider the IBM ISAM index in Figure 3.8. Assume that a personnel record with employee number 77000 is the third of four records on track 3 of cylinder 11. Describe a direct search through the index for that record.

3.14.   Consider the portion of the IBM ISAM file shown in Figure 3.9. Add the following records in the order shown. What would happen if the overflow track was full?

     a.   42000 Barber

     b.   39200 Madison

     c.   41800 Morgan

3.15.   Describe the splitting mechanism in the VSAM KSDS structure.

3.16. Compare the IBM ISAM and VSAM KSDS file organizations in term of:

    a. direct retrieval capability

    b. sequential retrieval capability

    c. method of record insertion

    c. retrieval performance after a substantial number of insertions have taken place

3.17. Consider the portion of the VSAM KSDS file shown in Figure 3.13. Add the following records in the order shown. What would happen if the free track was full?

    a. 42000 Barber

    b. 39200 Madison

    c. 41800 Morgan

3.18. Describe how a direct search works in a hashed file.

3.19. What are the prospects for a sequential search in a hashed file?

3.20. What is a hashing method?

3.21. Describe how the "division-remainder method" of hashing can be used to effect the direct retrieval of a record in a file.

3.22. What are the advantages and disadvantages of a hashed file vs. an indexed file?

3.23. What is a collision in a hashed file? What are synonyms? Describe a collision resolution technique.

3.24. Insert records with the following employee numbers into the personnel file shown in Figure 3.18.

    a. 32869.

    b. 00866.

3.25. A hashed file has space for 70 records, each 30 bytes wide. Each record has an additional 10 byte slot for a collision chain pointer, and there are an additional 15 record spaces for storing synonym records.

    a. Draw a diagram illustrating this situation.

    b. Store records with each of the following four digit keys, indicating the address each is stored at.

        i. 4000

        ii. 5207

        iii. 0360

        iv. 1410

4

Benefits of the Database Approach

Introduction

Now that we've taken a good look at the ways that simple linear files are built and accessed, it's time to pause and consider just how good these files are for use in handling the real world of data and data processing. But first, a point which we have been taking for granted has to be noted and emphasized. In speaking about simple linear files, we have been assuming that these files exist totally independent of each other; as yet, there has been no reason to assume otherwise. It will turn out, as we shall eventually see, that manipulating combinations of such files, in certain ways, can lead to a more powerful data storage concept (in fact to a legitimate database form). So, to distinguish between the two cases, we will, from here on, refer to the case that we have been discussing thus far as "independent linear files."

To be sure, independent linear files are just right in certain situations. But, as we shall see in this chapter, they are lacking, in several key respects, for the more complex data processing applications and environments which exist today.

Let's take a look at five key areas of discussion in that regard. They are:

1. Certain characteristics of today's data processing environment.
2. Problems associated with redundant data.
3. The ability to store data involved in multiple relationships.
4. Certain general issues of data management.
5. The concept of data independence.

Data Processing Environment Characteristics

Data as a Manageable Resource

In the earlier days of data processing most of the time and emphasis in application development was placed on the programs, as opposed to on the data and data structures. Hardware was expensive and limited in addressing scope. Programming was a new discipline and there was much to be learned about it in order to achieve the goal of efficient processing. Partial mechanization of the programming process, or even standardization of style were unknown. In this environment, the treatment of the data was hardly the highest priority concern.

As data processing continued to grow, a number of the ground rules began to change. Hardware became cheaper, software development took on a more standardized, "structured" form, and large backlogs of new applications to be implemented built up, making the huge amount of time spent on maintaining existing programs more and more unacceptable. It became increasingly clear that the way in which we handled (or mishandled) data in the past was one of the major factors in the program maintenance mess we found ourselves in. We found that

- Data was stored in different formats in different files
- Data was often not shareable among different programs that needed it, necessitating redundant files
- Data was often not easily recoverable or secure
- Programs were usually written in such a manner that if the way that the data was stored changed, the program had to be modified to continue working

Data was all too often inaccurate, inconsistent, or not up-to-date. Changes in everything from access methods to tax tables required programming changes.

At the same time, as an increasing amount of the enterprise's operational and strategic work became dependent on automated data processing, an increasing awareness that the data itself was an important *enterprise resource* evolved.

Money, capital equipment, inventories, and so forth are all important property to an enterprise. We have applied numerous management techniques to them (many of which, of course, have involved computers). Many people are now coming to the conclusion that data is also a manageable resource. A firm's data about its products, manufacturing processes, customers, suppliers, employees, competitors, and so on can, with proper storage and use, provide a significant competitive advantage.

At the intersection of all of the above happenings is the question of, "How?" We want to manage data as an enterprise resource, while at the same time improving its treatment in terms of the technicalities of data processing. It becomes clear, even before we reach the discussion of the specifics to come later in this book, that some sort of a uniform system to manage data as an enterprise resource is needed. The database environment, with its supporting software and accompanying management techniques, will provide the framework for treating data as a standardized, manageable, sharable resource.

Standardization and Specialization

In a data processing environment driven by independent applications, it is often difficult to maintain standards in programming and data storage conventions. Programmers tend to go their separate ways, especially when other programs are not directly dependent on their work. Unfortunately, a lack of standardization makes it difficult for anyone, often even the original programmer, to understand the program well enough to make required maintenance changes to it later on.

The sharing of data files among different applications and the use of consistent data description and access statements in the programs in the database environment forces a more careful and standardized look at the entire application development process. Now, whatever one programmer does may affect others too in terms, for instance, of data accuracy, update schedules, and performance. Standardization in programming techniques and storage schemes can only serve to make for a less error-prone environment.

In addition, the database environment leads to new levels of job specialization, which is really another form of standardization. Typically, a data administration function is formed to be responsible for the data. Within that function are people who specialize in database design, security, backup and recovery, performance, and so on. As the commitment to the new, data oriented environment increases, the application programming and operations groups develop a dependency on the data administration function to assume an increasing amount of the data oriented legwork of the

SALESPERSON NUMBER	...	SALESPERSON NAME	...
137		Baker	
186		Adams	
204		Dickens	
361		Carlyle	
.		.	
.		.	
.		.	

(a)

CUSTOMER NUMBER	...	SALESPERSON NUMBER	...
0121		137	
0839		186	
0933		137	
1047		137	
1525		361	
1700		361	
1826		137	
2198		204	
2267		186	
.		.	
.		.	
.		.	

(b)

Figure 4.1.   Separate files: (a) Salesperson, (b) customer.

application development and execution processes. This can include data collection and verification, monitoring, database design, integrity monitoring, security, backup and recovery; in effect a thorough custodianship of the enterprise's data. It doesn't happen overnight, but rather takes place as a gradual transition. But again, this kind of standardization— people and functional standardization in this case— can only lead to a more efficient error-free environment.

Redundant Data

Let's take a look at the problem of redundant data and its companion, the problem of integrity. First we will consider it in the context of one file, then in the context of many files.

Redundancy Within One File

Suppose that we are a sales organization and, of course, have to have a way of keeping track of our customers and our salespeople. Figure 4.1 shows two independent linear files, one for salespeople and one for customers. The Salesperson file is keyed on the SALESPERSON NUMBER field, and includes, as one of its other fields, the SALESPERSON NAME field. The Customer file is keyed on (the also unique) CUSTOMER NUMBER, and has, as one of its other fields, the SALESPERSON NUMBER: the number of the salesperson who is assigned to that customer account. There is one record per salesperson in the Salesperson file. A particular record contains the data that we hold about a particular salesperson, such as salesperson number, name, home address, home telephone number, and so on. There is a like situation for the data on each customer in the Customer file. This kind of data storage is said to be *nonredundant*, because the detail data on each entity is stored only once. That is as it should be.

If someone comes along and wants to know the name of the salesperson who is identified by a particular salesperson number (e.g., 186), he or she merely looks up that salesperson's record in the Salesperson file, Figure 4.1*a*, using the SALESPERSON NUMBER as the key, and reads off the name (Adams). Similarly, if someone wants to know the number of the salesperson who is responsible for a particular customer account, he or she goes to the Customer File, Figure 4.1*b*, and looks up that customer's record, using the CUSTOMER NUMBER as the key. So far, so good.

Now, what if someone comes along and wants to know the *name* of the

salesperson who services a particular customer account, identified by customer number. Can that information be obtained from only one of the files
in Figure 4.1? Clearly it cannot, since the customer number information
exists only in the Customer File, and the salesperson *name* information
exists only in the Salesperson File. The only way to answer that question
is to first look up that customer's record in the Customer File, find the
number of the salesperson on that account, then use that number to find
the person's record in the Salesperson File, and finally find his or her name
in the record. For example, in Figure 4.1, given customer number 1525,
we would access the fifth record in the Customer file, and find that the
responsible salesperson is salesperson number 361. We would then access
the record for salesperson number 361 in the Salesperson file, and find
Carlyle as the salesperson name. That kind of custom made, multicommand,
multifile access, is error prone in terms of programming, expensive in terms
of execution performance, and depending on the software involved, may
have to be coded separately for each such access combination.

Ah, but if we knew that we were going to make such queries, why did
we bother breaking the data up into two files in the first place. If it's all
contained in one file, in a meaningful way, then there are no costly multicommand, multifile accesses. Figure 4.2 shows the same data represented
in one file. Notice that we show the salesperson (by number) assigned to
a particular customer, just as we did in the two files in Figure 4.1. But now
the salesperson's name is carried along too. We can still answer the two
original simple questions that we put to the files in Figure 4.1. But now,

SALESPERSON NUMBER	CUSTOMER NUMBER	SALESPERSON NAME	. . .
137	0121	Baker	
137	0933	Baker	
137	1047	Baker	
137	1826	Baker	
186	0839	Adams	
186	2267	Adams	
204	2198	Dickens	
361	1525	Carlyle	
361	1700	Carlyle	
. . .	. . .	. . .	

Figure 4.2. Combined file.

in addition, we can answer the tougher, previously multifile question, "What is the name of the salesperson on a particular account?," with just the one file in Figure 4.2 and one command. Fine! Or is it? In the file in Figure 4.1*a*, there is one record per salesperson, each containing the particulars for a given person once. Indicating which salesperson services a particular account is simply a matter of attaching the salesperson's number to the single record that describes that customer in the file in Figure 4.1*b*.

But in the combined file of Figure 4.2, where all of the fundamentally different kinds of information are intermingled, the particulars of a specific salesperson must be repeated for every account that he or she services. A given salesperson may appear in several records in that file, and it makes no sense from a logical or a retrieval standpoint to specify, for example, the salesperson name for one customer that that salesperson services and not for another. To be complete, the data must be repeated in every appropriate slot. Thus, whereas in the two files of Figure 4.1, the name "Carlyle" is attached to the salesperson number "361" just once, in the combined file of Figure 4.2, the name "Carlyle" appears with salesperson number "361" in as many records as customers that Carlyle services.

This situation causes a number of problems. For one thing, it takes up a lot more storage space. (Try adding a home address field of 40 bytes and see how you feel about storing it once as opposed to, say, 50 times.) For another thing, it is rather unpleasant when it comes to updating. If Carlyle changes his (or her) name, the change must be recorded many times. The time consumed in doing that can be very costly, particularly if the records involved are scattered all over a disk. Also, there is the nagging doubt that all of the occurrences may not have been updated, due to anything from programming bugs to execution time system failures. When that happens, it's called an *integrity* problem.

There appears to be a trade-off, but then trade-offs are hardly rare in the computer field. In the two files of Figure 4.1, we have no redundancy (at least among the nonkey fields, strictly speaking), but a query of the type that we've been looking at requires a multicommand multifile access. In the combined file of Figure 4.2, we have eliminated the need for a multicommand multifile access for that type of query, but we have introduced redundancy among the nonkey fields. Neither of these situations is tolerable, for the reasons indicated previously.

The question is, can we have our cake and eat it too? And that brings us to one of the key features of the database environment. An *integrated* data management system, that is a true *database* system, is one in which data can be held nonredundantly (in the sense of the files in Figure 4.1) while at the same time, a query which requires a mixture of different kinds of data (such as the query that we've been looking at) can be specified in a single command from the highest level programming interface (*as if* the access was being made to the file in Figure 4.2). Any system that does not have this property really should not call itself a "database" system; "file management" system would be a more accurate term.

There are several approaches to designing a true database system, which revolve around several storage structures and different times and ways of "mixing" different pieces of data together. We will explore them later on.

Another benefit of the integrated approach is the encouragement that it gives to finding new uses for the data in the database. The richness of having so many different portions of the organization's data interconnected leads to many more usage possibilities than when they were stored separately.

Redundancy Among Many Files

There is another kind of redundancy which, while perhaps a bit more obvious than the one discussed previously, is not necessarily easier to combat, but for different reasons.

Frequently, certain data is needed by different departments in an enterprise in the course of their normal everyday work. For example, customer name and address may be needed by the sales department, the accounts receivable department, and the credit department. There will also generally be other pieces of information involving customers which are only needed by one or two departments. Typically the solution to this multiple need is redundancy. The sales department has its own stored file which, among other things, contains the customer name and address, likewise for the accounts receivable and credit departments.

While it's true that this keeps the departments from competing for the data, it opens up a can of worms, which is reminiscent of the problems that we encountered in single file redundancy. First of all, storing a piece of data three times takes three times the amount of storage as storing it once. In addition, every time the data must be updated, it must be changed in each file it resides in. This wastes processing time, causes control nightmares, and has the potential of leading to integrity problems if all of the data is not updated correctly and at the same time. Furthermore, the question arises as to whose responsibility it is to update the data in all of these different files, which are probably owned by widely separated departments.

Wouldn't it make more sense for such data to be stored just once, in a way that makes it accessible to all of the different groups that need it? This way there would be one group in charge of updating it, little wasted space, few integrity problems, and so on.

The database approach includes the concept of a common shared database with controlled management and update responsibility.

Multiple Relationships

In Chapter 2, we discussed the different ways that entities can relate to each other in terms of unary and multiple associations, and one-to-one, one-to-many, and many-to-many relationships, Figure 4.3. The question that we must now ask is, "How easily can we store data involving the two kinds of associations and three kinds of relationships in independent linear files?"

Roughly speaking, unary associations and one-to-one relationships are handled well by such files. After all, a key field and a simple non-key field in a record represent such a case, Figure 4.4. But when it comes to multiple associations and their resulting relationships, simple files leave something to be desired.

A multiple association can be represented "horizontally" with variable length records, Figure 4.5a. Unfortunately, that can cause program logic and space management headaches. Usually, if a programmer accesses a single record of a file, there is an action to be taken on the single value in one or more of its fields. In Figure 4.4, the programmer might read the record for employee 2186 and then might perform some action with the single social security number found in it. But what if that programmer accesses the record for manager Smith in Figure 4.5a, with the intention

```
    EMPLOYEE        EMPLOYEE
    SERIAL NO.  ⟷   SOC. SEC. NO.
                (a)


    EMPLOYEE        MANAGER
    SERIAL NO.  ⟵⟶   NAME
                (b)


    EMPLOYEE        SECURE
    SERIAL NO.  ⟵⟶   ROOM
                (c)
```

Figure 4.3. Relationships: *(a)* one-to-one, *(b)* one-to-many, and *(c)* many-to-many.

EMPLOYEE SERIAL NO	SOCIAL SECURITY NO	MANAGER	···
1234	111-000-2222	Smith	
1572	111-22-3333	Jones	
2186	222-11-5432	Jones	
4522	522-52-5221	Smith	
4991	333-55-9999	Doe	
5283	123-45-6789	Smith	
5542	654-32-1234	Smith	
· · ·	· · ·	· · ·	

Figure 4.4. Simple file.

of acting on the serial numbers of the people in that manager's employ? He or she must, under program control, manage the list of employee serial numbers found in it, performing the desired action on each one. That makes for a more complex error prone program. Also, working with variable length records can be a tricky business from a space management point of view. If a new employee is added to a manager's record in the file in Figure 4.5*a*, the new larger size of the record may preclude its being stored in the same place on the disk that it came from. Placing it somewhere else can cause performance problems in future retrievals.

A multiple association can be represented "vertically" with one partic-

MANAGER	EMPLOYEE SERIAL NO'S	···
Doe	4991	
Jones	1572 2186	
Smith	1234 4522 5283 5542	
· · ·		

Figure 4.5a. Multiple relationship representation: Horizontal representation.

MANAGER	EMPLOYEE SERIAL NO	···
Doe	4991	
Jones	1572	
Jones	2186	
Smith	1234	
Smith	4522	
Smith	5283	
Smith	5542	
· · ·	· · ·	

Figure 4.5b. Multiple relationship representation: Vertical representation.

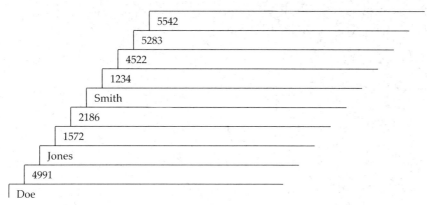

Figure 4.5c. Multiple relationship representation: Interspersed records.

ipant being repeated once for each of the other related participants, Figure 4.5*b*. But that introduces a form of redundancy: the name Smith appears once for each of that manager's employees. (It will turn out that when processed with "relational" constructs, files of the type in Figure 4.5*b* will qualify as the foundation of a legitimate database solution. Under these circumstances, the kind of redundancy found in Figure 4.5*b*, which concerns the key fields of two entities involved in a multiple association, will be acceptable. More about that later in Chapters 8 and 9.)

A multiple association can be represented with interspersed record types, Figure 4.5*c*. But this requires some fancy software devices to maintain the integrity of what are really two different files (represented by the two different record types) and still show the one (manager name) to many (employee number) relationship shown in Figure 4.5*c*. (Once again, going to all of that trouble, in fact, forms a kind of a database solution to be discussed later.)

One of the capabilities of database management systems is that they provide the means, naturally and easily, for all types of applications, of representing multiple associations and their attendant one-to-many and many-to-many relationships.

General Data Management Issues

There are several concerns about the way that we manage data which must be considered in any data processing environment, regardless of the file structures in use. These concerns are inherent in storing, managing, and accessing data. The areas are:

Security
Backup and Recovery
Concurrency
Auditability

Security

There are actually many aspects of security in a data processing environment, only some of which deal immediately and directly with access to data, which is our concern in this book. For example, to prevent an unauthorized person from gaining access to the system itself, sign-on passwords are often used. In a different vein, large doors, and, sometimes, armed guards are used to stop someone from blowing up the computer. There are several aspects of security which are specifically data related and thus are of interest here. The two key points involved are preventing people from seeing data that they are not entitled to see and preventing them from changing data which they have no business changing.

It is certainly possible to design and build systems which can protect the data in independent linear files. The problem is that unless everyone agrees to use this system, every programmer is left to his or her own devices, either omitting such security considerations, or reinventing the wheel for each application.

Backup and Recovery

Suppose an accident or an act of nature causes some unspeakable tragedy which mangles one of your disk packs. Or, suppose that an error in input is discovered which took place 10 minutes ago, and, in the real-time environment, affected other data as well.

Clearly, it is always advisable to have more than one copy of every data file. Furthermore, the copies must be kept in different buildings, or even different cities, to prevent a catastrophe from destroying all copies of the data. The process of copying a file, which must be done on a periodic basis to reflect changes in the data, is known as "backup", or "backing-up" the file. The process of using the file copy, plus other data, to correct either of the kinds of problems mentioned previously, is known as "recovery".

Here again, as with the security case, it is certainly feasible to have backup and recovery systems for independent linear file based data processing. But, again, this means that everyone in the environment must use the system, which is often contrary to the independent nature of the applications in such environments.

Concurrency

In a multiuser application, such as an airline reservations system with many reservations agents, a particular problem can surface regardless of the file structure in use, involving changing values of the fields in the records. When two users try to update the same record simultaneously (or as simultaneously as a multiprogrammed system allows), they have a rather nasty way of interfering with each other so that one of those two updates may wind up being ignored.

A common solution to this problem involves a technique called "lockout". Unfortunately as so often happens, the use of this technique itself causes other problems which did not previously exist and which have to be handled.

Once again, there is an important concern: Who or what software system should be responsible for implementing these protective devices?

Auditability

As more and more of an enterprise's data is stored and processed in automated data processing systems, it becomes an increasingly important focus of the auditing function. There is an endless list of reasons for management, accountants, and others, to ask who had access to, or made changes to, what data, at what point in time; not to mention what the new and old values of the data were.

The primary tool of the auditor is the audit trail. A permanent record of the nature of the changes made to the data. But here, as in the other three situations discussed, who or what should be responsible for the audit function?

Independent Files and General Data Management Issues

In all four cases, the key concept is that it makes sense to have a common way to deal with these areas built into the DBMS. This means that when a new application program is written, we can avoid the expense of the programmer having to write security, recovery, and so forth, routines from scratch, or trying to use specialized, but unconnected, software packages for these functions. It means that we can be confident that the routines work, since they are standard tested components of the DBMS. It means that the functions are standard for all application programs in the environment, which leads to easier management of them and economies of scale in assigning and training personnel to be responsible for these aspects. This kind of commonality is a hallmark of the database approach.

Data Independence

In the independent linear file data processing environment, decisions involving the way that the application program is written are usually made in concert with the choice of file organization and access method. The program logic itself is dependent upon the way in which the data is stored. In fact the *dependence* is often so strong that if for any reason the storage characteristics of the data should be changed in the future, the program itself must be modified, often extensively. That is a very undesirable characteristic because of the time and expense involved in such efforts. In practice, storage structures do and/or should change, to reflect improved storage techniques, new hardware, attempts at sharing data, and performance tuning, to name a few reasons. One of the reasons for the massive amounts of time spent on program maintenance is the typical level of dependency between programs and data.

What we would like to be able to do is separate out storage and access considerations from programming to as great an extent as possible. Today's DBMSs have been somewhat successful in this respect in solving certain aspects of the problem.

Conclusion

The use of independent linear files during the early days of automated data processing should be looked back upon, as a starting point and as a historical stopgap measure. It is clear that the independent linear files method of data storage, combined with an atmosphere of individual applications being implemented in a vacuum, carries with it a host of undesirable side effects. The solution, as we shall see more and more, is the database approach.

References

Date, C. J., *An Introduction to Database Systems,* 3rd ed., vol. 1, Addison-Wesley, Reading, MA, 1981.

King, J. M., *Evaluating Data Base Management Systems,* Van Nostrand Reinhold, New York, 1981.

Kroenke, D., *Database Processing,* 2nd ed., Science Research Associates, Chicago, IL, 1983.

Martin, J., *Computer Data-Base Organization,* 2nd ed., Prentice-Hall, Englewood Cliffs, NJ, 1977.

Ross, R. G., *Data Base Systems,* AMACOM, New York, 1978.

Questions and Exercises

4.1. Should data be considered a true corporate resource? Why or why not? Compare and contrast data to other corporate resources (capital, plant and equipment, personnel, etc.) in terms of importance, intrinsic value, and modes of use.

4.2. Defend or refute the following statement: "Data is the most important corporate resource because it describes all of the others."

4.3. How does the database environment change the way that we treat and think about data?

4.4. What are the two kinds of data redundancy, and what problems do they cause in the data processing environment?

4.5. Devise an example that demonstrates the problem of data redundancy within one file.

4.6. Describe the apparent trade-off between data redundancy and data integration in simple linear files.

4.7. In your own words, describe the key quality of a DBMS that sets it apart from other data handling systems.

4.8. Describe the situation in which data is held redundantly across several files.

4.9. Do you think that the single-file redundancy problem is more serious, less serious, or about the same as the multifile redundancy problem? Why?

4.10. Choose a functional part of a corporation and describe a few one-to-one, one-to-many, and many-to-many relationships among its entities.

4.11. In your own words, describe the problems involved in trying to handle multiple associations in simple, linear files.

4.12.   How important do you think it is to be able to handle multiple associations for data processing applications? Why?

4.13.   Describe the "general data management issues" outlined in this chapter. How important is it for a database management system to be able to handle them?

4.14.   What is data independence? Why is it desirable?

5

Database Management Systems Characteristics

The Nature of a Database Management System

Grasping the concept of a database management system requires some thought about the idea of a "middleman." There are many examples of middlemen in the world, with a number of variations.

Consider, for example, the idea of shopping for goods through a mail-order company, Figure 5.1. On one side is the consumer who wants to buy some merchandise, while on the other side is the company's warehouse which contains the merchandise. In the middle is a combination of the catalog describing the merchandise and the people and facilities of the company's catalog ordering department. The consumer cannot reach the merchandise in the warehouse without going through the catalog ordering department. This is an important point, because it allows the company to maintain strict inventory and accounting control over the goods in the warehouse. To allow the consumers direct access to the warehouse might well cause some serious control problems. Focusing in on the catalog brings up another interesting point about this situation. The catalog is, of course, not the merchandise itself, but a description of it. There may be 300 Brand X fishing reels in the warehouse, but, since they're all identical, a single catalog description of a Brand X fishing reel, together with the fact that there are 300 of them, is sufficient to describe the warehouse's stock. The consumer and the catalog ordering department both use the catalog as a means of knowing something about the fishing reels without actually going over to the shelf in the warehouse and touching them. That's important too. Eventually, the consumer places an order with the catalog ordering department. The department, consulting the catalog and other directory information, such as what aisle and shelf in the warehouse the goods are on, causes the goods to be shipped to the consumer, handling all of the accounting details along the way. The consumer receives his or her order, having dealt only with the "middleman" organization and its descriptive catalog.

Another example of a middleman is a long distance telephone infor-

Figure 5.1.   Mail-order department as middleman.

Figure 5.2. Long distance telephone information operator as middleman.

mation operator, who serves as the interface between a person seeking a telephone number, and the distant telephone directories unavailable to him or her, Figure 5.2. There are several noticeable differences between this example and the catalog buying example. For one thing, the "merchandise" in this case, the telephone numbers in the directories, is data. It is not exhaustible, like fishing reels on a shelf. An operator could give out the same telephone number an unlimited number of times and it would still be there to be given out again. Also, we could give everyone in the country direct access to every telephone book in the country by giving them each a copy of every telephone book. Without belaboring the physical problems involved in doing that, we will simply say that that solution would create a tremendous amount of redundancy. There is no need to give everyone a copy of every telephone book if the long distance information operators can serve as middlemen and funnel the information in their copies of the telephone books to those customers who need it, when they need it.

A third example of a middleman is a stockbroker, connecting potential buyers of stock with potential sellers through the mechanism of the stock markets, Figure 5.3. One difference between this example of a middleman

Figure 5.3. Stockbroker as middleman.

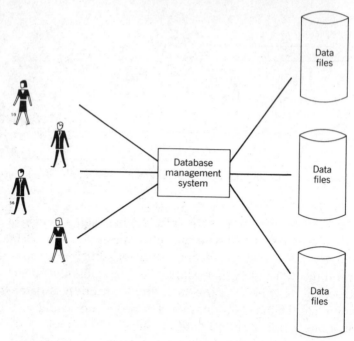

Figure 5.4.   Database management system as middleman.

and the two previous ones is that in this case the two parties on either side of the interface are functional equals, passing equally important data across the interface between each other. Also, this instance presents the clearest case of the three for keeping both sides strictly separated across the middleman interface. Can you imagine the anarchy of having all of the thousands of potential buyers and sellers of stock in one room together?

A DBMS is also a middleman. In the data processing environment it serves as the interface between data files and the people who seek the data in those files, Figure 5.4. Whether access to the files is sought in the form of an ad hoc query, typed in at a display terminal, or in the form of a formal printed report, the request must go through the DBMS, and the response must be passed back through the DBMS.

A bit more formally, a DBMS is a sophisticated piece of software which specifies how data may be structured, controls all access to the data, and provides certain other essential data services. The data structure, in some cases in concert with the way that the data is manipulated, must provide for data integration, reduction of data redundancy, and the expression of multiple relationships in the data. Access to the data is provided via a query facility, through calls embedded in a higher level language, or both. Other

DBMS supplied data services include security, backup and recovery, and concurrent update control.

Database management systems usually run under the control of a general purpose operating system, often taking careful advantage of the facilities of the operating system. They may have an entire computer system dedicated to them, or they may share a central processing unit (CPU) with other kinds of software facilities. A DBMS and its associated application programs may operate in a batch mode, may operate in an on-line multiterminal environment using an additional data communications facility, or may operate in both of these environments concurrently.

And the DBMS is the consummate middleman. As in the catalog buying example, the DBMS is the only means of accessing it's "merchandise," the data in the files. Like the long distance telephone information example it avoids a proliferation of copies of the same data. Like the stockbroker example it passes data in both directions across its interface, allowing data to be read from its files, and allowing new data to be placed in it, or existing data to be modified. As in all of the examples it provides a degree of security to the "materials" (data) that it is responsible for and creates order out of what might have been chaos.

Let's take a look at some of these ideas in a little more detail.

Data Definition Languages

Introduction

The term "data definition (or description) language," (DDL) is a broad label for the aspect of the DBMS that specifies the *way* that data may be stored. As basic as that statement sounds, there are really two views of the "way" that data is stored. At issue is the apparent conflict between the following two issues. One is the desire to have the programmer who is going to use the data perceive that it is stored in a relatively simple way. The other is the desire to have the data, as actually stored on the disk devices, take the fullest advantage of the complexities of the hardware and of the theories of database technology to accomplish all of the advertised benefits of the database approach. That distinction is important enough to warrant DBMS designers, at considerable expense, to create the capability of having two "views" of the data. We speak of the *logical view* of the data as the form that the programmer perceives it to be in, while the *physical view* reflects the way that it is actually stored on disk.

For this distinction to work, there must be a component of the DBMS which can convert requests for data coming from terminals or application programs based on the logical view, into the physical view form which is the way that the data is really stored on the disk. And for the DBMS to accomplish that, it must have at its disposal descriptions that it can "understand" of the way that the data is stored on the disk, and the way that the users or programmers perceive it. Such information is stored in special groups of records known as *control blocks*.

The Four Approaches to Structure

Introduction. Any particular DBMS is based on a data structure and data access mechanism. Whatever that structure and mechanism are, they must be able to store data in a nonredundant way, to handle multiple associations among the data, to integrate the data, and to provide direct as well as sequential access to the data. Over the years, many DBMSs have been developed for environments ranging from the largest mainframe computers to the smallest microprocessors. Yet every one of them is based on one of four fundamental approaches to DBMS data structure and data access mechanisms:

The hierarchical approach
The network approach
The relational approach
The pseudo-relational or flat-file integrated approach.

Explaining each of these four approaches will be the focus of a large part of the rest of this book. Nevertheless, a few introductory remarks are appropriate here.

Hierarchical Databases. Figure 5.5 shows a hierarchy of record types, representative of the type of structure found in a hierarchically based DBMS. The four record types in Figure 5.5 represent a firm's branch offices, cars assigned to each branch office, employees authorized to drive a particular car, and maintenance dates during which the car was serviced. Although not shown in the figure, each of these boxes really represents a collection of fields, as any record must. For example, each BRANCH OFFICE record contains a BRANCH OFFICE NUMBER field, a BRANCH OFFICE NAME field, a BRANCH OFFICE CITY field, and so on. The BRANCH OFFICE,

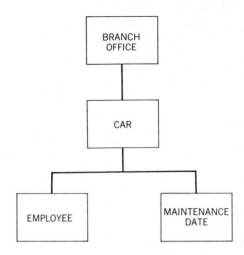

Figure 5.5. A data hierarchy.

CAR, and EMPLOYEE records are identified by unique key fields (e.g. BRANCH OFFICE NUMBER for BRANCH OFFICE).

A basic tenet of the hierarchical data structure is that each link connecting two record types represents a one-to-many relationship, in the downwards direction. Thus the structure in Figure 5.5 indicates that each branch office has several cars assigned to it, each car has several employees authorized to drive it, and each car has a multiple maintenance date history. Many-to-many relationships can be handled with a combination of hierarchies, as we shall see later.

The reduction of potential redundancy with this arrangement comes, first, from the fact that the details of a particular superior record (e.g., a BRANCH OFFICE record) are stored only once and can be integrated with the details of any occurrences of its subordinate records (e.g. CAR). For example, we would be able to combine the branch office address—which is stored only once in the one BRANCH OFFICE record occurrence for that branch—with details about any of the cars assigned to that branch. Also, it will turn out that the way that many-to-many relationships are accommodated through connected hierarchies saves on redundancy.

Network Databases. Figure 5.6 shows a network. As in the hierarchical case, each link between two record types in the network represents a one-to-many relationship between them. The direction of the relationship is shown by the double arrowheads in the figure. Again, many-to-many relationships require some additional constructs. Unlike the hierarchical case, it is common in networks, as we shall see in more detail later, to consider

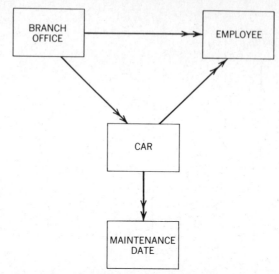

Figure 5.6.   A data network.

two connected record types and the link connecting them to be a substructure called a "set," which has certain valuable properties.

Database management systems that are based on the hierarchical or the network approaches are often called *navigational* systems. In both cases, data is stored as records of different types which are interconnected by address pointers. Programmers, using either of the hierarchical or network forms, can "navigate" through their structures. This means, for instance, that a program call to the database can be designed to find a particular branch office, a particular car in that branch, and to produce a list of the people authorized to drive it.

Relational Databases.   Figure 5.7 shows a relational database. At first glance it appears to consist of a few independent linear files, and, in fact, that's true from a structural point of view! Notice also that since the BRANCH OFFICE, CAR, EMPLOYEE, and MAINTENANCE DATE (for a given car) fields are unique, there is only one record for a given branch office (and it is in the Branch file), one record for a given car (in the Car file), and so on. This, of course, means that there is no redundancy among the *nonkey* fields. Since there is only one record for a particular branch office, all of the fields dependent on it such as BRANCH MANAGER, BRANCH ADDRESS, and so on, appear only once.

But what about the fact that the BRANCH OFFICE field appears in the Car file? Isn't that redundant with the BRANCH OFFICE field in the Branch

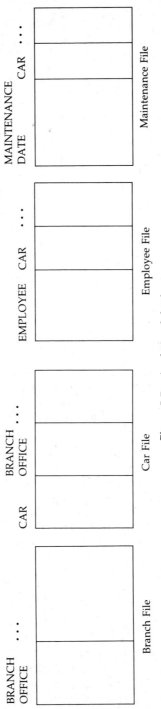

Figure 5.7. A relational database.

102

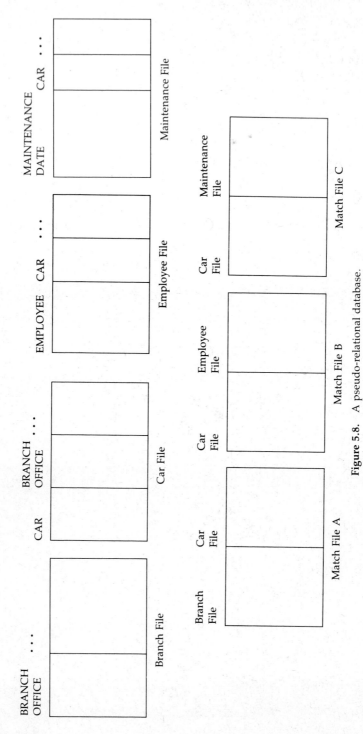

Figure 5.8. A pseudo-relational database.

file? In a sense it is, but in this case it is a necessary instance of redundancy. Since the record types or files in the relational database are not structurally interconnected as in the navigational approaches, the only way to integrate the files is to repeat the key field of one file in the other. If we didn't have the BRANCH OFFICE field in the Car file, how else would we know which cars were assigned to which branch offices? By the way, that's how one-to-many relationships are implemented in relational databases. Several different cars in the Car file may be shown to belong to the same branch office. Later on we will see that many-to-many relationships are handled in about the same way.

Although the files in the relational database concept are independent, there must be a way to integrate the data, to form useful combinations of data from different files. Put another way, there must be a functional equivalent of the idea of navigating through a hierarchy or network. There is such an equivalent, but as we shall see later, its power comes from execution time procedures involving those repeated key fields, rather than from the kinds of physical connective structures found in the navigational systems.

Pseudo-Relational Databases. Figure 5.8 shows a pseudo-relational database or flat-file integrated database. First, notice that the Branch File, Car File, Employee File, and Maintenance File are identical to the files of the relational database in Figure 5.7. The foregoing comments about eliminating redundancy in the flat files of the relational database apply here as well.

But the execution time procedures for integrating the data in the relational files do not exist here. There must be some physically built-in way of connecting the files. The lower half of Figure 5.8 shows three additional "match" files of two fields each. Such files indicate which records of one file are related to which records of the other file, effectively integrating the two files. For example, Match File A indicates which records of the Branch Office File and which records of the Car File are related, which really means which records of these two files have the same branch office numbers. This, in effect, allows the combining of detail data about a given branch office, with detail data about the cars assigned to it. Thus the pseudo-relational database combines the flat-file data structure of the relational database with the *concept* of accomplishing data integration with some kind of prestored, physical construct, as in the navigational systems.

Data Manipulation Languages

The term "data manipulation language" refers broadly to the mechanism used for retrieving data stored in a database. There are two basic ways of accessing the data in a database. One way is to have an application program issue an instruction to the DBMS to find certain data in the database and return it to the program. We speak of these instructions as being "embedded statements." The other way of accessing the data is for the person seeking the data to sit down at a display terminal and issue a command in a special language directly to the DBMS to find certain data and return it to the screen. We speak of that as a "query" operation. Either the embedded statement or query language approach to accessing data can be used with any of the four approaches to database structure.

Embedded Statements

The logic of a computer program, whether it's written in COBOL, PL/I, Assembler Language, or any other procedural language dictates that at various points in the execution of that program, data must be brought in from appropriate stored files, and data must be sent out to appropriate stored files. Thus, *embedded* in the program, at the proper logical places amongst the GOTO, IF-THEN-ELSE, A = B + C, and so on statements, are other statements which, when executed, cause the system to reach out to the disk drives (or tape drives, etc.) and transfer data into and out of the running program. When the program operates in the database environment, those I/O statements must be specially constructed to conform to the rules of the DBMS which, as we have discussed, will serve as the middleman between the program and the database.

Query Languages

There are situations that call for simply "looking something up" in the database. At such times, one would like to be able to send a command directly to the DBMS, instructing it to find and return the desired data, as opposed to having to plan, write, debug, and finally execute a program to accomplish the same thing. Such direct interaction with the DBMS through a terminal is the nature of a *query language*. Logic to interpret and carry out the query requests is packaged as a part of or an adjunct to the DBMS. The queries, generally, must be constructed according to a planned syntax.

Comparing Embedded Statements to Query Languages

There is a crucial point to be made in understanding the nature of data manipulation languages, and now is not too soon to make it. The concept of exactly what constitutes a "query" is partially dependent on whose point of view we are approaching the situation from. In a query language situation there is a general purpose processor which is capable of searching for and retrieving any data, as long as it is stored according to the prescribed DBMS structure, and as long as the construction of the query itself follows the proper conventions. Anyone using a query language should feel as if they are making a "query."

Now let's look at the embedded statement situation. Modern programming techniques in general, and DBMSs in particular certainly permit on-line terminal oriented operations. It is quite usual for executing programs with I/O statements written as embedded DBMS calls to accept requests for data from terminal devices, and update the database from data values typed in at these devices. The point is that the *programmer* was well aware, as he or she was writing the program in the first place, that he or she was not dealing with what we have been calling a "query language"—but if during execution of the program, you ask the *end user* what he or she is doing, the reply will be, "Querying the database." Any operation on data from a terminal can be termed a query, but one has to look at what is supporting it to determine if it is in the embedded statement or query language category.

Later in this book, we will look at some examples of both embedded statements and of query language calls.

Security, Backup and Recovery, and Concurrency

There are certain concerns about stored data that we should have regardless of the storage structure used and regardless of whether or not a DBMS is involved. One concern is the *security* of the data. As more and more of a company's business procedures are performed with the use of computers, the security of the data becomes ever more crucial. In addition to the need to keep all of its internal and customer records accurate, there are issues of protecting its new products and ideas, keeping its personnel and customer data confidential, and keeping its corporate budget and strategic planning information strictly within the company, to name a few issues.

We might ask such systems oriented questions as: Is the data protected against unauthorized access and unauthorized changes? Are the programs that do have legitimate access to the data protected against unauthorized modifications which could affect the data? Are the people who have legitimate access to some of the data in the database blocked from purposely or accidentally accessing the rest of the data?

Another concern is the ability to reconstruct the data if any part of it is inadvertently destroyed. The process of making a copy of a file for such purposes is referred to as a *backup* operation. The process of repairing a relatively small amount of damage to a file, or recreating a totally destroyed file, is called a *recovery* operation.

A third concern is the issue of *concurrency*. As we shall develop later, problems can arise when two or more users or programs attempt to update a particular piece of data simultaneously ("concurrently"). Without protections, the final result may not have taken into account all of the intended changes.

Since all three of these concerns are common concerns for all data, and since the procedures needed to handle them can be constructed in a very general manner, it is clear that such procedures should be built into any DBMS. To do otherwise would be to return to the earlier days of data processing when programmers were on their own for such issues with each new application they developed.

Data Communications Interface

In part of this chapter we discussed queries and query operations, and taking any necessary details for granted, we just assumed that interaction with the database was possible through a display terminal.

But, in fact, all of the detailed material discussed thus far in this book, and most of what is yet to come, concern the data, the DBMS and directly related topics of accessing the data. All of this *could* be done in a batch environment. But most DBMS environments today operate primarily in an on-line mode for fast access to data, immediate posting of changes to the data, and access to the data over a wide geographical range. The users and their terminals may all be clustered together near the computer itself, or they may be in far flung locations across the country or across the world.

The mechanisms needed to permit such an array of terminals, and in general the entire on-line environment, are not trivial and do not come free. Whether the data is in a database or not, such on-line terminal access to it requires a complex piece of software, usually called a "data communications driver," together with additional interfaces to the DBMS and to the application programs. (Note that the comment about "database or not" is in the same spirit as the similar comment about security, etc., in the last section.)

In the query language form of access, the DBMS must be prepared to receive messages from and send messages to terminals. In the embedded statement form, the application programs must not only have the capability of using special instructions for database access, but must also have the capability of using other special instructions to interact with the terminals. These instructions, inserted at appropriate places in the code according to the program logic, must be able to accept messages from the terminals, through the communications driver, and send messages back out again. The incoming messages, in their most basic form, will be requests for data in the database and instructions to change data in the database, and the outgoing messages will be the data being sent out to the terminals that requested it.

We will look at the issues of security, backup and recovery, and concurrency in more detail later in this book.

References

Date, C. J., *An Introduction to Database Systems*, 3rd ed., vol. 1, Addison-Wesley, Reading, MA, 1981.

King, J. M., *Evaluating Data Base Management Systems*, Van Nostrand Reinhold, New York, 1981.

Kroenke, D., *Database Processing*, 2nd ed., Science Research Associates, Chicago, IL, 1983.

Martin, J., *Computer Data-Base Organization*, 2nd ed., Prentice-Hall, Englewood Cliffs, NJ, 1977.

Ross, R. G., *Data Base Systems*, AMACOM, New York, 1978.

Questions and Exercises

5.1.   As described in this chapter, a database management system is a middleman between data and users. Think of another example of a middleman outside of data processing. Does it provide a total separation between the two parties? Do the two parties consider the middleman to be a help or a hindrance?

5.2.   What do you think are the benefits of having a middleman between data and its users in a data processing environment? Are there any disadvantages?

5.3. In your own words, what is a database management system?

5.4. Outline the capabilities that a database management system is expected to have.

5.5. What is the difference between the logical and the physical views of data stored in a database? What are the reasons for making the distinction?

5.6. What is the difference between a data definition language and a data manipulation language? How closely tied to each other are they?

5.7. What are the four approaches to database management system structure? At first glance, do you think that some of them are better than the others? Why or why not?

5.8. At first glance, do you think that all four of the database management system approaches are capable of fulfilling all of the promises of database?

5.9. What is the difference between an embedded data manipulation language and a query type data manipulation language?

5.10. In your own words, describe the circumstances under which someone might perceive an application that uses embedded statements to be in the realm of the query type language.

5.11. Give an introductory description of security, backup and recovery, and concurrency. How important do you think it is for a database management system to handle these concerns?

6

The Hierarchical Approach to Database

Introduction

The first approach to database management systems (DBMS) that we will look at is the hierarchical approach. Since one of the oldest and most widely used DBMSs is based on that approach, the thrust of this chapter will be to examine that DBMS: IBM's Information Management System (IMS).

In actuality IMS is composed of two parts. One part, Data Language/I (DL/I), is the database facility itself, including the data structure rules and the programming language interface. The second part, called the Data Communications Facility, is the communications driver (the software that defines an interactive environment) and allows messages and requests for data to be sent from terminals to the central computer and replies sent back to the terminals. IMS is not its own operating system, but runs under IBM's OS/MVS family of large scale operating systems. DL/I can also use the Customer Information Control System (CICS) as a communications driver in either the OS or DOS (a medium scale operating system) environments, or it can run as a batch only system, although that is not common today. In practice, the acronyms IMS and DL/I are used interchangeably to refer to the database portion of the system. This is the portion that will be discussed in this chapter.

IMS is a full-scale database management system capable of handling very large files and a very large number of simultaneous users. Of course, it has the ability to integrate data, reduce redundancy, and handle multiple relationships in the data. It also includes facilities for backup and recovery, security, and concurrent processing protection.

Hierarchies

Before looking at IMS, we should set a firm foundation in what a *hierarchy*, or *tree* (we'll use the words interchangeably) is. Figure 6.1 shows an abstract tree or hierarchy. It is simply an arrangement of points called *nodes* (numbered 1-11 in the figure) connected by *branches* or *edges* (the straight lines in the figure) with the following restrictions. There is one special node called the *root* which is always drawn at the top of the diagram. Node 1 is the root node in the tree in Figure 6.1. The tree branches downwards from the root; each node is capable of branching into several nodes at the next level downwards. As a result, every node (with the exception of the root) is connected upwards to only one node in the tree. For example, node 3 is connected upwards only to node 1. Node 9 is connected upwards (immediately) only to node 6.

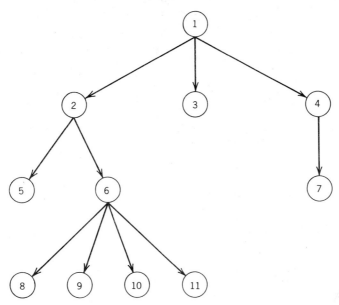

Figure 6.1.   A tree or hierarchy.

The nodes that come downwards directly out of a given node are called its *child nodes.* Conversely, each of those child nodes thinks of the node that it came from as its *parent node.* For example, in Figure 6.1, nodes 2, 3, and 4 are child nodes of node 1. Nodes 5 and 6 are child nodes of node 2. Node 1 is the parent of nodes 2, 3, and 4. Node 2 is the parent of nodes 5 and 6. We might speak of all of the nodes below a given node as its *descendants.* Thus the descendants of node 1 are nodes 2 through 11. The descendants of node 2 are nodes 5, 6, 8, 9, 10, and 11. A node with no branches coming out of it downwards (e.g., nodes 3, 5, and 8) is called a *leaf* or *terminal node,* as distinguished from nodes 1, 2, 4, and 6 which are called *nonterminal nodes* or *intermediate nodes.* Nodes that have the same parent (e.g., nodes 5 and 6) are called *twins* or *siblings.*

Actually, the use of the word "tree" here and the accompanying terminology, derive directly from trees in everyday life. Figure 6.2 shows a picture of a tree turned upside down. On top is the root and branching downwards are the branches, nodes, and leaves. Figure 6.3 shows a family tree, with all of the concepts of children, descendants, parents, and so forth. George and Mary (nee Smith) Jones have three children, John, Susan, and Marsha, and so on.

That the concept of the tree can be used to manage stored data may be a bit mysterious at this point, but we shall gradually develop that idea in the succeeding pages.

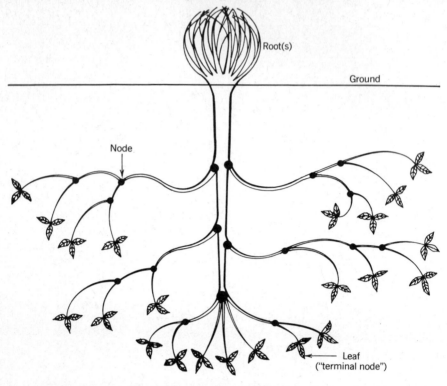

Figure 6.2. A real tree upside down.

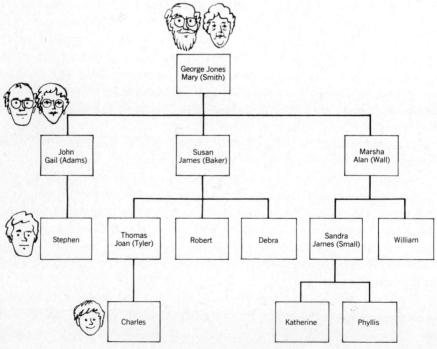

Figure 6.3. The Jones family tree.

IMS Physical Structure

Now that you know what a hierarchy is, let's begin the discussion of IMS by describing how data can be stored in that form and what the advantages are of doing so. We'll use an example that involves baseball teams. We have to maintain information about each team in the league, including information about all of the players on the team, all of the coaches on the team, the various pieces of prior work experience that each coach has, and the bats (each bat has a unique serial number) that each team has.

Simple Hierarchies

The Baseball Teams Hierarchy   Figure 6.4 shows the Baseball Teams hierarchy. The first thing to realize is that each node of this tree represents a different *record type,* called *segments* in IMS. The TEAMS record or segment, like any record, consists of a number of fields that describe the team: TEAM NAME, TEAM CITY, TEAM MANAGER, and so forth. The words in the boxes in Figure 6.4 are record or segment names; the field names are not shown at this point in order to keep the figure relatively simple.

Every branch in the tree in Figure 6.4 represents a one-to-many relationship. Thus for a given team there are many players, many coaches, and many bats. For a given coach there are many pieces of work experience. (By the way, "many" in this context really means 0, 1, or more than 1; for example, a coach might have no applicable pieces of work experience, one, or more than one.)

Still Figure 6.4 just shows the overall outline of how we are going to

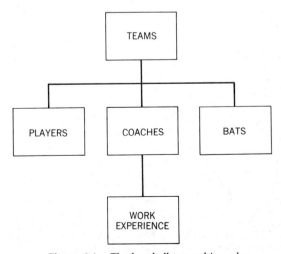

Figure 6.4.   The baseball teams hierarchy.

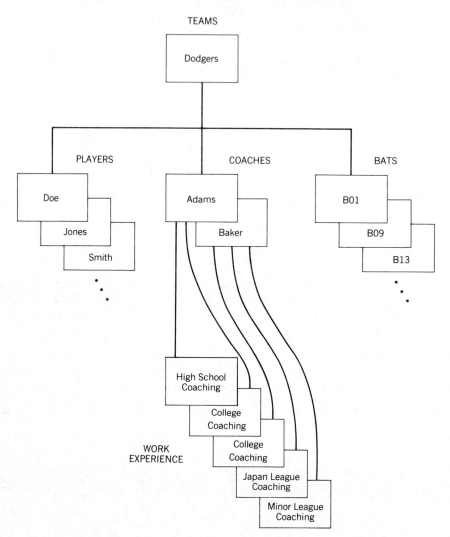

Figure 6.5. The Dodgers occurrence of the baseball teams hierarchy.

store information about baseball teams. It does not show the details of what the storage for one team would look like. Figure 6.5 shows the *occurrence* of the Teams hierarchy for the Dodgers. Such a hierarchical occurrence, which is called a *database record* in IMS, consists of a single occurrence of the root node, and all of its subordinate segment occurrences. All of the database records of the same hierarchy put together are called a *database*. Carrying that definition one step further, several databases spoken of together are also, informally, but usually, called a "database" or "databank."

Thus in Figure 6.5 we find the Dodgers occurrence of the TEAM record on top, the Doe, Jones, and Smith occurrences of the PLAYERS record attached underneath it, and so on. Coach Adams has high school and college coaching experience; Coach Baker has college, Japan League, and minor league coaching experience. (The connecting lines in Figure 6.5 are intended only to show the one-to-many relationships, not the physical storage arrangements—that will come next.) Following the earlier remarks, the words in the boxes in Figure 6.5 are record or segment occurrence names (or key field values—you can look at it either way). Although it's not shown, we understand that the Doe record really includes fields that describe his player serial number, his name, his hometown, and so forth.

Something else to notice about this hierarchic arrangement, which may not be immediately apparent, is the savings in what would otherwise be redundant data. Whatever information we have about the Dodgers that is stored in the Dodgers segment, for example, the name of the team manager, *applies to all of its subordinate segments*. For example, at one time or another we may want to know Doe's manager, Jones' manager, or Smith's manager. Since they're all on the same team, they all have the same manager and in fact we do not have to store his name redundantly with each player. The information is kept once, up above in the Dodgers segment. Part of the sense of data integration in the hierarchical arrangement is that, within a database record, data in a superior segment applies to all of the occurrences of its subordinate segments.

Once again this brings us to one of those places where the logical must give way to the physical. The previous discussion *sounds* good, but how do you convince a computer that bunches of record occurrences of different types are arranged in the tree-like form we've been describing? That's neither obvious nor trivial, but it is very important. Here are two fundamental methods.

Sequential Storage of Hierarchies.   One way of storing IMS hierarchical occurrences is to kind of flatten them, in a controlled way, and store them sequentially. Figure 6.6 shows a schematic of a section of computer memory (it could be either primary or disk memory) containing the Dodgers database record of Figure 6.5. The segment occurrences are laid out in a particular sequence which is a variation of a technique known as "preorder sequential traversal." Essentially, it's a top-to-bottom, left-to-right, and front-to-back listing. Notice that we start at the top of the tree and store the Dodgers segment first. Then we travel downwards and to the left and pick up the segment for player Doe. With nothing below Doe, we move "back" through Jones and Smith. Then we move towards the right and get coach Adams and his subordinate segment occurrences, and so on. Could we reconstruct

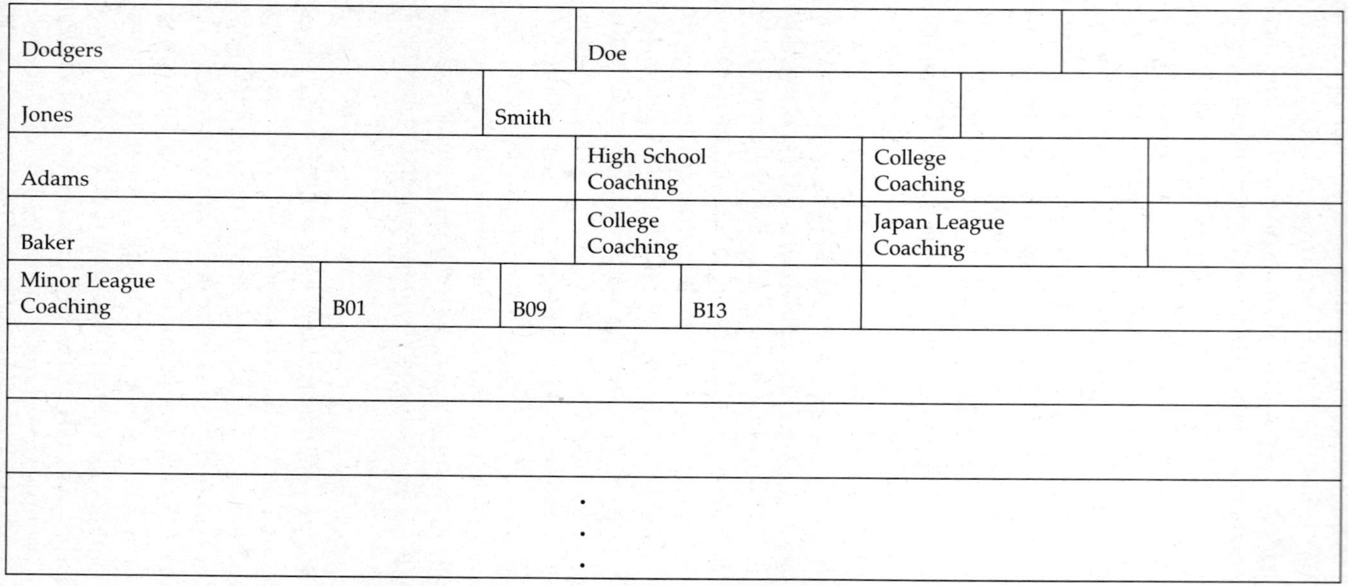

Dodgers	Jones	Smith	Doe								
Adams	High School Coaching		College Coaching								
Baker	College Coaching		Japan League Coaching								
Minor League Coaching	B01	B09	B13								

. . .

Figure 6.6. Sequential storage of the Dodgers team occurrence.

the tree from the stored form in Figure 6.6? Yes, but we would have to include some other information along the way, such as the segment type and segment length of each stored occurrence. (By the way, the empty spaces at the end of each line in Figure 6.6 are not directly germane to this discussion but add some realism to it. They indicate that there may be space boundaries in the disk storage medium and only records that entirely fit in a storage unit may do so. If not they must be placed in the next "line.")

This seems like a workable arrangement for storing a database record, and in fact it is quite appropriate for certain kinds of applications. Unfortunately it has a couple of drawbacks which make it inappropriate for use in most database applications, especially those requiring fast, on-line response to queries. One problem is that the way the segment occurrences are laid out so tightly in sequence makes it difficult to insert new data into the middle of a database record. For example, if a new player joins the team, there is no space left to insert his segment occurrence amongst those of the players already on the team.

The other problem has to do with rapid access to a specific segment occurrence. Let's assume for the moment that we can get to all of the root segment occurrences on some kind of a direct basis (we'll further develop this later). With the sequential storage arrangement, there is no way to get to any of the subordinate segment occurrences (i.e., all of the nonroot segment occurrences in the database record) except by methodically and slowly moving sequentially through the stored segments, starting with the root until you find the segment that you were looking for. For example, in Figure 6.6, if you know that Baker is one of the coaches on the Dodgers, and you want to find out about his prior experience, you have to read through the segments for Dodgers, Doe, Jones, and so on, until you finally reach Baker and his experience segments. There has to be a better way!

Pointer-Based Storage of Hierarchies.   The better way for achieving rapid access to a specific segment occurrence is based on the use of pointers to connect together the different segment occurrences of a database record. Figure 6.7 shows the Dodgers database record stored physically with two kinds of pointers, known as *child pointers* and *twin pointers.* Those terms follow the usage for the words child and twin that we developed earlier. A child pointer (called "physical child first" pointer in IMS) points from a given node to the first occurrence of one of its child segment types. Thus in Figure 6.7, there is a child pointer from Dodgers to Doe, the first of its players, to Adams, the first of its coaches, and to B01, the first of its bats. Also there is a child pointer from Adams to High School Coaching, and

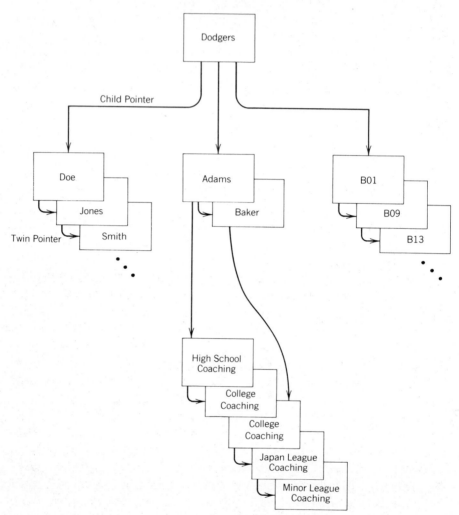

Figure 6.7. Child and twin pointer storage of the Dodgers team occurrence.

from Baker to College Coaching, in each case the first of their pieces of work experience. Each collection of segment occurrences of the same kind, *that belong to the same occurrence of the parent segment type,* are connected together by twin pointers ("physical twin forward" pointers in IMS). Doe, Jones, and Smith are all players on the Dodgers, and so are connected together by twin pointers (the arrangement is called a *twin chain*). Coaches Adams and Baker are chained together under Dodgers, as are all of the Dodgers' bats. Similarly, the High School Coaching segment and the (first) College Coaching segment are chained together under coach Adams, as are the (second) College Coaching segment, the Japan League Coaching segment, and the Minor League Coaching segment under coach Baker.

New segment occurrences can be added physically anywhere on the disk, as long as the appropriate pointers are updated and added to maintain the proper logical structure of the database record. Incidentally it does help, for performance reasons based on minimizing the amount of travel of the disk access arm mechanism, to insert the new segment in an open space as close to the other members of its twin chain as possible.

And this arrangement is much better for fast access of the subordinate segments. Again assuming that we can get to the Dodgers segment directly, locating Baker's pieces of experience is readily accomplished. First we follow a child pointer from Dodgers to Adams (the system can distinguish one child pointer from another, so with the proper command it will get to Adams and not to Doe or to bat B01). Then we follow a twin pointer from Adams to Baker, a child pointer from Baker to the first of his pieces of work experience, and a series of twin pointers to the rest of his pieces of work experience.

As options for performance reasons, IMS also provides pointers that go backwards through a twin chain and pointers that go from a segment occurrence to the last segment occurrence on its subordinate twin chains.

Logical Relationships

Introduction. We have seen that a single hierarchical structure can be a very powerful data storage form. But it also can be limiting, both in the degree of data integration that it permits, and in the fact that it cannot directly handle many-to-many relationships.

Figure 6.8 shows two hierarchical structures. The one on the left is the Teams hierarchy that we have been looking at. The one on the right is another hierarchy, the Players hierarchy. The Players hierarchy has one database record (remember, that means one root occurrence and all of its subordinate occurrences) for every player in the league. Stored with each player are his annual statistics, arranged as one segment occurrence per year, and information about the positions he is qualified to play.

As you look at those two hierarchies side-by-side, it might strike you as strange that a PLAYERS segment appears in both hierarchies. On the left it represents the players on a given team, while on the right it is an independent list of all of the players in the league. Let's assume that the fields in each of those two PLAYERS segments are identical (PLAYER SERIAL NUMBER, PLAYER NAME, PLAYER HOME ADDRESS, etc.). Then it might seem that an alternative to the two hierarchies in Figure 6.8 would

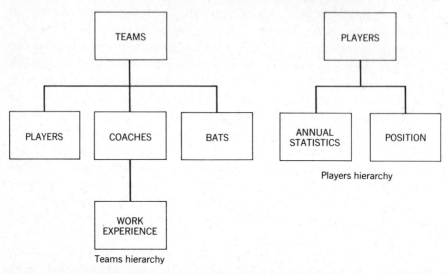

Teams hierarchy

Players hierarchy

Figure 6.8. The Teams and Players hierarchies.

be the single hierarchy in Figure 6.9 with the players' annual statistics and position information folded in under the PLAYERS segment in the Teams hierarchy. Is that a better solution?

It turns out that there are advantages to both the storage arrangements of Figure 6.8 and of Figure 6.9. (For the following discussion, remember that the assumption made earlier in this chapter—direct access can only be made to the root of each database record— still holds).

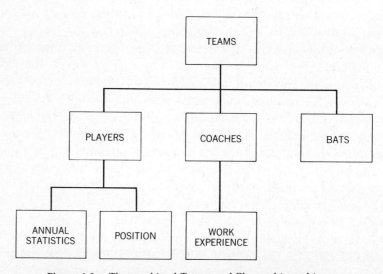

Figure 6.9. The combined Teams and Players hierarchies.

There are a couple of advantages to the two hierarchy arrangement in Figure 6.8. It may well be necessary, for some applications, to be able to reach PLAYERS segment occurrences directly. In the two hierarchy arrangement of Figure 6.8, PLAYERS can be reached directly, since the PLAYERS segment is the root of its own database. In the single hierarchy of Figure 6.9 PLAYERS cannot be reached directly (although later on we shall see an embellishment to the system which would allow that). Also in Figure 6.8, a player in the league who is not currently affiliated with a team can still exist quite comfortably in the Players hierarchy which is independent of teams. In the single hierarchy of Figure 6.9, a player can only exist if he is affiliated with a team. (We might fix that by having a special team called "unaffiliated players," but in general you can see that that sort of thing might be a problem.)

On the other hand, there are a couple of advantages to the single hierarchy arrangement in Figure 6.9. The most obvious is the one that we have already alluded to: by moving the player annual statistics and position information over to the Teams hierarchy we eliminate the redundancy of having each PLAYER segment appear twice, once in each of the two hierarchies. And with the single hierarchy arrangement we achieve a higher degree of data integration. Suppose we want a report detailing all of the player position information for all of the players for a given team. Even though we have not gone into data accessing in IMS yet, you can see that in the two hierarchy arrangement of Figure 6.8, we would have to use the Teams hierarchy to find out who all of the players are on that team and then use that information to inquire about the position information for those players in the Players hierarchy. In the single hierarchy of Figure 6.9, we can gather all of that information in a much more direct manner.

So which arrangement do we use? What we would really like is "to have our cake and eat it too." We would like the more flexible access and less restrictive storage benefits of the two hierarchy case and, at the same time, the reduced redundancy and higher degree of data integration of the single hierarchy case. In fact, there is a facility in IMS which brings together the best of both of those worlds, and it is called *logical relationships*.

Figure 6.10 shows what is known as a unidirectional logical relationship. We have replaced the PLAYERS segment in the Teams hierarchy with a special kind of pointer segment known as a *logical child segment*. We can jump from that logical child segment in the Teams hierarchy to the PLAYERS segment in the Players hierarchy, effectively finding all of the players on a given team, just as we could with the old PLAYERS segment in the Teams hierarchy. In fact, do we have our cake and can we eat it too? Since the Players hierarchy remains as it was we can find players directly (it's

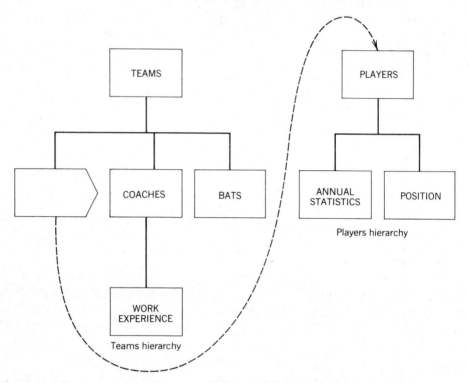

Figure 6.10. A unidirectional logical relationship.

still the root of its own hierarchy) and handle the case of a player not currently on a team. Since the player information only appears in one of the two hierarchies we have eliminated the players redundancy that we were concerned about. Finally, using the logical relationship we can start at the TEAMS segment of the Teams hierarchy and cross over to the Players hierarchy, picking up all of the player, annual statistics, and position information that we desire. That takes care of the broader level of data integration that we talked about before.

Implementation. How does that really work on the disk? Figure 6.11 shows part of the Dodgers database record from the Teams database, together with the root portions of the Doe, Jones, and Smith database records from the Players database. The logical child segment behaves like any other segment type in the Teams hierarchy. Thus its first occurrence under a given team is reached via a child pointer, and the rest are reached via a twin chain as shown. But there is now an additional pointer, housed in

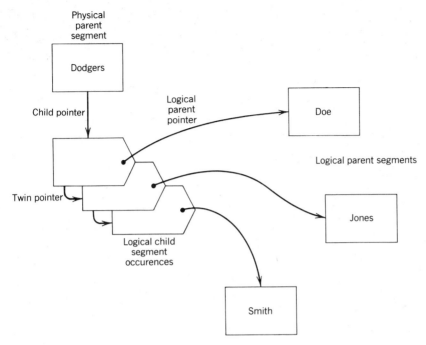

Figure 6.11. An occurrence of the logical relationship.

the logical child segment (called a *logical parent pointer*) which jumps over to the other database. Incidentally because the logical child segment is really a part of the Teams hierarchy, we refer to its parent segment, TEAMS, as its *physical parent*, and the segment that it points to in the other hierarchy, PLAYERS, as its *logical parent*.

As an aside, why did we bother setting up an entire new segment type, the logical child segment, to effect the logical relationship? In going from Dodgers to the logical child occurrences and over to the PLAYERS occurrences aren't we just following one pointer (the child pointer out of Dodgers) to another pointer (the logical parent pointer) to finally get to the destination? Why not just have one pointer in Dodgers that points directly over to its players? The answer is that we can't do that because we don't know how many players there are on the Dodgers and so we wouldn't know how much room to leave for all of the pointers that we would have to put in the Dodgers segment. Setting up the logical child segments as we have done allows for any number of players, lets the system use its normal methods for insertions and deletions, and simplifies the application programming. It also allows for something called "intersection data."

Intersection Data. We long ago settled the matter that simple attribute data, like a team's manager, is stored as a field in the appropriate segment. But there is another kind of attribute data. Often there is descriptive information about the relationship *between* two entities and that kind of information cannot go into either of their segments. Consider, for example, the number of years that a player has played on a particular team. Could that information be stored in the team's segment? No, because there are many players on that team and it would be impractical to store such information in its segment. What about in the player's segment? If we now consider this database to hold historical data, we have the same problem: a player may have played on several different teams over many years. The answer is to take advantage of the logical child segments. One of the things that Figure 6.11 shows is that there is a different occurrence of the logical child segment *for every related team and player*. Thus the logical child occurrence that connects two entity occurrences is the natural place to store such *intersection data*. Figure 6.12 shows how we would represent intersection

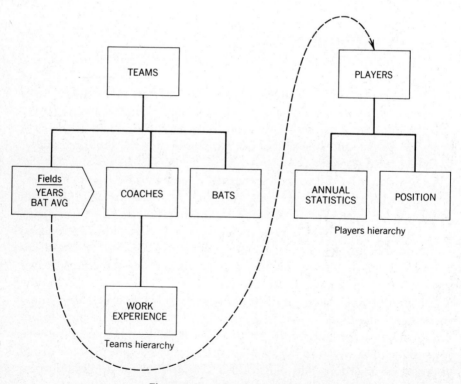

Figure 6.12. Intersection data.

data in the general structure. By the way, that's the first time that we've seen fields—intersection data is represented as fields—in any of this series of figures. (BAT AVG is that player's batting average calculated over all of the years that he played for that team.)

Many-to-Many Relationships. Hierarchies, as we have shown, are quite adept at handling one-to-many relationships. But as it turns out, a single simple hierarchy cannot handle many-to-many relationships. Look at Figure 6.5 once again. Both coaches Adams and Baker had college coaching experience. Let's assume for the moment that there are no fields other than the EXPERIENCE NAME field in those WORK EXPERIENCE segments, making the two College Coaching segments identical. If that's the case, then isn't it redundant to carry the identical College Coaching segment under two different coaches?

Yes, it is. But what is the alternative? If we had both Adams and Baker, either through child or twin pointers, point to a single College Coaching segment, then we would get all mixed up over whether the Japan League Coaching and Minor League Coaching segments, connected to the College Coaching segment via a twin chain, belonged to Adams or to Baker. The reason that happens is that the situation described really involves a many-to-many relationship. Now we're saying that for a given coach there are many pieces of work experience and for a given piece of work experience, there are many coaches who have it. Thus for the reason shown, a simple hierarchy can't handle a many-to-many relationship.

The solution to the problem of handling many-to-many relationships in

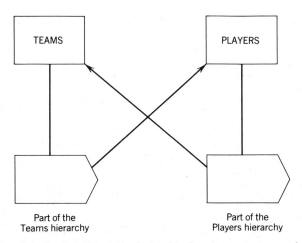

Figure 6.13. A bidirectional logical relationship for a many-to-many relationship.

IMS is to use another form of logical relationship called a *bidirectional logical relationship*. Figure 6.13 shows the root segments of the Teams and Players hierarchies, each with a logical child pointing to the other. Again, consider the data to be historical in nature so that we are interested in keeping track of all of the teams that a particular player has ever played on, and of all of the players who have ever played on a particular team. This is a many-to-many relationship which can be implemented in IMS by the dual or bidirectional logical relationship structure shown.

Once again moving to a view of the actual storage, Figure 6.14 shows

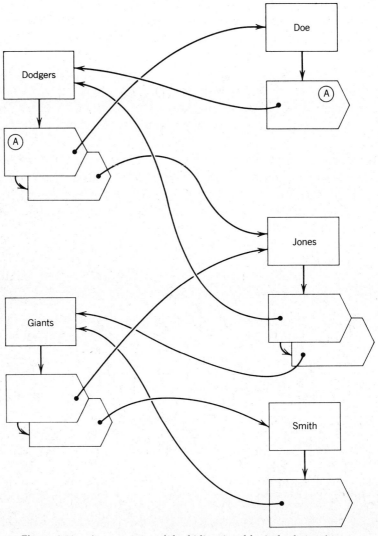

Figure 6.14.   An ocurrence of the bidirectional logical relationship.

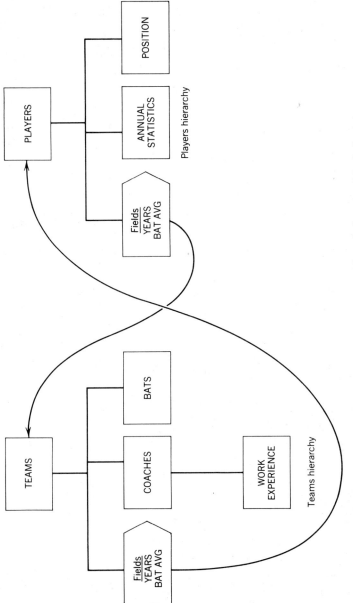

Figure 6.15. The Teams and Players hierarchies connected by a bidirectional logical relationship.

127

an occurrence of that bidirectional logical relationship. The Dodgers have had Doe and Jones on their team. The Giants have had Jones and Smith on their team. Conversely, Doe has played for the Dodgers, Jones has played for the Dodgers and for the Giants, and Smith has played for the Giants. The child, twin, and logical parent pointers operate as before, but in both directions.

With this arrangement, there are two logical child occurrences for every match-up between a player and a team, specifically one under the player involved and one under the team involved. The two boxes labeled "A" in Figure 6.14 both connect the Dodgers with Doe. We will note in passing that if intersection data exists, such as the number of years that a player has played for a team in this example, it is stored in both of the appropriate logical child segments and if it ever changes in one place, the system automatically updates it in the other.

Figure 6.15 shows the entire Teams and Players hierarchies connected by the bidirectional "physically paired" logical relationship. It also includes the YEARS and BAT AVG fields as sample intersection data. Note that there is another, structurally more complex form of bidirectional logical relationship (called "virtually paired") in which intersection data resides on only one side of the relationship.

Logical vs. Physical Databases

Incidentally did it sound strange a little while ago when we were talking about a logical child segment's "logical" and "physical" parents? Were we saying that the logical child segment can have *two* parent segment types, a physical parent and a logical parent? Doesn't that violate the fact that in a tree a node can have only one parent? Yes and no.

The two separate structures in Figure 6.8 are both clearly hierarchies. The combined structures shown in Figures 6.10, 6.13, and 6.15 are, technically, restricted networks. We will discuss networks as a database storage form in Chapter 7. Suffice it to say for now that a network is a more complex form than a hierarchy (in fact a hierarchy is a limited kind of network). What is important about this in terms of IMS is that while, technically, the use of logical relationships creates networks in the underlying physical structure, *programmers always write their programs based on hierarchies.*

All of the IMS database structures that we have looked at thus far are known as IMS *physical databases.* Programmers (we will look at IMS programming shortly) write their code based on IMS *logical databases.* Logical databases are really, merely descriptions of what the programmers should consider the data to look like. Segments of logical databases map onto seg-

Figure 6.16. A logical database derived from a single physical hierarchy.

ments of physical databases, which contain the actual data. An IMS logical database, in the simplest case, is a subtree of an IMS physical hierarchy, that is, it consists of a node and some or all of its descendants. The starting node, that is, the root of the logical database, must be either the root of the physical database or a node which has a secondary index (to be discussed later) pointing into it. Figure 6.16 is a logical database derived from the Teams physical database. Compare Figure 6.16 with Figure 6.8 to see the mapping between the two. Figure 6.17 is a logical database derived

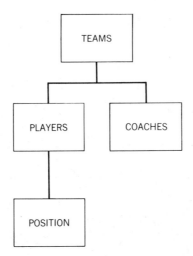

Figure 6.17. A logical database derived from two physical hierarchies connected by a logical relationship.

from the Teams and Players physical hierarchies and the logical relationship
between them. Compare Figure 6.17 with Figure 6.10 and see how the
logical relationship connecting the two physical databases becomes a branch
in the logical database.

There are a couple of advantages to the concept of logical databases.
One is simplicity in that the programmers always work with hierarchies
and not networks. Another is the ability to have different programs access
data from the same physical database(s), with each program being restricted
to only those segments (and even only those fields) that it really needs.

Access Methods

In Chapter 3, we discussed access methods for simple linear files. Several
times thus far in this chapter there has appeared the expression, "assuming
that we can reach the root occurrences directly." The time has come to
make some meaning out of that expression and discuss access methods in
the hierarchical context.

There are four main "IMS Access Methods". They are:

1. Hierarchic Sequential Access Method (HSAM)
2. Hierarchic Indexed Sequential Access Method (HISAM)
3. Hierarchic Indexed Direct Access Method (HIDAM)
4. Hierarchic Direct Access Method (HDAM)

The choice of IMS Access Method really determines two things. One is
whether the individual database records will be stored using the sequential
or pointer based storage techniques. The second is the type of access that
the system will construct to the root occurrence of each database record.
Figure 6.18 outlines all of the possibilities.

In HSAM the database records are constructed using the sequential storage technique. As far as access to the root occurrences goes, there is no

	Access to Root	Database Record Structure
HSAM	Sequential	Sequential
HISAM	Indexed	Sequential
HIDAM	Indexed	Pointer-Based
HDAM	Hashed	Pointer-Based

Figure 6.18.   IMS access methods.

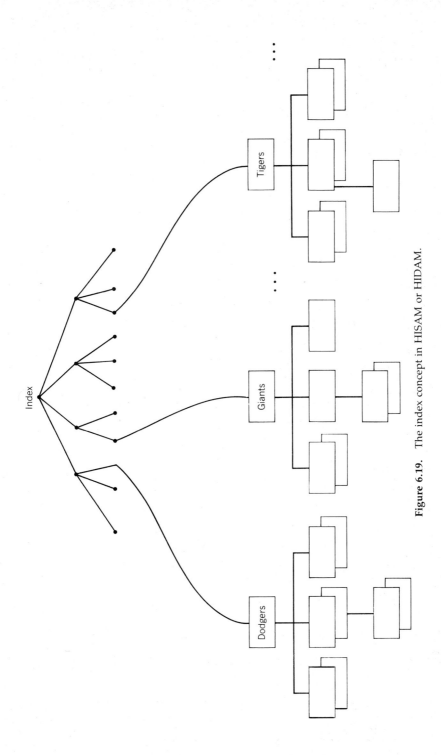

Figure 6.19. The index concept in HISAM or HIDAM.

direct access capability. The database records are simply stored one after the other on the disk in sequence based on the key field in the root segment. Lacking any direct access capability HSAM is used, for example, for archival storage.

As in HSAM, in HISAM the database records are constructed using the sequential storage technique. But in HISAM, the database records are directly accessible via an index which points to the key field of the root occurrences, Figure 6.19. The index used today is usually the VSAM-KSDS index that we discussed in Chapter 3. Since that is really an indexed-sequential structure, not only are the database records directly accessible by the key of the root segment, but they are also stored in physical sequence by that field too.

In HIDAM the database records are constructed using the child pointer, twin pointer arrangement (or another method known as hierarchic pointers). Here as in HISAM, the VSAM-KSDS index is used to access the roots. The combination of direct, indexed access to the roots, plus pointer based construction of the database records makes HIDAM a candidate for use in on-line, fast response systems.

In HDAM the database records are constructed using the pointer based method. The root occurrences are directly accessible, but this time using a hashing based access method. That means that with HDAM, access to the root occurrences is normally faster than with HIDAM, but since hashing is used, the database records are in no particular order, sequential or otherwise, on the disk. The fastest access method is generally considered to be HDAM.

One final note about this topic, Figure 6.19 is really a rather profound diagram. It shows the use of the tree concept *both for index construction and for data storage* simultaneously. The VSAM-KSDS index is based on the tree concept, as is the method of storing the actual data in the IMS database records. The distinction between those two uses of the tree, and the fact that they can be used in tandem are important, interesting, and often overlooked.

Secondary Indexes

Using the IMS Access Methods, direct access to database records can be achieved through the key field of the root segment. But there are many circumstances in which additional direct access is required. This can either take the form of direct access to the root segment via a field other than the key or direct access to any field of any other segment. For example, going back to the Teams hierarchy in Figure 6.8, we might want direct access to

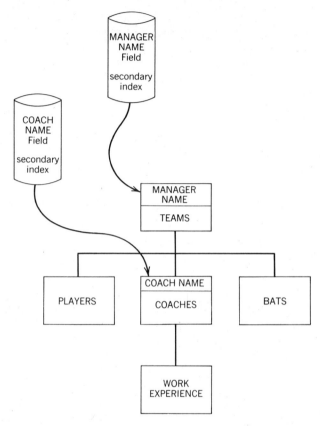

Figure 6.20. Secondary indexes.

the TEAMS segment via the MANAGER NAME field or direct access to the COACHES segment via the COACH NAME field.

Such additional direct access can be accomplished by the use of a *secondary index*. While the values of the key fields used in the IMS Access Methods must be unique, the fields on which secondary indexes are built need not be unique. Figure 6.20 shows the Teams hierarchy with secondary indexes pointing to the two fields suggested. The secondary indexes themselves are organized as additional VSAM-KSDS indexes.

A side effect of the use of secondary indexes is additional flexibility in the creation of logical databases. We mentioned earlier that without the use of secondary indexes, the root of a logical database must be the root of a physical database. However, with the use of secondary indexes, the root of a logical database may be either the root of a physical database or a segment pointed to by a secondary index. Loosely speaking, the root of a logical database must map onto a physical segment that can be accessed

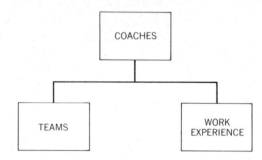

Figure 6.21. A logical database based on a secondary index.

directly. If the root of a logical database is a segment pointed to by a secondary index, the structure of the logical database must conform to certain rules. Figure 6.21 shows a logical database based on the physical database of Figure 6.20. Relying on the Coach Name secondary index, the COACHES segment is set up as the root of the logical hierarchy. The subordinate segments in the logical hierarchy fall into two classes. They may be any of the logical root's descendants in the physical hierarchy (the WORK EXPERIENCE segment in this case). Or they may be the segments in the unique path of segments from the indexed segment (COACHES) back to the root of the physical database (which qualifies only the TEAMS segment in this example). In this arrangement, the system uses an optional pointer called the "physical parent" pointer to point upwards in the physical hierarchy, for example, from COACHES to TEAMS in Figure 6.20, so that logically COACHES can have TEAMS as a subordinate segment type in Figure 6.21.

Let's note in passing that since a secondary index orders the values of the field that it indexes, it can be used for sequential retrieval too. For example, the COACH NAME Field secondary index of Figure 6.20 could be used to retrieve all of the league's coaches in alphabetic order, regardless of what teams they are working for. The problem with that is performance: since the coaches were stored relative to the teams that they work for, their storage was done without regard to keeping coach names that are close in alphabetic order near each other on the disk. Using the secondary index to retrieve them sequentially will cause a great deal of disk access arm movement and poor performance will result.

Control Blocks

We're about to discuss how programmers use IMS and its data (the "data manipulation language"). But first, we must mention the link within the

IMS system between the data structures and the application programs that will use them.

It's well and good to talk about hierarchies, logical relationships, and so on and about how they are physically stored and accessed. But how does the IMS system, as the middleman between the data and the programs, know what the nature of the data is and how it is stored. The answer is with a set of instructions given to IMS, known as *control blocks.*

There are several kinds of control blocks in IMS, and it is interesting to see how they mesh with the concepts and structures that we have been talking about. One is called the Physical Data Base Description (Physical DBD). Physical DBDs describe the physical storage structures, including what the segments are, how they are arranged in hierarchies, key fields, logical relationships, secondary indexes, IMS access methods, and optional pointer choices. Interestingly, the way that the hierarchical structure is specified is by indicating the parent of each listed segment. Since one of the characteristics of the tree structure is that every node has exactly one parent, except for the root which has none, that method is an unambiguous way of specifying to the system what the tree structures look like.

Then there are several kinds of control blocks which describe what we have called the logical databases, that is, the way that programmers perceive the data. First there is the Logical Data Base Description (Logical DBD) control block. It selects those segments of individual or logical relationship connected physical hierarchies which will form the programmers' hierarchical views. The Program Communication Block (PCB) is a control block which picks out subtrees from the Logical DBDs (the rules about which segments may be roots in the logical structures hold here too) for specific program uses. Any given IMS program ties to one Program Specification Block (PSB) which lists all of the PCBs needed by that program.

DL/I Language Interface

Introduction

In terms of data manipulation, DL/I is what we referred to earlier as an "embedded" language. DL/I statements that access the data in the IMS database are embedded in COBOL, PL/I, or Assembler language application programs. In effect, the DL/I statements function as macro or subroutine calls to the IMS database management system, instructing it to retrieve or store data in the IMS databases. Let's take a look at how this works.

The Calling Mechanism

The DL/I call statement contains a number of parameters, each designed to perform a specific function in communicating between the program and the database during the data transfer operation. The parameter that sets the tone for this call statement is the "Function Code," which specifies what kind of data transfer statement it is. It distinguishes among the four basic kinds of such operations: (1) retrieval, (2) update, (3) insertion, and (4) deletion and among some variations within them as we shall soon see.

Once you have specified what kind of operation this is to be, you must indicate what portion of the database it is to operate on. For that purpose, the DL/I call statement includes a PCB name. Remember a PCB is a control block which defines a portion of the database from the programmer's point of view.

Also there must be a defined storage area in main memory which serves as the actual transfer point for data. When a retrieval operation is specified, that is the place that the program knows the requested data will be placed after it is found in the database. Also on an insertion or update operation, that is the place that the program is to put the new data for the system to pick up and transfer to the database. In DL/I that is called the "Input/Output Area" or "I/O Area".

In addition, there is other information that the system passes back for the program's use after a call is made. This includes a list of the key field occurrences of the segments that the system encounters from the root segment down to the segment being sought. The list of key field occurrences is placed in a designated storage area (called the "Key Feedback Area".) The system also sends back a status code providing further information about the result of the call.

Last but not least in the call statement are the "Segment Search Arguments" (SSAs). These are parameters which guide the system through the hierarchy specified by the PCB, to the place where the desired operation is to take place. In the following example we will further explain all of these parameters and concepts.

Figure 6.22 is a more detailed description of the Teams hierarchy of Figure 6.4. In this case it is a logical database which encompasses the entire Teams physical database. It not only shows the segments in the hierarchy but also the fields in the segments. Both the segment and field names are abbreviated in ways suitable for use in program statements. The leftmost field in each segment is a unique key field. In DL/I the root segment must have a unique key field, but the subordinate segments may or may not have one. Figure 6.23 is the occurrence of the Teams hierarchy for the Dodgers (the Dodgers

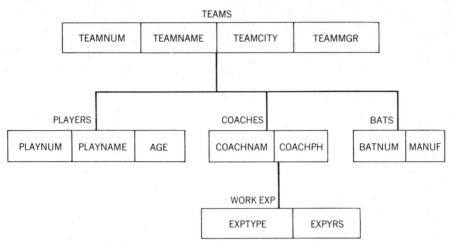

Figure 6.22. The teams hierarchy showing segment names and field names.

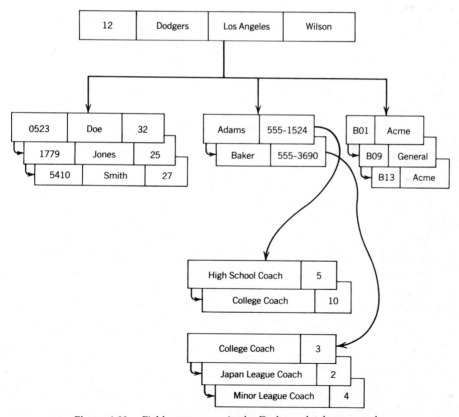

Figure 6.23. Field occurrences in the Dodgers database record.

137

database record) first shown in Figure 6.5, but this time including the field occurrences. As shown it is structured with child and twin pointers. We will assume that the IMS Access Method chosen is either HIDAM or HDAM so that the key field of the root segment is either indexed or hashed for direct access.

Direct Retrieval

The simplest kind of DL/I statement is the Get Unique statement, which has a function code of "GU". It is designed to find a specific segment occurrence directly and return it or several of its fields to the calling program. The nature of the direct retrieval is based on locating the root segment of a logical hierarchy. Again, this means that that segment either maps to a segment that is the root of a physical hierarchy (and is accessible either by a hashing algorithm or an index) or is a segment that has a secondary index pointing to it. Let's take a look at it in the context of our baseball example.

Suppose you want to find the root occurrence of the Dodgers database record because you want to find out what are its homecity and manager's name. Assume that at the point you need the information, you know that the Dodgers are team number 12. At the appropriate point in your program's logic, you would issue the following DL/I call: (Note: for simplicity, all of the following examples will show only the function code and segment search arguments).

GU TEAMS (TEAMNUM = 12)

The expression "TEAMS (TEAMNUM = 12)" is called a Qualified SSA. Remember that the PCB denoted in the call (not shown in this example) specifies *which hierarchy* you are interested in. The segment name (TEAMS) in the SSA specifies *which segment type in that hierarchy* you are interested in. The field name and value (TEAMNUM = 12) in the SSA specifies *which occurrence of that segment type in that hierarchy* you are interested in. Thus the expression "GU TEAMS (TEAMNUM = 12)", with the Teams hierarchy specified in the PCB, says to the system, "Go to the Teams hierarchy and find the occurrence of the TEAMS segment which has a TEAMNUM field value of 12, and return that segment to the program." In this case, since the field involved in the SSA (the "search field") is a unique key field, then of course, there will only be one segment involved.

Since TEAMNUM is a unique key field, and in fact, is the key field of the root segment, this call will be quite straightforward. The system will determine which IMS Access Method the database is stored with, and thus determine whether the database records are stored with an index based on the key of the root (TEAMNUM) or are stored directly with a hashing algorithm based on the key of the root (TEAMNUM). The system will find the TEAMS segment for Dodgers and return

12   Dodgers   Los Angeles   Wilson

to the designated I/O Area.

You can also issue a Get Unique call with a search field that is not the key of the root segment (and is not a field that has been indexed with a secondary index). In that case the system will do a sequential search through the database records of that database looking for the requested segment. Obviously this can be a very time consuming process, therefore the database design and the DL/I calls must take it into account.

The following is an example with multiple SSAs. Suppose you know that Baker, a coach on the Dodgers, used to be a minor league coach and you want to find out how many years he coached in the minors. You would issue the following DL/I call:

```
GU TEAMS (TEAMNUM = 12)
   COACHES (COACHNAM = Baker)
   WORKEXP (EXPTYPE = Minor League Coach).
```

Look at Figure 6.22 and notice that each of the three SSAs refers to a record type at a successive level downwards in the hierarchy. Again since the first SSA refers to the key field of the root segment, the system will find the Dodgers root directly. Then following the instructions in the succeeding SSAs, it will move from the Dodgers database record, following along the child and twin pointers, to the COACHES occurrence for Baker, then to the WORKEXP occurrence for Minor League Coach. Note that if any of the search fields in the lower level SSAs are not unique, the system will choose the first occurrence that it comes to which satisfies the condition within the higher level SSA constraints. It will return the last segment named in the SSA list to the I/O Area:

Minor League Coach   4.

The Key Feedback Area will contain:

12   Baker   Minor League Coach

which are the key fields of the three segments designated by the SSAs and accessed during the search. The EXPYRS field in the retrieved segment has the value 4, and that is the answer to the question.

SSAs can also be "unqualified". Suppose we know that each coaches' set of work experiences are ordered from earliest to most recent, and you want to find Baker's earliest piece of work experience, not knowing in advance what type it is. You would issue:

```
GU TEAMS (TEAMNUM = 12)
    COACHES (COACHNAM = Baker)
    WORKEXP
```

The system would home in on Baker under Dodgers and pick up the first of his pieces of work experience with no qualification.

What if you issue a Get Unique and the segment that you specify in the SSAs is not there? This is where the status code comes in. For each DL/I function code, there are a number of status codes that can be returned by the system after a call with that code is issued. In the situation of the missing segment described here, a status code indicating "Not Found" would be returned. After every DL/I call the application program must include instructions to test for the status codes that are appropriate possibilities for the function code used in that call.

Sequential Retrieval

IMS is also capable of conducting sequential searches through the database. In their simplest form, such sequential searches consist of retrieving all or some of the segments on a twin chain. However, sequential searches can involve occurrences of different segment types in a database record and even segment occurrences in more than one database record. It is important to note that when the latter happens, the order of retrieval is preorder sequential: top-to-bottom, left-to-right, and front-to-back, regardless of whether the actual storage of the segment occurrences is accomplished physically sequentially in preorder sequential order or is accomplished with child and twin pointers.

In the direct retrieval situations that we just saw the search always started at the beginning of the database. In sequential retrieval we will establish a position at a particular record in the database and work from there. That position, which can be set with either a GU call, or with one of the sequential type calls, which we are about to look at, is held with a "current position" pointer which the system takes responsibility for maintaining. Loosely speaking, it means the system always keeps track of exactly "where it is in the database" at any given time.

As a final note before looking at a few examples, let's consider how a program can use the data returned to it as the result of IMS sequential retrievals. In the direct retrieval case, the program issued a single request and got back a single segment occurrence. In an in-line fashion, the program's logic could make whatever use of the data it was supposed to. But in the sequential retrieval case, the program must plan to process multiple occurrences of the same segment type (on a twin chain) or even occurrences of different segment types. Thus the IMS calls involving sequential retrieval statements must be in the midst of some kind of loop in the program logic to process one occurrence, then another, then another, until all of the intended occurrences have been processed.

Suppose you wanted to retrieve all of the occurrences of all types of segments under the Dodgers root. You would first issue:

GU TEAMS (TEAMNUM = 12)

which would accomplish two things. First of all it would get you the information in that root segment occurrence, and second it would establish the system's current position pointer at that segment occurrence. Then to get all of the subordinate segment occurrences, you would issue the "Get Next" statement in some kind of a program loop:

GN

Each time that (very simple) GN call statement is executed in the loop, the system will return another segment in preorder sequential order. First will be the PLAYERS segment for Doe, then Jones, then Smith, then the COACHES segment for Adams, followed by his two WORKEXP segments, then Baker, followed by his three WORKEXP segments, then the three BATS segments. If the GN call was executed one more time, the next segment occurrence to be returned would be the root segment of *the next database record.* To stop that from happening, the program must continually check the status code returned by the system. After GN calls the system will indicate whether the current position pointer has moved up a level in the database record, has retrieved a segment type different than the last one, or has reached the end of the database. Of course the program can also check to see the type of segment retrieved which would also answer the question of whether it has gone on to the next database record (i.e., if the segment type retrieved is a root).

For example, as a variation on this theme, if you issue

GN COACHES

in a loop, you will retrieve all of the COACH segment occurrences starting from the point that the current position pointer is at, to the point that your program ends the execution of the loop.

While the GN statement is obviously useful, it may have struck you that it seems a bit uncontrolled in the way that it can jump from segment type to segment type. What is needed is a way to more carefully limit the range of a sequential retrieval call. In fact, it is quite common to have application situations in which we want to focus on a single, particular segment occurrence, and consider only its subordinate occurrences, and no other record occurrences in the database. To accomplish this in DL/I there is another function code called "Get Next Within Parent" (GNP).

Let's say that you want to find all of the players on the Dodgers. First you would "establish parentage" (which can be done with either a GU or GN call) by issuing:

GU TEAMS (TEAMNUM = 12).

Then you would loop through:

GNP PLAYERS

After you have retrieved the last of the players on the Dodgers (Smith), the next pass through that loop will produce a status code indicating that there are no more occurrences of that segment type within the parentage setting (no more players on the Dodgers).

If you want to find all of the subordinate segment occurrences of all types under the Dodgers root, you would again establish parentage at Dodgers and then loop through

GNP

This time in preorder sequential order, you will pick up all of the subordinate segment occurrences under Dodgers, from Doe to bat number B13, and then on the next pass through the loop the system would return the status code indicating that you have reached the end of the parentage bounds.

Insertion, Deletion, and Update

Insertion.   When a new segment occurrence is to be inserted, the program must place it in the I/O Area. Then a DL/I Insert call must be issued with the lowest level SSA left unqualified. For example, if you want to insert a new player under Dodgers, you would place the new segment occurrence in the I/O Area and issue:

```
ISRT TEAMS (TEAMNUM = 12)
     PLAYERS
```

If the segment occurrence being inserted is a root, then the system uses the appropriate indexing or hashing technique to insert it into the correct place in the database. If it is not a root, then the system will insert it into the appropriate twin chain in one of several ways. If the segment type has a unique key field on which sequence is being maintained, then the system will insert the segment into the place that will maintain that sequence based on the inserted segment's key field value. If the segment type has no key field, then it will be placed either at the beginning of the twin chain (referred to as "first" in the syntax), the end of the twin chain ("last"), or at the point in the twin chain that the system's current position pointer is currently at (hopefully somewhere in that twin chain) ("here"), depending on specifications made in the control blocks. If the segment has a non-unique key field, then the same "first, last, or here" rules apply within the equi-key value segments on that twin chain.

Deletion. Deletion is simply a matter of specifying a particular segment occurrence by having the system's current position pointer point to it and then issuing a DLET call. That pointer would ordinarily be positioned with a retrieval call: GU, GN, or GNP. However, there is a potential problem, not just with IMS, but with any shared data situation in which multiple users may try to simultaneously change a record. It requires the use of slightly different function codes in this context. We will discuss that problem later under the heading of "concurrency." Suffice it for now to say that there is a set of commands parallel to Get Unique, Get Next, and Get Next Within Parent, known as "Get Hold" commands which are used when that situation may be a factor. They are Get Hold Unique (GHU), Get Hold Next (GHN), and Get Hold Next Within Parent (GHNP). Thus to delete the segment occurrence for bat number B09, you would issue:

```
GHU TEAMS (TEAMNUM = 12)
     BATS (BATNUM = B09)
DLET
```

There is a potential complication on a delete operation, which has to do with logical relationships. First let's look a little bit closer at deletions within our single physical hierarchy example. If we delete the segment for coach Adams, we should reasonably expect the system to also automatically delete his experience segments, and it will. There's no point in keeping around a coach's experience segments if he no longer exists. In fact, this is a characteristic of the hierarchical structure: other than a root occurrence, every segment occurrence must be attached to a parent occurrence at all times.

But what if the DL/I call refers to a logical database which involves two physical databases connected by a logical relationship. Refer back to the logical hierarchy in Figure 6.17 and to the two connected hierarchies in Figure 6.12 on which that logical hierarchy is based. If we delete the Dodgers root segment occurrence, should all of the players on the Dodgers be deleted from the database too? After all they are connected under Dodgers in the logical hierarchy in Figure 6.17. On the other hand in the physical hierarchies of Figure 6.12, they stand alone as occurrences of a physical root segment type. The answer depends on the application situation. We might want them to be deleted or we might not want them to be deleted. The system is general enough to allow for that decision to be made in advance in the control blocks. In IMS this is called "rules coding,"and there are such "rules" for insertion and update as well as for deletion.

Update. The update operation in DL/I is called "Replace" and has a function code of REPL. The mode of operation is a cross between those of Insert and Delete. The updated segment is placed in the I/O Area (as in Insert). The segment to be updated is located in the database with the current position pointer, and the Get Hold commands are used (as in Delete).

Additional Topics

Command Codes. Certain parameters (called "command codes") can be added to DL/I call statements. They are capable of expanding the range of function of the DL/I calls. Here are two examples.

As we have seen, a multi-SSA call retrieves only the segment named in the last SSA. There is a parameter which signals a "path call" which retrieves all (or any additional specified) of the segments in the unique path of segments between the first and last specified SSAs. For example, the call:

```
GU TEAMS*D (TEAMNUM = 12)
    BATS (BATNUM = B09)
```

would return:

12   Dodgers   Los Angeles   Wilson   B09   General

in the I/O Area. "D" is the parameter for the path call and is not required on the last SSA since it is always returned.

The parameter "L" will find the last occurrence on a twin chain. For example:

GU TEAMS (TEAMNUM = 12)
    BATS*L

will return:

B13   Acme

in the I/O Area.

Multiple "Current Position Pointers".   We have described the current position pointer as a place keeper within a database. There are application situations in which one such pointer is not enough. For instance, a program may need to keep track of the last occurrence of each of several different segment types that it accessed. Two techniques, known as "multiple positioning" and "multiple PCBs" allow for a range of options in having the system maintain multiple current position pointers. Those options include a separate such pointer for each segment type in a hierarchy and even multiple positions within the segment type.

Application Development Facility (ADF)

The Application Generator Concept.   A *transaction* in IMS is a message sent by a user from a terminal into the computer, which triggers a program to begin some processing and eventually return the results to the terminal. Some transactions are associated with complex and protracted processing. But many transactions are simple requests to display the data in a segment, insert or delete a segment, or update the data in a segment. Certainly the program logic and code needed to perform those simple functions will differ little from one such request to another, albeit different data, hierarchical structures, and screen displays will be involved. It seems a shame to have to have programmers write such code from scratch, "reinventing the wheel" every time a new program which must process such simple transactions is written.

This situation is common to any database (and in general to any large scale file processing) environment. One response to it has been the development of *application generators.* An application generator allows a programmer to implement simple display, insert, delete, and update application functions at a simpler, higher level than that provided by ordinary COBOL or other standard language code. Typically an application generator contains standard routines for performing those simple functions. The generator plugs a description of the database involved and a description of the nature of the output required (such as the screen layout) for a specific application into those standard routines and produces code to accomplish the requested functions.

For DL/I applications, IBM offers the Application Development Facility (ADF) for the IMS/DC environment, and the functionally similar Development Management System (DMS) for the CICS environment.

Application Development with ADF.   Application development with ADF is an alternative to writing programs in COBOL, PL/I, or Assembler that access IMS databases. It is important to understand at this point that ADF has absolutely nothing to do with designing or creating IMS databases. Like a COBOL program with embedded DL/I calls in it, ADF is strictly a vehicle for accessing existing DL/I databases and displaying or manipulating the data in them.

ADF contains standard processing routines for database manipulation which are tailored by the application developer for the particular application. The tailoring is done by supplying the system with descriptive specifications called "rules." The rules describe the structure of the databases to be accessed, the nature of the transactions, security considerations of which users can perform what functions on what data, edit and audit functions which check to make sure that data being input into the database fall within expected value ranges, and error messages for given situations. The rules are specified as lines in tables, and thus ADF is called a "table driven" system.

In addition for more complex functions, users can execute COBOL, PL/I, or Assembler code in a "special processing" mode while remaining under the ADF umbrella.

Using ADF.   Figure 6.24 is the first image that the ADF user sees on his or her display screen (after a simple sign-on screen). This "Primary Menu" screen is a system generated, standard screen which presents the user with several options. For database access the user would select option "D", indicating that he or she wants to execute an IMS transaction. The user would then also select a transaction mode. The transaction modes on the Primary Menu screen represent the four simple functions that we have been discussing. The reason that there are six modes listed is that a dis-

```
                          P R I M A R Y    M E N U
       OPTION:        TRANSACTION MODE:       IDENTIFIER:
                      KEY:

          OPTIONS                              TRANSACTION MODES
   A - PROJECT MESSAGE SENDING                 1 - DELETE
   B - PROJECT MESSAGE DISPLAY                 2 - INITIATE
   C - SESSION TERMINATION                     3 - REMOVE
   D - TRANSACTION SELECTION                   4 - ADD
   F - PROJECT / GROUP SWITCH                  5 - UPDATE
   H - USER MESSAGE SENDING                    6 - RETRIEVE
   I - USER MESSAGE DISPLAY

                              FOR OPTION  - IDENTIFIER IS
                                   D      - TRANSACTION ID
                                   F      - PROJECT/GROUP
                            A,B,C,H,I   - (NOT USED)
```

Figure 6.24. An ADF Primary Menu. (Reprinted by permission from *IMSADF GIM* (GB21-9869-2) by IBM Corp.)

tinction is made between deleting or inserting a root segment ("delete" and "initiate") and a nonroot segment ("remove" and "add"). The term "retrieve" indicates a simple display of data while "update" means display and permit changes.

Having indicated the type of operation to be performed, the system then moves the user to the "Secondary Option Selection" screen, Figure 6.25.

```
      S E C O N D A R Y   O P T I O N   S E L E C T I O N    PAGE:
                                                             LAST

   INITIATE   SELECT:        KEY:
   ACTION:                   SELECT 'C' TO RETURN TO PRIMARY MENU
   P3 - PAY/PERS YTD
   P5 - PAY/PERS YTD
   P7 - PAY/PERS SAVINGS BOND
   P8 - PAY/PERS MISC.LEAVE
   PA - PAY/PERS PERS+EDUC
   PB - PAY/PERS POSITION
   PC - PAY/PERS APPOINTMENT
   PD - PAY/PERS SEPARATION
   C2 - CLASS/COMP GRADE
   C4 - CLASS/COMP POSN+HOLDER
   T3 - TIME+ATTEND ACCT CHG
   T4 - TIME+ATTEND LEAVE
   M2 - PAYROLL PROCESS
   D2 - DEPT/PAYR PROCESS
   A1 - PAY CHK RECON
   EA - EMPLOYEE APPOINTMENT
```

Figure 6.25. An ADF Secondary Option Selection Menu. (Reprinted by permission from *IMSADF GIM* (GB21-9869-2) by IBM Corp.)

```
                        PRPS PAYROLL/PERSONNEL APPLICATIONS
                          PRIMARY KEY SELECTION SCREEN
        INITIATE      TRANSACTION:   EMPLOYEE APPOINTMENT
        OPTION:       TRX:   2EA   KEY:

        *** ENTER THE FOLLOWING KEY INFORMATION ***
            EMPL SOC-SEC NUMBER-----------
            PAY-PERS KEY PERSONNEL--------
            PAY-PERS KEY EDUCATION--------
            PAY-PERS KEY POSITION---------
            PAY-PERS KEY APPOINT----------
```

Figure 6.26.   An ADF Primary Key Selection Menu. (Reprinted by permission from *IMSADF GIM* (GB21-9869-2) by IBM Corp.)

Using this screen the user selects the transaction that he or she wishes to execute, from among those transactions which he or she is authorized to execute. The transaction includes directions both on what is to be done, and which segment *type* of which database it is to be done to.

Figure 6.26 shows the "Primary Key Selection Screen," which is the next one that the user sees. It specifies what the key field(s) are of the segment type that will be accessed by the requested transaction and allows the user to enter values for those key fields. This tells the system which *occurrence* of that segment type the user wants to see or work on.

Finally the segment occurrence in question is displayed, Figure 6.27. If the segment occurrence exists already, the display will show the actual field values along with the field names. If not then it will just show the field names (in preparation for an insert operation, for example). The format of this final display can be a system default arrangement or can be specified by the application developer in a very easy way.

```
                PRPS PAYROLL/PERSONNEL APPLICATIONS

                 EMPLOYEE APPOINTMENT (PAGE 1 OF 2)
        INITIATE         TRANSACTION:   EMPLOYEE APPOINTMENT
        OPTION:       TRX:   2EA   KEY:   548586513B5B5B5B5
        *** ENTER DATA FOR UPDATE ***
        SOCIAL SECURITY NUMBER:   _____
        POSITION NUMBER:   _____
        TITLE CODE:   GRADE:___   STEP:___   SALARY:        .00  HOW-PAID:  _____
        EMPLOYEE NAME LAST:_____  FIRST:_____  MI:___  JRSR:  _____
        PRIOR SERVICE:     0      YEAR LAST WORKED:  _____
        PROBATION CODE:____       DATE PROBATION END:_____  FLAS:_____
        TYPE APPOINTMENT:_____    FULLPART TIME:  ____   HIRE DATE:_____  MAIN:_____
        PAY-PERS KEYS: :   PERSONNEL(P9):  B5   EDUCATION(PA)  :  B5
                           POSITION (PB):  B5   APPOINTMENT(PC):  B5
          NEXT SCREEN:ENTER,OR STOP PROCESS:E,OR RETURN TO BEGINNING:R   1
```

Figure 6.27.   An ADF Data Display. (Reprinted by permission from *IMSADF GIM* (GB21-9869-2) by IBM Corp.)

References

IBM Corporation, *IMS Application Development Facility (IMSADF) General Information Manual*, IBM Form No. GB21-9869, 1980.

IBM Corporation, *DL/I Functions for Application Design*, IBM Form No. SR20-4680, 1981.

IBM Corporation, *IMS/VS Version 1 Application Programming Reference Manual*, IBM Form No. SH20-9026, 1978.

IBM Corporation, *IMS/VS Version 1 Data Base Administration Guide*, IBM Form No. SH20-9025, 1980.

Kapp, D., and Leben, J. F., *IMS Programming Techniques*, Van Nostrand Reinhold, New York, 1978.

Walsh, M. E., *Information Management Systems / Virtual Storage*, Reston Publishing, Reston, VA, 1979.

Questions and Exercises

6.1.   Describe a hierarchy. Describe an example of a hierarchy in a corporation.

6.2.   Describe the basic form of an IMS hierarchy. What do the nodes represent? Conceptually how are multiple associations handled? How does it provide for the reduction of data redundancy?

6.3.   How would we modify the Baseball Teams hierarchy in Figure 6.4 to maintain information on each team's season ticket holders?

6.4.   Carefully explain the difference between a segment type and a segment occurrence.

6.5.   Compare the advantages and disadvantages of pointer-based storage and sequential storage of data in IMS hierarchies.

6.6.   In the Baseball Teams hierarchy of Figure 6.4, is it necessary to have a team number field in the PLAYERS segment? Why or why not?

6.7.   Redraw the Dodgers occurrence of the Baseball Team hierarchy in Figure 6.7 to reflect the following. (Note: players and coaches are kept in alphabetic order.)

  a.   The addition of coach Doogan, who has been a high school and college coach

  b.   The addition of player Evans

  c.   The addition of player Turner

6.8.   Describe the meaning of the hierarchy shown in terms of the real world environment that it represents (what is the nature of the data that can be stored in it, what kinds of applications might use it?).

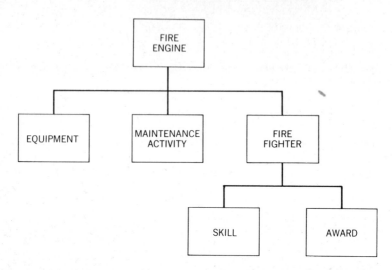

6.9.   In your own words, describe the advantage of a logical relationship in reducing redundancy, promoting data integration, and so on

6.10.   Why are the combined Teams and Players hierarchies in Figure 6.9 an incomplete solution to the redundancy of the two PLAYER segment types in the hierarchies of Figure 6.8?

6.11.   What are the advantages of the unidirectional logical relationship in Figure 6.10?

6.12.   Define and describe the purpose of a logical child segment. What is intersection data? Why does it belong in the logical child?

6.13.   How can logical relationships be used to represent many-to-many relationships in IMS databases?

6.14.   Describe the meaning of the database shown in terms of the real world environment that it represents (what is the nature of the data that can be stored in it, what kinds of applications might use it?).

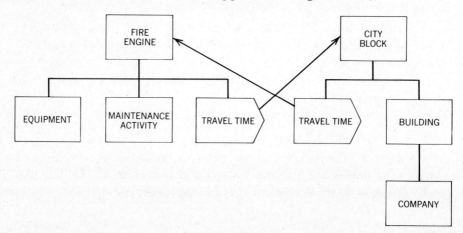

6.15.   What is the difference between an IMS logical and physical database? What are the advantages of making the distinction?

6.16.   What is an IMS Access Method? Describe Figure 6.19 in your own words.

6.17.   What are secondary indexes and what do they accomplish? If there is already direct access to the root segment, what is the purpose of having a secondary index based on a field in the root segment?

6.18.   What is a control block? What kind of information do control blocks contain?

6.19.   What are the major IMS data manipulation statements? Do they cover all of the types of data manipulation functions that you might need?

6.20.   Refer to the IMS database record in Figure 6.23 (an occurrence of the hierarchy shown in Figure 6.22) and indicate the results of each of the following IMS calls.

    a. GU TEAMS (TEAMNUM = 12)
           PLAYERS (PLAYNUM = 5410)

    b. GU TEAMS (TEAMNUM = 12)
           BATS (BATNUM = B09)

    c. GU TEAMS (TEAMNUM = 12)
           BATS (MANUF = Acme)

    d. GU TEAMS (TEAMNUM = 12)
           COACHES (COACHNAM = Adams)
           WORKEXP (EXPYRS = 10)

    e. GU TEAMS (TEAMNUM = 12)
           COACHES (COACHNAM = Adams)
           WORKEXP (EXPYRS = 13)

6.21.   Refer to the IMS database record in Figure 6.23, which is an occurrence of the hierarchy shown in Figure 6.22.

    a. Write a DL/I call to find out how many years coach Adams of the Dodgers was a college coach.

    b. Write a DL/I call to find out if a player named Murray is on the Dodgers team.

6.22.   Refer to the IMS database record in Figure 6.23 (an occurrence of the hierarchy in Figure 6.22) and indicate the results of each of the following IMS calls or call sequences. In each case, assume that

           GU TEAMS (TEAMNUM = 12)

has just been executed. Loop indications are for COBOL or PL/I programs.

    a. Start of loop
        GN PLAYERS
      end of loop

    b. Start of loop
          GNP PLAYERS
       end of loop

    c. Start of loop
          GNP BATS (MANUF = Acme)
       end of loop

    d.   GN COACHES
       start of loop
          GNP WORKEXP
       end of loop

6.23. Refer to the IMS database record in Figure 6.23, which is an occurrence of the hierarchy shown in Figure 6.22. Write DL/I calls with loops if necessary (see the style in the previous exercise) to get:

    a. All of the coaches on the Dodgers
    b. All of Dodgers coach Adams' coaching experience
    c. All of the coaching experience of each of the Dodgers coaches

6.24. Refer to the IMS database record in Figure 6.23, which is an occurrence of the hierarchy shown in Figure 6.22. Write DL/I calls with loops if necessary to:

    a. Insert new coach, Turner, into the Dodgers database record.

    b. Delete all of coach Adams experience.

    c. Update player Jones' age to 26

6.25. What is an application generator? What are the advantages of using one? Are there any disadvantages?

7

The Network Approach to Database

Introduction

Another approach to database management systems is based on structures called networks. Over the last two decades many DBMSs have been developed which are implementations, to a greater or lesser extent, of the network oriented DBMS specifications developed by the Conference on Data Systems Languages (CODASYL) and its Data Base Task Group (DBTG) and Data Description Language Committee (DDLC). The Conference on Data Systems Languages is "an organisation composed of volunteer representatives of computer manufacturers and users in industry and the Federal Governments of Canada and the United States of America" (the reason for the unusal spelling of the word "organization" is that the specifications are published by the "EDP Standards Committee of the Secretariat of the Canadian Government").

The CODASYL work on uniform specifications for a DBMS began in the late 1960s. Reports or sets of CODASYL specifications have been produced from time to time; some of the most notable came out in 1971, 1973, 1978, and 1982. The different commercially available "CODASYL DBMSs" are based on some percentage of the specifications in one or more of the CODASYL reports.

In keeping with the spirit of this book to provide a thorough and accurate understanding of the *fundamental concepts* of database, we will discuss the CODASYL approach to database management systems as a general topic. We will not differentiate between the different CODASYL specification versions or the different commercial implementations. What we will do is describe the general features and objectives of the CODASYL approach.

Networks

To begin with, let's take a look at what is meant by the term *network*. A network is really a very general kind of a structure: simply, in the abstract, it is a set of *points* connected together in some way. For convenience we will refer to the connection between two points as an *edge*. Didn't the concept of a tree fit that definition? Yes, it did but with further restrictions. In fact, a tree is merely a restricted kind of a network.

In practice we deal with networks frequently in everyday living. Figure 7.1 shows one such common network: a network of highways connecting cities. Another example is the telephone network. Also we speak of a "network of friends" in which the people interact with each other.

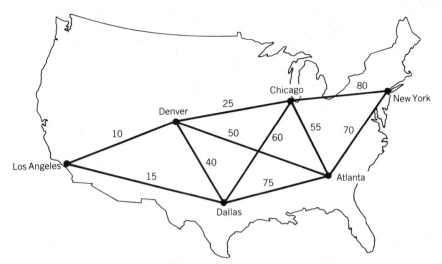

Figure 7.1. A network of cities and highways.

Defining the following terms now will help later. Two points are *adjacent* if they are connected by an edge. Thus Chicago and Denver are adjacent in Figure 7.1 since they are connected by Highway 25. An edge is *incident* to a point if it touches it. Highway 15 is incident to Dallas. The *degree* of a node is the number of edges incident to it. The degree of Atlanta is 4 because Highways 70, 55, 50, and 75 are all incident to it. A *path* is a serially connected series of edges, such as Highways 10, 25, and 80, connecting Los Angeles to New York. A *cycle* is a path that begins and ends at the same point. The path of Highways 25, 55, 75, and 40 is a cycle because it begins and ends at Denver.

Understanding the differences between trees and more general networks is important to the coming discussion. There are a couple of ways of distinguishing a tree from a more general network, and while such a discussion can quickly become rather complex, we will try to keep it as simple as possible.

Ordinarily, a tree is a network that has no cycles. Refer back to Figure 6.1 and convince yourself that for each and every point on that network, which we call a "tree," there is no way to begin a path at a point, to traverse a series of edges, and to return to the starting point without having to back track over at least one edge at least once. Contrast that with the structure of Figure 7.2 which shows a cycle connecting nodes 1, 2, and 3.

But it is also possible to have a network which *is not a tree and yet has no cycles*. In talking about the trees of Chapter 6, we established the root as the node at the "top" of the structure and always worked downwards

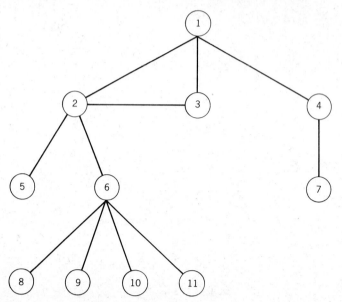

Figure 7.2. A network with a cycle.

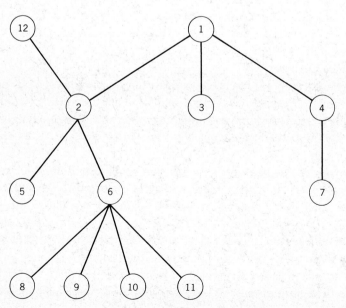

Figure 7.3. A network with no cycles.

from it. In effect, we established a *direction* on the branches or edges: downwards (which also corresponded very conveniently to a one-to-many relationship in that same direction for DL/I). Once we have established such a downwards direction on the edges of a tree, another characteristic of the tree is that *a node may not have more than one parent.* Figure 7.3 is a copy of Figure 6.1 with a new node added (number 12). It represents a network (which is not a tree) that has no cycles. If all of the edges are considered to point downwards on the page, then clearly, node 2 has two "parent" or superior nodes, rendering that structure invalid as a tree, but still perfectly valid as a network.

Now just as we did for trees and IMS, let's see how a network can be used to store data in the CODASYL DBMS concept.

CODASYL Physical Structure

To describe how data can be stored in the form of a network we will use the same baseball example that we used in the IMS discussion.

The Set Concept

Introduction. The basic building block of a CODASYL network is the *set.* A set consists of two record types in a one-to-many relationship to each other. Figure 7.4 shows the COACH TEAM set; a given team has a number of coaches on it. We will follow the convention, often found in CODASYL literature, that the link between the two record types of a set is shown as a single-headed (rather than a double-headed) arrow, although it represents a one-to-many relationship. Unlike in the description of IMS, we will leave

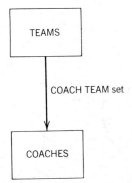

Figure 7.4. A CODASYL set.

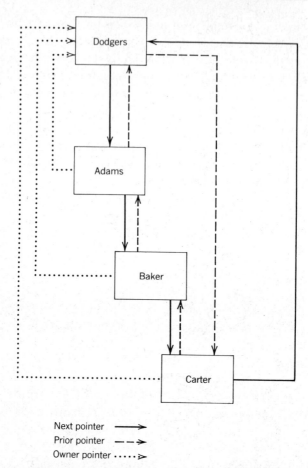

Next pointer ——————▷
Prior pointer — — —▷
Owner pointer ·····▷

Figure 7.5.   An ocurrence of the COACH TEAM set.

the arrow heads in here because as we shall soon see, the direction of the one-to-many relationship will not always be downwards in the diagrams as it is in IMS.

The record type on the "one side" of the one-to-many relationship (TEAMS) is called the *owner record type*, while the record on the "many side" (COACHES) is called the *member record type*.

Storage of Sets.   Just as we have previously spoken of record occurrences and hierarchical occurrences, here we can speak of set occurrences. A set occurrence consists of one occurrence of the owner record type of the set, and all of the occurrences of the member record type associated with it. Figure 7.5 shows an occurrence of the COACH TEAM set. The Dodgers have three coaches, Adams, Baker, and Carter. Figure 7.5 also shows the usual way that CODASYL set occurrences are stored: with pointers. The main (and the only required) pointer is the "next" pointer, shown as solid lines in Figure 7.5. With next pointers, the owner record occurrence (Dodgers) points to the first member record occurrence (Adams). That member record occurrence points to the next one, and so on until the last member record occurrence (Carter) of the set points back to the owner record occurrence.

Notice that except for that last next pointer that goes from the last member record occurrence back to the owner record occurrence, the chain of next pointers looks just like the child-twin pointer arrangement in IMS. By the way, you might be tempted to look at the chain of next pointers and yell, "cycle," and you would be right. They do form a cycle. Just remember that here we have a cycle of *record occurrences* within a set occurrence, while the essence of the discussion about cycles earlier in this chapter was geared towards cycles of *record types*, a discussion which we will come back to a little later on.

There are two optional types of pointers illustrated in Figure 7.5, which in practice are used for some of the more complex network arrangements and processing. The "prior" pointer (shown as dashed lines) operates the same way that the next pointer does, but it goes in the opposite direction. The "owner" pointer (shown as dotted lines) points from each member record occurrence to the owner record occurrence of that set.

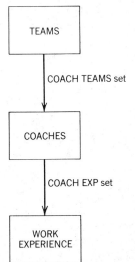

Figure 7.6. A record as the member record type of one set and the owner record type of another.

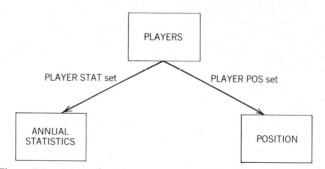

Figure 7.7. A record as the owner record type of two different sets.

From Sets to Networks. Sets can be combined in many different ways to form networks of a wide range of shapes and sizes. Figure 7.6 shows two sets. In the familiar spirit of one-to-many relationships, the COACH TEAMS set records the coaches on a team, while the COACH EXP set records the pieces of work experience of a particular coach. Note that the COACHES record type is the member record type of the COACH TEAMS set and at the same time is the owner record type of the COACH EXP set. Figure 7.7 shows two sets that have the same owner record type: PLAYERS.

Notice that the networks shown in Figures 7.4, 7.6, and 7.7 (Figure 7.4 can be looked upon as a network consisting of one set) appear on the surface to be indistinguishable from trees. Now look at Figure 7.8 which shows three sets. The COLLEGE set indicates all of the players in the league who came from a particular college, the ON TEAM set shows all of the players on a team, and the HOME set shows all of the players in the league who were born in a particular state. In that structure, all three sets have the same member record type, PLAYERS. Borrowing from the IMS terminology

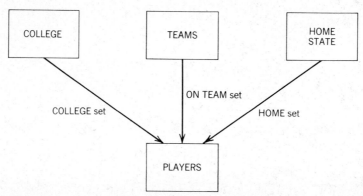

Figure 7.8. A record as the member record type of three different sets.

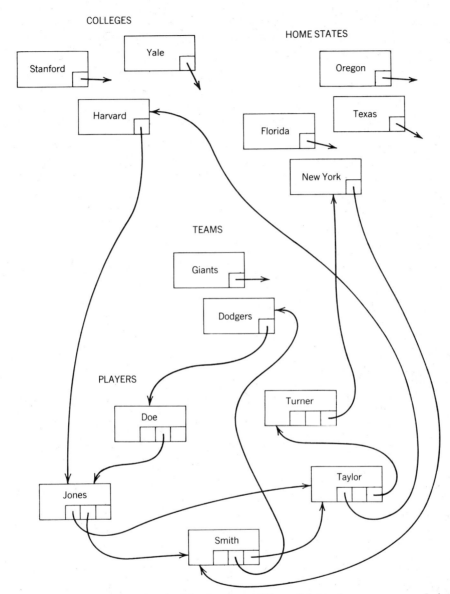

Figure 7.9. An occurrence of each of the three sets of Figure 7.8. In player occurrences: Left pointer slot is for college chain; middle pointer slot is for team chain; and right pointer slot is for home state chain.

we might say that the PLAYERS record has three "parent" record types (which, of course, can't happen in IMS). Thus the structure is not a tree but a more general network.

Figure 7.9 shows the pointer arrangement for an occurrence of each of those three sets. A record occurrence participates in (and must have a "next" pointer slot for) one chain of record occurrences for each set it is in. In the structure in Figure 7.8, the PLAYERS record is the member record type of each of the three sets, meaning that a player can be shown to have graduated from one college, to be playing for one team (currently, presumably), and to have been born in one state. In the PLAYERS occurrences in Figure 7.9, the leftmost of the three pointer slots is for the COLLEGE set, the middle is for the ON TEAM set, and the rightmost is for the HOME set. The diagram shows that Jones and Taylor graduated from Harvard; Doe, Jones, and Smith play for the Dodgers; and Smith, Taylor, and Turner were born in New York. If all of the data were shown, we would see what college chain Doe is on, what home state chain Jones is on, and so forth.

Figure 7.10 shows another network structure that is not a tree. It can maintain the players on a team in the TEAM PLAYER set, the coaches on a team in the TEAM COACH set, and the coaches who coach a particular player in the COACHED BY set. But if we also wanted to maintain the opposite of the COACHED BY set, that is, the players that a coach is responsible for coaching, then the two together would form a many-to-many relationship, which leads to the following discussion on "juncture records."

Juncture Records

Thus far we have not said anything about storing data in many-to-many relationships in CODASYL networks. In fact (in a way similar to the sit-

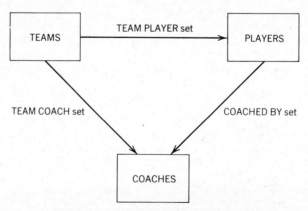

Figure 7.10.   Another network structure.

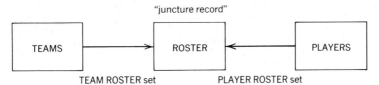

Figure 7.11. A many-to-many relationship in CODASYL.

uation in IMS) CODASYL network structures cannot directly represent many-to-many relationships. We would say that within one set a member record occurrence can be associated with a single owner record occurrence. In Figure 7.4 a coach can only be associated with one team; there can be no historical data on all of the teams that a coach has worked for during his or her career. Many-to-many relationships are developed in CODASYL networks through the introduction of a new record type, variously known as a *juncture,* "link," "intersection," or "connection" record. Instead of a single many-to-many linkage between two record types being represented in one set, there will be two sets. One set will have one of those two record types as its owner record type and a newly created juncture record as its member record type. The other set will have the other of the two record types as its owner record type and that same juncture record as its member record type. The arrangement is actually quite similar in spirit to the logical relationship structure in IMS.

Figure 7.11 shows the many-to-many relationship between TEAMS and PLAYERS, on the same historical basis that we dealt with in the last chapter, represented in the CODASYL network form. The TEAM ROSTER set and the PLAYER ROSTER set taken together form the many-to-many relationship. There will be a ROSTER record occurrence for each instance of a particular player having played on a particular team or viceversa. Figure 7.12 (which demonstrates the same relationships shown in Figure 6.14) shows occurrences of the two sets described in Figure 7.11. The ROSTER record occurrences and the pointers are labelled for reference in the following discussion. The ROSTER record occurrences, drawn in the middle of Figure 7.12, each have two next pointer slots, since the ROSTER record type is the member record type of both of the sets involved. In each occurrence, the left-hand pointer is for the TEAM ROSTER set, while the right-hand pointer is for the PLAYER ROSTER set. The Dodgers have had both Doe and Jones as players, at one time or another, while the Giants have had Jones and Smith. Conversely, Doe has only played on the Dodgers, Smith only on the Giants, and Jones on both.

Figure 7.12 also provides a good illustration of the need for the optional

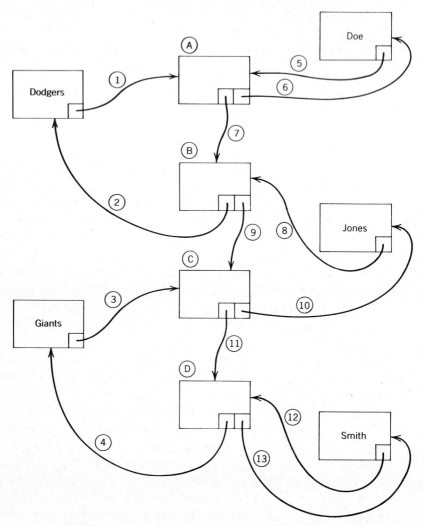

Figure 7.12. Occurrences of the two sets shown in Figure 7.11.

"owner" pointer. Remember that all of the pointers shown in Figure 7.12
are next pointers. Suppose you start out at the Jones occurrence and want
to find out what all of the teams he has played on are, and other information
about those teams stored in the TEAMS record occurrences. Pointer 8 from
Jones leads the system to ROSTER occurrence B. The system could at that
point, loosely speaking, hold its place at B and follow pointer 2 to Dodgers,
yielding one of the teams that Jones has played on. But this is only because
B happens to be the last of the players on the Dodgers chain and thus

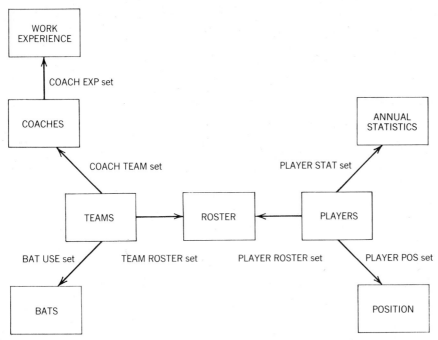

Figure 7.13. The Teams and Players example in network form.

points over to Dodgers. The more general and problematic case is illustrated by following pointer 9 to the next roster record occurrence on the Jones chain, roster record C. In order to get to the teams record associated with roster record C (the Giants), the system must follow pointer 11 and then pointer 4 (and in general possibly many more pointers on a longer chain). In so doing it passes through ROSTER occurrence D which has absolutely nothing to do with Jones. On the other hand if the ROSTER occurrences had owner pointers, then from C it could simply use an owner pointer to directly find the Giants, which is the owner record of that occurrence of the TEAM ROSTER set.

Figure 7.13 (including the ROSTER record of Figure 7.11) shows the full Teams and Players network. Remember that intersection data will be stored in the juncture record. This network is the CODASYL equivalent of the IMS structure shown in Figure 6.15.

Schemas and Subschemas

Following commonly used DBMS conventions, the CODASYL specifications allow for a distinction to be made between the actual stored data and the view of it that the programmer sees. In addition, they suggest another intermediate level of view. Described as being at the "conceptual level," this view describes the overall database and can involve several physically separate networks.

In CODASYL, the description of the actual stored data is called the *internal schema*. The description at the conceptual level is called the *logical schema*. The description of a program or programmer's view of the data is called a *subschema*. For purposes of security and clarity, a connected portion of a CODASYL network can be described in a subschema and presented to a programmer for a particular application. The programmer need not be aware of the rest of the actual stored network defined in the schemas.

Access Methods

Options.   The various versions of the CODASYL specifications and various implementations of them have provided for a variety of ways to store and access record occurrences. As we look at the alternatives, bear in mind that in CODASYL every record type may, although need not be, treated independently in terms of access from all of the other record types. We shall now explain this further.

One common CODASYL file organization has the occurrences of a record type being stored using a hashing algorithm based on their keys. When stored in this way, access is said to be "via calc." As is usual for a hashing driven organization, this method provides very fast direct access but no physical sequencing of the data.

Another method of storage and access for the occurrences of a record type is referred to as "via set." The record type involved must be the member record type of a set. The point of this method is to store the member record occurrences of a set occurrence physically near the owner record occurrence of the set. Access to those member record occurrences must be through the owner record occurrence of that set. Those occurrences cannot be retrieved independently.

Another method, known in CODASYL as "direct," has been dropped from the latest set of specifications but may still be found in some implementations. In this arrangement all record occurrences are assigned a relative address called a "data base key." A program can discern and maintain data base key values and, at a later time, refer directly to a record occurrence by its data base key. This method is also a convenient way of creating a sequential file.

Some implementations permit indexed sequential storage. Some also include secondary indexes as options.

Usage Comments. Remember that each record can be treated independently in terms of access if that makes sense for the application set that will use the data. In theory every record type of a network can be stored "via calc" using a hashing method. The record occurrences of the different record types will be scattered over a wide physical range of disk cylinders and packs, but will be related to each other in the usual CODASYL set oriented way with (at least) next pointers. In this arrangement, fast direct access can be had to any occurrence of any record type. However, navigating through the network from occurrence to occurrence will be relatively slow because of the scattering of data characteristic of hashing.

The way to avoid that problem is to store one of the record types with a hashing algorithm, and to store the others connected to it, and in turn, others connected to them "via set." This will allow fast direct access to one of the records, and then, since they are stored physically close by on the disk, relatively fast sequential access to the occurrences connected to it in the network. However, in so doing, we give up direct access to those other records (unless secondary indexes are permitted). Referring back to Figure 7.6, if COACHES records are stored via set relative to TEAMS records and WORK EXPERIENCE records are stored via set relative to COACHES records, then a team and its descendants will be stored physically near each other which may well be a plus for performance depending on the nature of the applications using the data.

This is a standard common sense kind of tradeoff situation. Similar arguments can be made in other systems, including IMS.

CODASYL Language Interface

Introduction

The CODASYL organization is responsible for maintaining standards for the COBOL language. As a result of this orientation, the intention of the CODASYL database specifications was for the databases to be accessible by COBOL programs. While a variety of methods of language access have been built into and around various CODASYL database implementations, they are fundamentally intended to be embedded type functions in COBOL programs. We will explore the various statements involved in such access, but first we must look at a few preliminary topics.

Preliminary Topics

Set Membership Class. An occurrence of a record type, which is the member record type of a particular set, can exist in the database without being in an occurrence of that set (without being associated with an occurrence of the owner record type of the set). For example, referring back to Figure 7.4, a coach can have a record in the database without being in an occurrence of the COACH TEAM set; it simply means that he or she is temporarily unemployed.

For that reason, the CODASYL database designer must specify certain characteristics of the record types relative to the sets of which they are the member record type. Those characteristics will guide the system in whether or not certain record and set manipulation statements can act on the particular records and if so how. There are two "storage class" options and three "removal class" options. A given record type can have any combination of storage class and removal class for a given set in which it is the member record type. In general it can have different such combinations for each set of which it is the member record type. Let's look at those options now as one of the necessary areas to cover before we look at the data manipulation statements a little later.

Storage Class. A record's "storage class" (also called "insertion class") guides the DBMS in its actions when inserting a new occurrence of a record into the database, when that record acts as the member record occurrence of a set.

One possibility is for a record type to be declared *automatic* relative to a set of which it is the member record type. Then when an occurrence of that record is inserted into the database, the system will automatically link it into an occurrence of that set (associate it with—that is, connect it to—an occurrence of the owner record type). Of course, the program must indicate which occurrence of that set it is to be associated with. The other choice is *manual*. If a member record type of a set is declared to be manual, then when an occurrence of it is inserted into the database it will not be linked into an occurrence of the set. Subsequently if it becomes necessary, this will have to be done by a separate command which we will describe later.

Removal Class. A record's "removal class" (also called "retention class") gives or denies the system permission to obey application program commands to move member record occurrences already associated with a set occurrence out of that set occurrence.

If a record type which is the member record type of a particular set is declared *fixed* for that set, then it must always stay in the occurrence of that set in which it was originally inserted. It cannot be moved to a different occurrence of that set unless, as a brute force measure, it is deleted from the database entirely and reinserted with a new set occurrence association.

If a record type is *mandatory* for a particular set, then it must always be in the chain of some occurrence of that set, but not necessarily the one it was originally associated with.

If a record type is *optional* with regard to a given set, then it can be disassociated (disconnected) from the occurrence of the set that it was in, remain in the database, and not be reassociated with another occurrence of that set.

Currency. In the discussion on IMS, we developed the concept of the system place-keeper or internal pointer which always maintains a sense of current position in the database. This concept is highly developed in the CODASYL specifications and a fairly large number of such current position pointers, each referring to a different substructure of the network, can be maintained. Remember that the system maintains a different set of position pointers for each user of each program simultaneously.

The CODASYL equivalent of the basic IMS current position pointer is called the *current of run-unit*. It always indicates the last record occurrence (of any record type) reached in the network. The *current of record* indicates the last occurrence of a particular record type touched upon. There is such an indicator for each different record type. The *current of set* is for the last record occurrence reached in a given set. Again there is one such pointer for each set, all simultaneously maintained. The *current of realm* is for the last record occurrence reached within a large subset of the network known as a "realm" or "area."

The FIND Statement

The first CODASYL statement that we will look at is the FIND statement. We will discuss it and all of the other CODASYL language statements with an example network which parallels the IMS example used in Chapter 6. Figure 7.14 is a network structure which represents the same data as the

Teams hierarchical structure that appeared in Figure 6.4. Figure 7.15 shows the fields in the records of that network structure, just as Figure 6.22 did for the hierarchical case. Figure 7.16 shows the same actual data in the network as Figure 6.23 did in the hierarchy. The pointers in Figure 7.16 are all next pointers.

One word of caution before we begin: different versions of the CODASYL specifications and different CODASYL implementations have used somewhat different command syntax constructions. There are two main families of such syntax constructions. We will try to stick to one of them but will mention the other occasionally as well.

Informally stated, the purpose of the FIND statement is to locate and have the system point to a particular record occurrence in the database. More formally, the FIND statement locates a particular record occurrence and sets the current of run-unit indicator to it. (It normally also sets the current of record for the record type involved, the current of set for the set involved, and the current of realm for the realm involved.) The FIND statement does not retrieve the record from storage— that requires a GET statement after the FIND statement, as we will discuss. Before a FIND

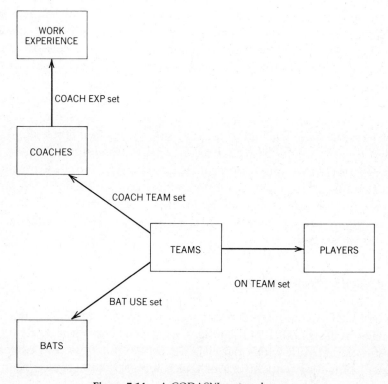

Figure 7.14. A CODASYL network.

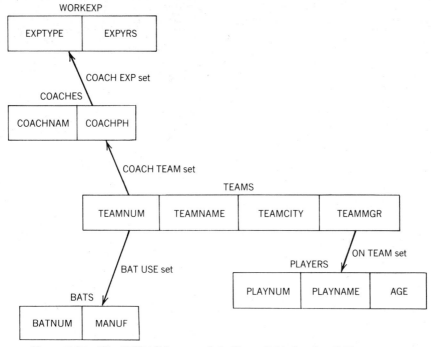

Figure 7.15. The CODASYL network in Figure 7.14 showing field names.

statement is executed, the program must set the proper variables in the
subschema defined in the COBOL program's Data Division to indicate *which
occurrence* of the record type written in the FIND statement is to be located.
By way of comparison, this function was performed in IMS by the segment
search arguments withing the command itself.

Let's start with a simple example of direct record location. Assume that
the TEAMS records are stored directly with a hashing algorithm, which
we called the "calc" mode. To find the Dodgers record in the database you
would first "MOVE" the value 12 to the TEAMNUM field in the TEAMS
record description in the subschema, and then issue:

FIND ANY TEAMS.

Variations on the same theme include:

FIND TEAMS RECORD

and

FIND ANY TEAMS USING TEAMNUM IN TEAMS.

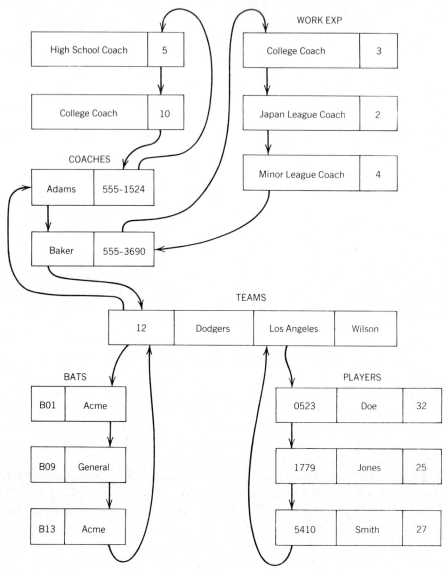

Figure 7.16.   A partial occurrence of the network in Figure 7.14.

As a result of this command, the Dodgers record will be the current of run-unit, the current of record for record type TEAMS, the current of set for the ON TEAM, COACH TEAM, and BAT USE sets, and the current of realm for whatever realm it is in.

    If the records were stored in CODASYL's "direct" mode, and you know the unique positional identifier for a particular record occurrence, then you would issue a command that would look like:

FIND TEAMS; DB-KEY IS identifier.

The CODASYL specifications also support the concept of finding a record occurrence within a specified set occurrence. To do that, the first thing that has to be done is the establishment of the set occurrence involved. The easiest way to do this is to specify the owner record occurrence of the desired set. If a particular record type is the owner record type of a particular set then each occurrence of that owner record type establishes an occurrence of the set.

For example, suppose you want information about the bats that the Dodgers use. The first thing you would do is select the occurrence of the BAT USE set in which Dodgers is the owner record occurrence. You can do that by doing a simple FIND of the Dodgers record, which among other things, establishes the (one and only) set occurrence of the BAT USE set that Dodgers is in as the current of set. Having done this, if for instance, you wanted the first BATS record associated with Dodgers, you would issue:

FIND FIRST BATS RECORD WITHIN BAT USE

where BATS is the name of the record type and BAT USE is the name of the set. If you wanted the last of the bats associated with Dodgers you would replace FIRST with LAST. NEXT would get you the next one on the chain (compare with the IMS Get Next command); PRIOR would get you the previous one; an integer represented as a constant or an integer variable would get you that number occurrence (first, second, third, etc.) counting from the first member record occurrence of the set (and going backwards if the number is negative).

You can also find a record occurrence within a set occurrence based on the value of one of the fields of that record occurrence. For example, if you wanted to find the record for Dodger's bat B09, you would first establish the BAT USE set occurrence that has Dodgers in it as the owner record, as the current of set, and then you would issue:

FIND BATS WITHIN BAT USE USING db-id

where db-id would identify B09 as the search key.

What if you wanted to find all of the Dodger's bats manufactured by the Acme Company? You can't use the command form just discussed, because if several BATS record occurrences have the same search field value, then *every time* you issue that command you will find the *first* occurrence with that field value. Another command form is needed, and obviously, the command must be set up within a program loop to process all of the record occurrences with the specified search key value (all of the Dodgers' bats made by the Acme Company). First you establish the proper set occurrence (again, the occurrence of the BAT USE set with Dodgers in it) as the current of set. Then you FIND the first Acme manufactured Dodgers' bat using one of the command structures discussed. Then to find the rest of the Dodger's Acme bats, you issue within a program loop:

FIND DUPLICATE WITHIN BAT USE USING db-id

where again db-id establishes the search key.

Another FIND variation within a set is to locate the owner record occurrence of the current of set as:

FIND OWNER WITHIN BAT USE.

For systems supporting the realm concept there are similar commands for finding record occurrences within a realm as opposed to within a set. Included in these are commands to find the FIRST, LAST, NEXT, PRIOR, or integer identified record occurrence of a given record type within a realm.

Finally, it may be necessary to reestablish a record occurrence as the current of run-unit. The term reestablish is used because in this case the record was previously "found" and is at the moment the current of some record, set, or realm. But due to subsequent FIND statements, which involved other records, it is not at the moment the current of run-unit. For example, to find the last referenced bat in the BAT USE set you would issue

FIND CURRENT BATS WITHIN BAT USE

or

FIND CURRENT OF BAT USE SET.

As a final note remember that as was the case with IMS, exception conditions must be tested for after a CODASYL command is issued. Examples of these conditions include end of set or realm reached, no record found (which matches the selection criteria specified), current of run-unit is not correct record type, and so forth.

The GET Statement

The GET statement brings a record occurrence, or selected fields of a record occurrence, into the user's "user work area" (UWA) in main memory. If you simply issue:

GET

then the system retrieves the record occurrence which is the current of run-unit. If you issue, to retrieve a TEAMS record for example:

GET TEAMS

then the system not only retrieves the current of run-unit, but also checks to see if it is in fact an occurrence of the TEAMS record type. While there are different capabilities and limitations among the different systems, it is fair to make the broad comparison that in CODASYL a FIND statement followed by a GET statement accomplishes the same thing that a Get Unique or Get Next (depending on the circumstances) statement does in IMS.

Record Maintenance Statements

The STORE, ERASE, and MODIFY statements serve as maintenance commands for records in the database (although as you will see, there are side effects of these commands that do affect set membership). After this section we will discuss maintenance commands for sets.

The STORE Statement. The STORE statement inserts new records into the database. The program must first move the appropriate data for the new record into the UWA, and then, for example, issue:

STORE TEAMS

to insert a new TEAMS record. Of course, the system will handle the necessary details of insertion depending on whether the records of the record type involved are stored with a hashing algorithm, an index, or a relative address.

Remember too, that the system will automatically add that record occurrence to the sets which that record type participates in (the COACH TEAM, BAT USE, and ON TEAM sets to continue the example) *if* the storage class for that record in those sets was declared to be "automatic" in the schema (see the earlier discussion on storage classes). A word of caution: for those automatic set connections to be made to the correct occurrences of those sets, those set occurrences must be specified before the STORE statement is issued. There are variations on how this can be done, (it comes under a heading known as "Set Selection") but it can be done by setting variables in the schema or by issuing FIND statements to set the current of set indicators.

The ERASE Statement.   The ERASE statement deletes records from the database. In the various versions and implementations of the CODASYL specifications there have been a number of variations of the ERASE statement with various restrictions. We will discuss two such variations.

Suppose a team drops out of the league entirely. In addition to the TEAMS record, and depending on the circumstances, you might or might not want to delete the descendants of that record, namely the BATS, PLAYERS, COACHES, and WORKEXP records as shown in Figure 7.15. If, for example, you make Dodgers the current of run-unit, and then issue:

ERASE ALL TEAMS

then the Dodgers and all of its descendant record occurrences, that is everything shown in Figure 7.16 will be erased from the database.

If, on the other hand, you issue:

ERASE Dodgers

(without the parameter "ALL"), then the rules for the removal class of a record type in a set will be considered. For example, let's say that BATS in the BAT USE set are fixed. This means that the bats assigned to the Dodgers can never be used by another team and, as common sense would dictate, they will be deleted with the Dodgers. Assume that Players in the ON TEAM set are optional. Then the players can exist independently in the database, without having to be assigned to a team, so they will be taken out of the ON TEAM set, but otherwise left alone. And what if COACHES in the COACH TEAM set are mandatory? Then coaches may move from team to team but must always be in *some* team. Since the ERASE Dodgers statement doesn't say which team to reconnect the coaches to, this causes a problem, and in fact, would invalidate this entire command, leaving the database as it was before.

The MODIFY Statement.   Updates to stored records are accomplished using the MODIFY statement. For example, if you want to change some data in a TEAMS record, you issue a FIND and then a GET statement to bring the record into the UWA, you change the appropriate data fields, and then you issue:

MODIFY TEAMS.

Set Maintenance Statements

The CONNECT, DISCONNECT, and RECONNECT statements serve as set maintenance commands as follows.

The CONNECT Statement.   The CONNECT statement links an existing record occurrence, which is the current of run-unit, into the set occurrence which is the current of set (for the desired set type). For example, what do you do if Stanton, an existing, but currently unemployed player joins the Dodgers? First you would issue a FIND statement to set the current of set indicator to the occurrence of the ON TEAMS set that has Dodgers as its owner record occurrence. Then you would issue a FIND statement to make Stanton the current of run-unit. Finally, you would issue:

CONNECT PLAYERS TO ON TEAMS.

The DISCONNECT Statement.   If a record is currently a member record occurrence of some set occurrence, it can be DISCONNECTed from that set, but still remain in the database, whether or not it is involved in any other sets. For example, to fire Stanton from the Dodgers, you would first make Stanton the current of run-unit and then issue:

DISCONNECT PLAYERS FROM ON TEAMS.

Remember the removal class rules. For the foregoing statement to make sense, it must have a removal class of optional specified for that set.

The RECONNECT Statement.   The RECONNECT statement allows you to move a record occurrence from one occurrence of a set to another occurrence of the same set. For example, suppose that Stanton is currently on the Dodgers, but is traded to the Giants. First you would identify the occurrence of the ON TEAMS set which has Giants as the owner record occurrence as the target set occurrence (based on the "set selection" rules).

Next you would make Stanton the current of run-unit. Then you would issue:

RECONNECT PLAYERS WITHIN ON TEAMS

Here again, the removal class option specified must be taken into account. Obviously a RECONNECT statement would be in direct contradiction with a removal class of fixed for that record type in that set. It must be either mandatory or optional.

References

CODASYL Journal of Development, January, 1978, CODASYL Data Description Language Committee, may be ordered from: Materiel Data Management Branch, Department of Supply and Services, 4th Floor, Core B1, Place du Portage, Phase III, 11 Laurier Street, Hull, Quebec, K1A 0S5, Canada.

Date, C. J., *An Introduction to Database Systems,* 3rd ed., vol. 1, Addison-Wesley, Reading, MA, 1981.

King, J. M., *Evaluating Data Base Management Systems,* Van Nostrand Reinhold, New York, 1981.

Kroenke, D., *Database Processing,* 2nd ed., Science Research Associates, Chicago, IL, 1983.

Martin, J., *Computer Data-Base Organization,* 2nd ed., Prentice-Hall, Englewood Cliffs, NJ, 1977.

Olle, T. W., *The Codasyl Approach to Data Base Management,* Wiley, New York, 1978.

Ross, R. G., *Data Base Systems,* AMACOM, New York, 1978.

Questions and Exercises

7.1.   Describe a network. Describe some portion of or activity in a corporation that can be described as a network.

7.2.   What is the distinction between a tree and a network? Which is a subcategory of the other?

7.3.   What is a CODASYL set? What kind of data and data relationships is a set capable of holding? What are the pointer options for storing occurrences of sets?

7.4.   Describe the basic form of a CODASYL network. What do the nodes represent? How are sets incorporated into the structure? Conceptually, how are multiple associations handled? How does it provide for the reduction of data redundancy.

7.5.   Redraw the partial network occurrence in Figure 7.9 to reflect the following. (Note: players are kept in alphabetic order.)

a. Doe and Smith attended Stanford

b. Doe's home state is New York

c. Taylor and Turner play for the Giants

7.6. What is a juncture record? How are many-to-many relationships handled in CODASYL networks?

7.7. Why are juncture records really necessary? Can't many-to-many relationships be handles in CODASYL networks without them? Explain.

7.8. What are schemas and subschemas in CODASYL database management systems? What is the distinction between them and what are the advantages of making that distinction?

7.9. What are the access method options for storing CODASYL networks? For a given node in a network, what are the trade-offs between those options?

7.10. How would you modify the Teams and Players network in Figure 7.13 to:

a. Maintain information on each team's season ticket holders?

b. Maintain information on each coach's skills?

c. Maintain a variety of data about the colleges that players attended? (Several players may have attended a particular college and a given player may have attended more than one college.)

7.11. Describe the meaning of the CODASYL network shown in terms of the real world environment that it represents (what is the nature of the data that can be stored in it; what kinds of applications might use it?)

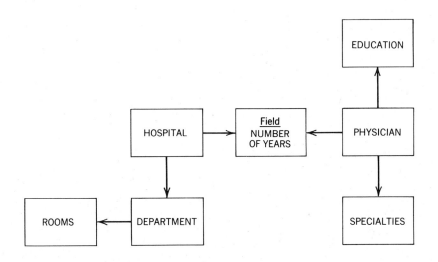

7.12.   Discuss the concepts of storage class and removal class in CO-DASYL networks. What are they? How do they relate to each other? Why are they necessary?

7.13.   What are the major CODASYL data manipulation statements? Do they cover all of the types of data manipulation operations that you might need?

7.14.   Refer to the occurrence of the CODASYL network of Figure 7.15, which is shown in Figure 7.16. Indicate the results of each of the following CODASYL statement sequences.

   a.   MOVE 12 to the TEAMNUM field in the TEAMS record
         FIND ANY TEAMS
         GET

   b.   MOVE 12 to the TEAMNUM field in the TEAMS record
         FIND ANY TEAMS
         FIND FIRST COACHES RECORD WITHIN COACH TEAM SET
         GET

   c.   MOVE 12 to the TEAMNUM field in the TEAMS record
         FIND ANY TEAMS
         FIND COACHES WITHIN COACH TEAM USING Adams
         GET

   d.   MOVE 12 to the TEAMNUM field in the TEAMS record
         FIND ANY TEAMS
        start of loop
         FIND NEXT PLAYERS RECORD WITHIN ON TEAM
         GET
        end of loop

7.15.   Refer to the occurrence of the CODASYL network of Figure 7.15, which is shown in Figure 7.16. Write CODASYL calls with loops if necessary (see the style in the previous exercise) to:

   a.   Get the record for coach Baker
   b.   Get coach Baker's first experience record
   c.   Get all of the coaches on the Dodgers
   d.   Get all of coach Baker's pieces of experience
   e.   Add a new player, Turner, to the Dodgers
   f.   Delete player Jones from the database
   g.   Update player Jones' age to 26

      h.   Remove player Jones from the Dodgers

      i.   Transfer player Jones from the Dodgers to the Giants

  7.16.   What are the CODASYL record maintenance statements? Do they cover the full range of record maintenance activities?

  7.17.   Discuss the CODASYL set maintenance statements. What do they do? Why are they necessary?

8

The Relational Approach to Database

Introduction

In 1970, Dr. Edgar F. Codd of IBM published a paper entitled, "A Relational Model of Data for Large Shared Data Banks." This paper marked the beginning of the field of relational database. During the ensuing years, the relational approach to database has received a great deal of publicity. Yet it has only been within the last few years that commercially viable relational database management systems have been on the market. Relational database has been very tempting in concept, but until fairly recently, very elusive when it has come to applying it in a real world environment. And there are many people who feel that this approach is the one that holds the greatest promise for the future.

The saga of relational DBMSs is one of the most fascinating stories in this still young field of database. How they compare with hierarchical and network DBMSs in terms of operation, performance, and overall philosophy, is not only interesting, but highly instructive for a true understanding of some of the most basic concepts in database.

We will begin this chapter with an easy to understand basic foundation in relational database concepts and operations. Then we will make some comparisons between the relational and the navigational approaches. Next we will describe a widely used commercial relational database language. Finally, we will look at another available system which is a relational DBMS with a novel approach to the user interface.

Relational Database Concepts

Review of the Database Premise

We began the discussion of database in Chapter 4 with the separate simple, linear files of Figure 4.1 and the combined file of Figure 4.2. For convenience, those two figures have been repeated as Figures 8.1 and 8.2. Let's review the situation concerning the files in those figures. The two files represented in Figure 8.1 are simple linear files. SALESPERSON NUMBER is the unique key field of the Salesperson file. CUSTOMER NUMBER is the unique key field of the Customer file. There is one record for each salesperson in the Salesperson file, and one record for each customer in the Customer file. These two files have the highly desirable property of being conceptually simple, and in addition, have no data redundancy among their nonkey fields. For a given salesperson, his number, his name (and presumably his

SALESPERSON NUMBER	...	SALESPERSON NAME	...
137		Baker	
186		Adams	
204		Dickens	
361		Carlyle	
. . .		. . .	

(a)

CUSTOMER NUMBER	...	SALESPERSON NUMBER	...
0121		137	
0839		186	
0933		137	
1047		137	
1525		361	
1700		361	
1826		137	
2198		204	
2267		186	
. . .		. . .	

(b)

Figure 8.1. (a) Salesperson file and (b) Customer file.

address, telephone number, etc.) are listed exactly once in the Salesperson file. The same can be said for the customer data in the Customer file.

The problem with these two files is the seeming inability to integrate data in any way short of brute force application programming. In order to find the *name* of the salesperson responsible for a given customer, the application programmer must find the record for that customer in the Customer file, pick up the salesperson number in it, and use that piece of data as entry to the Salesperson file to find the record for that salesperson, which contains his name.

The other choice, the combined file of Figure 8.2 solves the data integration problem—the above query can be answered with the retrieval of a single record—but introduces extensive and unacceptable data redundancy.

SALESPERSON NUMBER	CUSTOMER NUMBER	SALESPERSON NAME	· · ·
137	1021	Baker	
137	0933	Baker	
137	1047	Baker	
137	1826	Baker	
186	0839	Adams	
186	2267	Adams	
204	2198	Dickens	
361	1525	Carlyle	
361	1700	Carlyle	
· · ·	· · ·	· · ·	

Figure 8.2. Combined file.

We asserted that a true DBMS must both provide a data structure that allows data to be stored nonredundantly, while also making it appear to the application programmer that the data is highly integrated. In Chapters 6 and 7 we showed how that goal can be accomplished through the use of two nonlinear data structures: hierarchies and networks.

If you stop to think about it, the ability of the hierarchical and network DBMSs to hold data nonredundantly and at the same time provide an integrated atmosphere was directly a product of the data structures in use. As we saw in Chapters 6 and 7, the hierarchies and networks did hold data nonredundantly. The data about a given baseball team could be stored just once, and then be associated with each of the players, for example, on the team by the way that their records were linked together. This interlinking of records also provided a sense of data integration, which the programmer could take advantage of by navigating through the structures with the proper commands in his or her application programs.

Another Solution to the Database Problem

What is a Relation?   While the hierarchical and network solutions to the problem form the foundation for tracking much of the world's commerce today, many people have longed for the relative simplicity of simple, linear files in the database environment. They've thought, wouldn't it be nice to be able to treat data as if it were stored in simple linear files and still have the system provide some kind of data integration capability. This desire is precisely the driving force behind relational database.

To begin with, let's consider the data structure used in relational databases. That's easy. As implied previously, the data appears to be stored in what we have been referring to as simple linear files. Whether or not the actual physical storage is arranged that way or just makes it appear so is unimportant. Following the conventions of the area of mathematics that relational database is founded on, we will begin calling those simple linear files *relations* or *tables*. We will assume that no two rows, records, or *tuples* of a relation are identical. Technically, the columns, fields, or *attributes* of a relation can be arranged in any order without affecting the meaning of the data. A relation always has a field or a group of fields which serve as its (unique) key. This must be true, since we know that no two tuples can be identical and so, as a worst case, all of the relation's fields could serve as the key if necessary (but that situation is rare in practice). With that understanding, it's convenient to think of keys in terms of single fields and we shall do so for now. If a relation has more than one unique field then they are each called *candidate keys* and the one among them that is chosen as "the key of the relation" is called the *primary key*. If in a collection of relations that make up a relational database an attribute serves as the key field of one relation and also appears as a field of another relation, then it is called a *foreign key* in that latter relation. The concept of a foreign key is an important one that we shall explore shortly.

So a relational database is simply a collection of relations. In terms of the way that we think about the data, the relations are quite independent, as opposed to the tightly pointer-connected structures in the hierarchic and network based approaches. Assuming that the relations, like those in Figure 8.1 (we'll start referring to those two files as relations now), are designed well, there is no redundancy among the non-key fields. The question of how to design relational databases will be deferred until Chapter 10, but we will make appropriate comments about it as needed in this chapter as well.

By the way as with any database approach, there is the issue of access methods based on the relational structure. Since a relation is fundamentally thought of as a simple linear file, any of the access methods that we've discussed in this book are applicable. The tuples of a relation can be stored with a hashing algorithm, with an index, or in a simple sequential arrangement (without an index). We will see shortly that the nature of relational operations would render the exclusive use of a sequential access method unacceptable in practice. As will also become clear, efficiency in relational

SALESPERSON NUMBER	SALESPERSON NAME	COMMISSION PERCENTAGE	YEAR OF HIRE
137	Baker	10	1975
186	Adams	15	1971
204	Dickens	10	1963
361	Carlyle	20	1963

(a)

CUSTOMER NUMBER	SALESPERSON NUMBER	CITY
0121	137	New York
0839	186	Hartford
0933	137	Boston
1047	137	Boston
1525	361	Newark
1700	361	Washington
1826	137	New York
2198	204	New York
2267	186	New York

(b)

Figure 8.3. (a) Salesperson relation and (b) Customer relation.

DBMSs usually depends on direct access to a number of the attributes of a relation. Thus relational DBMSs typically allow for indexes to be created over several or even all of the attributes of a relation.

Extracting Data from a Relation. Given a relational database consisting of one or more relations, we have to begin to think about how to extract data from it. Without any special tools for extracting data from a relation, the problem reverts to simply writing a program in some programming language to retrieve data from a simple linear file. If that was as far as we could go, then there would be no field of relational database to talk about! But the crucial point is that an inherent feature of a relational DBMS is the capability to accept high level data retrieval commands aimed at simple linear files or relations and process them, *even to the extent of matching records in different files,* as in finding the *name* of the salesperson on a particular customer account. Let's see what that might look like, first in terms of single relations then across multiple relations.

Since a relation is simply a rectangular arrangement of values, it would seem to make sense to want to approach one horizontally, vertically, or in a combination of the two. To take a horizontal slice of a relation implies retrieving one or more tuples or rows of the relation. That's nothing more than fancy language for retrieving one or more records of a file. Taking a vertical slice of a relation means retrieving one or more attributes or columns of the relation for all of its tuples. In combination, we can retrieve one or more attributes of one or more tuples, the minimum of which is a single attribute of a single tuple, or a single field of a single record. That's as fine a sense of retrieval as we would ever want.

Using terminology from a database formalism called "relational algebra," and a relaxed free-form command style for now, let's look at two commands called "Select" and "Project," which are capable of the kinds of horizontal and vertical manipulations that we just discussed. For a database, we'll use the relations in Figure 8.3, which are the same two relations as those in Figure 8.1, except that we have now added some more nonkey fields and eliminated the dot-dot-dots that indicated additional unknown attributes and tuples. To begin with, suppose that we want to find the record for salesperson number 204. In a very straightforward way, our command might be:

Select tuples from the Salesperson relation in which SALESPERSON NUMBER = 204.

The result would be:

SALESPERSON NUMBER	SALESPERSON NAME	COMMISSION PERCENTAGE	YEAR OF HIRE
204	Dickens	10	1963

Notice that the result of the Select operation is itself a relation, in this case consisting of only one tuple. The result of a relational operation will always be a relation, whether it consists of many tuples with many attributes or one tuple with one attribute (i.e., a single value).

Perhaps we want all of the records with a common value in a particular (nonunique) field:

Select tuples from the Salesperson relation in which COMMISSION PERCENTAGE = 10.

The result of that operation is:

SALESPERSON NUMBER	SALESPERSON NAME	COMMISSION PERCENTAGE	YEAR OF HIRE
137	Baker	10	1975
204	Dickens	10	1963

Of course we might want to retrieve the entire file, perhaps with a command like

Select all tuples from the Salesperson relation.

To retrieve what we referred to earlier as a vertical slice, we will use the Project operator. To retrieve the number and name of each salesperson in the file we issue:

Project the SALESPERSON NUMBER and SALESPERSON NAME over the Salesperson relation.

The result will be a long narrow relation:

SALESPERSON NUMBER	SALESPERSON NAME
137	Baker
186	Adams
204	Dickens
361	Carlyle

If we project a nonunique field, then a decision must be made at some level as to whether or not we want duplicates (although, since the result is itself a relation, technically we can't have any). For example, whether:

Project the YEAR OF HIRE over the Salesperson relation.

produces:

YEAR OF HIRE
1975
1971
1963
1963

or

YEAR OF HIRE
1975
1971
1963

would depend on the particular implementation involved.

More powerful still is the combination of the Select and Project operators. Suppose we apply them serially, with the relation that results from one operation being used as the relation that the next operation operates on. Let's say that we want the number and name of the salespersons working on a 10% commission. We would issue the following two commands:

Select tuples from the Salesperson relation in which COMMISSION PERCENTAGE = 10. Project the SALESPERSON NUMBER and SALESPERSON NAME over that result.

This produces:

SALESPERSON NUMBER	SALESPERSON NAME
137	Baker
204	Dickens

The following combination illustrates the ability to retrieve a single value. Suppose that we want to know the year of hire of salesperson number 204. Since we know that SALESPERSON NUMBER is a unique field, we know that we will be dealing with only one tuple. Since we are seeking one attribute from that tuple, we know that we will wind up with a single value:

Select tuples from the Salesperson relation in which SALESPERSON NUMBER = 204. Project the YEAR OF HIRE over that result.

The result is the single value:

YEAR
OF
HIRE

1963

Extracting Data Across Multiple Relations.   It will be within the context of extracting data across multiple relations that we will enter upon a discussion of data integration in the relational database approach. Look at the relations in Figure 8.3 and think back to the earlier example of data integration: Find the name of the salesperson on a particular account. The suggested solution to that problem thus far has been to find the account record in the customer file, read the salesperson number in that record, and use that number to find the record for the salesperson in the salesperson file.

Wouldn't it be nice if the same system which is capable of retrieving data based on the kinds of Select and Project commands that we've looked at, is also capable of doing that kind of multiple relation search? In fact, using an operator called *Join*, together with Select and Project, we can solve the multiple relation data integration problem.

Continuing with our relaxed command style, let's issue commands to find the name of the salesperson responsible for customer number 1525:

Join the Salesperson relation and the Customer relation, using the SALESPERSON NUMBER of each as the join field. Select tuples from that result in which CUSTOMER NUMBER = 1525. Project the SALESPERSON NAME over that result.

Let's examine the first sentence, which represents the join command. Remember how we had picked up the SALESPERSON NUMBER attribute value in one relation and used it to search for the needed record in the other relation? We were able to do that precisely because that field existed in both relations! (Even if the two attributes had different names, like "SALESPERSON NUMBER" in one relation and "EMPLOYEE NUMBER" in the other relation, we could still perform the same operation because they represent the same kind of information. Technically we would say that they have the same "domain of values.") The join operation will take advantage of the common SALESPERSON NUMBER field (which for the purposes of this command is called the "join field") and look for tuples in the two relations with the same value for the join field. When it finds such a pair of records it takes all of the fields of both records and creates a single new record out of them in the resultant relation. It is truly an exhaustive operation, comparing every tuple of one relation against every tuple of the other relation, looking for a match in the join fields. So the result of the join command, the first of the three commands in the command sequence we're executing, is:

SALES-PERSON NUMBER	SALES-PERSON NAME	COMMISSION PERCENTAGE	YEAR OF HIRE	CUSTOMER NUMBER	SALES-PERSON NUMBER	CITY
137	Baker	10	1975	0121	137	New York
137	Baker	10	1975	0933	137	Boston
137	Baker	10	1975	1047	137	Boston
137	Baker	10	1975	1826	137	New York
186	Adams	15	1971	0839	186	Hartford
186	Adams	15	1971	2267	186	New York
204	Dickens	10	1963	2198	204	New York
361	Carlyle	20	1963	1525	361	Newark
361	Carlyle	20	1963	1700	361	Washington

Notice that the first and sixth attributes are identical. They represent the SALESPERSON NUMBER attribute from the Salesperson and Customer relations respectively. Remember that two tuples would not be combined together to form a tuple in the resultant relation unless those two join field values were identical in the first place. This type of join is called an "equi-join." If, as seems reasonable, we eliminate one of the two identical columns in the process, we call the result a "natural join."

To continue with the command sequence to eventually find the name of the salesperson responsible for customer number 1525, first we issue the Select command that we wrote previously, using the relation that re-sulted from the join. This produces:

SALES-PERSON NUMBER	SALES-PERSON NAME	COMMISSION PERCENTAGE	YEAR OF HIRE	CUSTOMER NUMBER	SALES-PERSON NUMBER	CITY
361	Carlyle	20	1963	1525	361	Newark

Finally, we issue the third command, the Project, and get:

SALES
PERSON
NAME

Carlyle

Notice that we could have streamlined this process. We were dealing with only a single customer and there is only one tuple for each customer in the Customer relation, with CUSTOMER NUMBER as the unique key field. Thus we really only had to look at one tuple in the Customer relation to solve the problem. We'll talk about the use of information like that to increase the overall efficiency of the process later in this chapter, within the context of the Structured Query Language system.

A variation on the join concept is called the "outer join" (as opposed to the previously mentioned "inner join"). In an outer join, all of the tuples of one of the relations appear in the resultant relation regardless of the presence or absence of a join field match in the other relation. If a particular tuple's join field doesn't match that of any tuple in the other relation, then in the resultant relation that tuple will appear with null values where the values from the matching tuple in the other relation, had there been one, would have gone.

Comparison Between the Relational and the Other Approaches

Points of Comparison.   One way of comparing the relational approach with the others is through the concept of the join. While we have thus far spoken of joins only in the relational context, we can discuss them and revisit the closely related issue of data integration in the context of the hierarchical and network systems as well. A second way is in the comparative effort to design a database and to modify it after it is in use.

A third way of comparing the relational and nonrelational approaches is by their performance characteristics. This discussion will explore the reasons behind relational database only recently becoming commercially viable. And a fourth mode of comparison involves potential integrity exposures at the time of insertion and deletion operations.

A Join Is a Join Is a Join.   Figure 8.4 shows the same Salesperson and Customer data model set up in a hierarchical or network form. The comparison between the relations of Figure 8.3 and the structure of Figure 8.4 is very important and drives to the heart of the database concept.

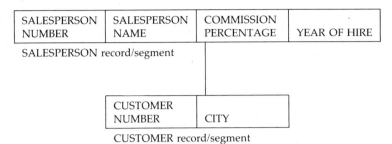

SALESPERSON NUMBER	SALESPERSON NAME	COMMISSION PERCENTAGE	YEAR OF HIRE

SALESPERSON record/segment

CUSTOMER NUMBER	CITY

CUSTOMER record/segment

Figure 8.4. Salesperson—customer hierarchy or network.

Regardless of what the underlying structure is in the DBMS being used for a particular application, one fundamental concept of data integration remains the same: Records describing different entities in the application environment must in some way be capable of being associated with each other. Fundamentally this is not a deep concept in computer science, but rather is the way the world around us works. A salesperson is responsible for several customers. A customer has a salesperson assigned to him or her to place an order with. The world revolves around such relationships. And yet, when we try to model the world in a data directed, automated data processing environment, those relationships translate into the concept of data integration.

Return to Figure 8.3 and think about how such relationships leading to data integration are maintained in the relational (or for that matter, the simple linear file) environment. With independent relations, the information recording which tuple(s) of a relation have a meaningful association with which tuples(s) of another relation must exist explicitly. The SALESPERSON NUMBER attribute obviously belongs in, and in fact does appear in the Salesperson relation. In addition, while it may be something that at first glance we might take for granted, the fact that SALESPERSON NUMBER also appears in the *Customer* relation is crucial to making sense out of the application environment. That's how we know which customers a salesperson is responsible for and which salesperson a customer turns to to place an order. That the SALESPERSON NUMBER attribute was in fact placed in the Customer relation when these structures were being designed is a nontrivial point, which will be discussed under the heading of "database design" in Chapter 10 of this book.

Now focus your attention on the hierarchical or network equivalent in Figure 8.4. There too, salespersons are associated with customers but in a different way. They are related implicitly by the design of the hierarchical structure, and explicitly by the child and twin or next pointers which are created when actual data is loaded according to the defined structure. Notice that the Customer Record in Figure 8.4 is missing the SALESPERSON NUMBER field. It's *not needed* because when the data is loaded according to that structural form *physical pointers* will be created which will tie the customers to their responsible salespersons.

But that leads to another crucial question: Does the concept of the join exist in hierarchical and network databases? The answer, as you should be able to surmise at this point, is *yes* (at least informally). And now, here is a key point in the comparison between relational and nonrelational databases:

> In hierarchical and network databases joins are performed implicitly at the time that the hierarchies and networks are designed, and explicitly with pointers when the data is loaded according to those structures. The power of data integration is primarily a function of the data structure.
>
> In relational databases joins are performed "on the fly," at execution time by the DBMS according to commands given to the system at that time. The data structure, that is, the relations, must have join fields present in the right places, but fundamentally the power of data integration is an execution time function of the DBMS.

Data integration is *the* fundamental concept in database, and one way or another, the join is the implementation vehicle for it.

Flexibility in Design and Modification.   As we will see in Chapter 10, there are two prominent, as well as several less prominent, methods for designing a database. Each method has proponents who feel that the one that they favor is easier to use. This is really a part of a larger argument that often flares up about which approach to database is more "natural" in terms of the way that they model real world application situations. Database experts have been known to go on for hours arguing that question to no agreement, because it is a matter of opinion. "Natural" is not a technical term and we will not pursue that argument here.

Nevertheless, we will note in passing that there are many people who feel that relations are easier to design and inherently simpler to manage than hierarchies or networks. One thing that occurs when a relational database is designed is the proper distribution of join fields in the relations, based on the way the application environment operates. This assures that any semantically correct (makes sense in terms of the application) query that requires a join will find the join fields in the right places when it needs them. But join operations, particularly brute force joins that require full file scans of one or both files, can be painfully slow for large files.

When designing a hierarchical or network database, decisions must be made as to which of the integrating associations are actually designed into the structure. In the hierarchical and network environments, the performance of join oriented accesses that are based on relationships that have been designed into the structure (and are ultimately implemented with pointers) can be very fast, although accesses based on relationships that have not been designed into the structure can be extremely slow.

Later modifications to the database, depending on their nature, can often be made more easily in a relational database too. Here we're not talking about adding additional record or tuple occurrences to a database, but rather changing or expanding the number of record *types*. For example, an entirely new relation can be added to a relational database without affecting existing query forms or the existing relations. Adding new record types to hierarchical or network databases may require fitting them into existing structures, reloading the data into the database and resetting pointers, and may affect queries in existing application programs.

But it is also important to note that if the nature of the change involves an underlying change in the application, like the salesperson number no longer being unique or more than one salesperson now being responsible for a customer, then the database may have to be redesigned regardless of which approach to database was taken.

Performance Characteristics.   At last it's time to answer the question of why relational DBMSs have only recently become commercially viable. Recall the explanation of the join earlier in this chapter, and the example in which we joined the two relations of Figure 8.3. As sample relations, the Salesperson relation has only four tuples and the Customer relation has only nine tuples. The thought of comparing every tuple of one of those relations with every tuple of the other to accomplish the join seemed so reasonable that you probably didn't give it a second thought. But what if we attempted to join a 1 million tuple relation with a 3 million tuple relation. How long do you think that would take—even on a large fast computer? It might well take much longer than a person waiting for a response at a terminal would tolerate.

On the other hand, in a typical relational database application environment, many queries to the database will deal with only one relation and will not require a join operation at all. Still, what about the queries that do? Modern, sophisticated relational database systems rely on either special hardware devices for performance enhancement, or on clever software techniques to speed-up the join process by, for example, reducing the scope of the join in terms of the number of tuples involved. They also take advantage of the general increase in speed of computer processors that has developed continually over the years. We will discuss the hardware devices in Chapter 14 of this book, and the software techniques later in this chapter under the Structured Query Language heading.

And what is the comparative situation with hierarchical and network databases? The key point here revolves around the fact that data integration is accomplished at the time the data is loaded and is maintained by all of the physical pointers that interconnect the records. Hierarchies and networks may appear to be complex structures and may present problems in future database structure modifications, but you can't beat physical pointers for speed. That's the other side of the coin: the reason, at least vis-à-vis performance, that hierarchical and network based DBMSs *have* been commercially successful from the advent of the database era.

Integrity Exposure on Insertion and Deletion.   Let's say that our example company gets a new customer account and it is assigned to a particular salesperson. If IMS is our DBMS, and the data structure is as represented in Figure 8.4, then we can only add the new CUSTOMER segment as an attached segment to the applicable SALESPERSON segment, which makes sense in the overall scheme of things. In the network environment we can force the situation with the specification of "automatic" as a set insertion parameter. But in the relations of Figure 8.3, there is nothing inherent in the data structure to force a tuple for a particular salesperson to exist in the Salesperson relation, just because someone inserts a customer record into the Customer relation with that salesperson recorded in it. That is a potential integrity exposure that the system or the application program must handle. The formal term involved is "referential integrity." Similarly, a salesperson record can be deleted, leaving the value referring to it in the customer record with nothing to reference.

By the way, note that under certain application circumstances the ability to add a tuple to a relation without regard to referential integrity considerations can be an advantage. For example, we might want to add a new customer to our Customer file without specifying who the salesperson is or specifying a salesperson who for some reason does not yet exist in the Salesperson file. Nevertheless, there are many who feel that for a relational DBMS to address a full spectrum of operational application systems, referential integrity as a system function will be a necessary requirement of relational DBMSs in the future.

Structured Query Language (SQL)

Introduction

As an example of a relational database language we will look at IBM's Structured Query Language (SQL). This is a relational language which is derived from an earlier IBM research project in relational database called "System R." It is currently embodied in two IBM relational DBMSs: SQL/Data System (SQL/DS) which runs under IBMs DOS and VM operating systems, and Database 2 (DB2) which runs under the MVS family of larger operating systems. Other companies too are basing relational DBMSs on SQL.

In keeping with the spirit of this book, we will not be concerned with the differences between the different SQL implementations (they are relatively minor anyway) but rather will concentrate on the basic principles and general syntax involved. We will use the term SQL to refer to the language and the collective systems. We also note in passing that SQL/DS and DB2 are both full fledged DBMSs, with provisions for backup and recovery operations, security checks, and so forth, but these topics will not be discussed in this chapter. As we did in the chapters on hierarchical and network database concepts, we will concentrate on the structural and language aspects here, and postpone a discussion of those other concepts for a later chapter. (Note that the following subject matter on the SQL data structure and optimizer applies to the IBM implementations of the SQL language and is not an inherent feature of SQL as such.)

The SQL Data Structure

There are only a couple of points to mention about the SQL data structure, beyond repeating what by now should be obvious: the data appears to be stored as simple linear files or relations. In the SQL terminology they're called "tables."

The tables are accessed either sequentially or through indexes. An index can reference one or a combination of columns (in SQL the term "column" is used instead of "field") of a table. A table can have several indexes built over it. An index can reference a column whose values are unique or are not unique. When the data in a table changes, SQL automatically updates the corresponding data in any indexes that are affected by that change.

The concept of logical versus physical databases is implemented in SQL. A physical table is called a "base table." A logical table is called a "view" and is a subset of one or more base tables. A view may consist of a subset of the columns and/or a subset of the records of a table. As is typical of implementations of the concept of a logical database, the creation of a view in SQL does not entail the physical duplication of data in a table into a new table. Instead, information describing the nature of the subset is kept in one of several system "catalogs." If a query references a view (queries can be issued to either base tables or views), the information about the view in the catalog will map from it to the physical table where the required data is actually stored.

The SQL Optimizer

Prior to responding to a query from a user, SQL attempts to figure out the most efficient way of answering that query. Informally, the flavor of what it does is as follows.

SQL is geared towards taking maximum advantage of its indexes. That, of course, makes it incumbent upon the person designing the SQL tables to include an appropriate set of indexes based on the anticipated types of queries. Let's digress for a moment on that point. First of all, remember that SQL will answer queries regardless of whether or not indexes which might speed things up exist. Secondly, bear in mind that the helter skelter creation of a large number of indexes may impact performance. If a SQL database is at all volatile, that is, it has a significant amount of insert, delete, and update activity, then the automatic facility in SQL which updates the indexes will tend to slow down the overall system—the more indexes, the more slowing down will take place.

The optimizer checks to see if the query involves columns that have indexes built over them and, if so, notes other factors about the column values. For many select type operations it will clearly take advantage of those indexes, going directly to only those records that are required. If a join is involved in the query, the system tries to figure out the way that it can take the greatest advantage of any appropriate indexes. For example, if the query calls for a join operation, and the join columns (join fields) in each table are either in sorted order, or have indexes built over them, then comparing every record of one table against every record of the other is unnecessary. The system can simply start at the top of each table (or index if the table is not in order by the join column) and move downwards, keeping track of the current value in each, as if performing a merge operation. Another example involves the case where a join requires only a single record from one table, which must be matched against one or many records of another table. Clearly, if that single record from the first table can be found directly with an index, then the system is saved from having to go through all of the records of that table, as it would have to in a brute force join. Our original example of finding the name of the salesperson responsible for a particular customer account is an instance of that case.

Note in passing that the system also makes sure that the specified columns are in fact in the specified tables, that the user is authorized to see that data, that numeric columns are not being compared to alphabetic columns, and so forth. All of that information is stored in the collection of system catalogs.

The SQL Language

In this section we will explore many of the commands in the SQL language in the context of the baseball example that we've used before. The six tables in Figure 8.5 represent most of the structure of the original example. The player statistics and position data is missing, but on the other hand many more occurrences of the records in the rest of the structure are shown. Both changes are strictly for instructive purposes and do not imply anything about the capabilities of the system. Compare Figure 8.5 with Figure 6.15. Notice how the TEAMS, COACHES, WORKEXP, BATS, and PLAYERS tables correspond directly to segments in the IMS structure. The TEAMS and PLAYERS tables have unique key columns (unique key fields), TEAM-NUM and PLAYNUM respectively. Since it is possible to have two different coaches with the same last name on two different teams, uniqueness in the COACHES table is obtained by a combination of the TEAMNUM and COACHNAM columns. It then follows that uniqueness in the WORKEXP table requires the combination of the TEAMNUM, COACHNAM, and EXPTYPE columns, since in addition to the foregoing comment, a coach can have several pieces of experience. Bat numbers are only unique within a team, so the TEAMNUM and BATNUM columns are required for uniqueness in the BATS table. The AFFILIATION table in the relational database serves the same purpose as the logical relationship in the IMS database: it represents the many-to-many relationship showing, historically for players, which teams they have played on during their careers, and for teams, which players they have had on their rosters during their existence. Note how the YEARS and BATAVG columns in the AFFILIATION table represent the same "intersection data" that appeared in the IMS logical child segments. Look over the relations of Figure 8.5 and convince yourself that the data is highly nonredundant. Each team is described just once, as is each player, and so forth.

SQL commands can be issued either as ad hoc query commands or as

TEAMS Table

TEAMNUM	TEAMNAME	TEAMCITY	TEAMMGR
12	Dodgers	Los Angeles	Wilson
15	Giants	San Francisco	Johnson
20	Yankees	New York	Simpson
24	Tigers	Detroit	Corbin

TEAMS Table

TEAMNUM	COACHNAM	COACHPH
12	Adams	555-1524
12	Baker	555-3690
15	Taylor	555-4820
20	Jackson	555-2444
24	Victor	555-9327
24	Dooley	555-7321

COACHES Table

TEAMNUM	COACHNAM	EXPTYPE	EXPYRS
12	Adams	High School Coach	5
12	Adams	College Coach	10
12	Baker	College Coach	3
12	Baker	Japan League Coach	2
12	Baker	Minor League Coach	4
15	Taylor	College Coach	15
24	Victor	Minor League Coach	12

WORKEXP Table

TEAMNUM	BATNUM	MANUF
12	B01	Acme
12	B09	General
12	B13	Acme
15	B01	Acme
20	B03	United
20	B04	Modern
24	B18	General
24	B21	United

BATS Table

Figure 8.5. The Baseball relational database.

PLAYNUM	PLAYNAME	AGE
358	Stevens	21
523	Doe	32
1131	Johnson	28
1779	Jones	25
2007	Dobbs	27
4280	Cohen	25
4319	Ross	24
5410	Smith	27
6564	Linton	24
8093	Smith	21
8366	Gomez	33

PLAYERS Table

PLAYNUM	TEAMNUM	YEARS	BATAVG
358	15	5	0.300
358	20	3	0.320
523	12	10	0.257
1131	20	1	0.283
1779	12	1	0.223
1779	15	7	0.246
1779	24	2	0.240
2007	24	3	0.290
4280	15	1	0.195
4280	20	3	0.227
4319	15	4	0.298
5410	12	6	0.307
6564	20	12	0.310
6564	24	3	0.280
8093	12	5	0.250
8093	20	2	0.240
8093	24	8	0.265
8366	20	7	0.283

AFFILIATION Table

Figure 8.5. *(continued)* The Baseball relational database.

data access commands embedded in COBOL, FORTRAN, PL/I, or Assembler Language programs. In this section we will assume that SQL is being used in the ad hoc query mode. The syntax in the embedded mode is functionally the same as in the query mode with some additions that you might expect. We will mention one or two examples of these differences as we proceed through the explanation of the commands. You should also realize that when an SQL command is used in the embedded mode and returns a multituple relation as its result, it is up to the program to process that result, one tuple (or record) at a time as required.

SQL Single Table Retrievals

Let's begin with some simple select and project type commands. Actually in SQL, all of the retrieval type commands, including those that we have previously spoken of as select, project, and join, will be performed with the SELECT command. For clarity we will indent and place different parts of the commands on different lines, although SQL commands can be written as a continuous string at a display terminal. To retrieve the entire TEAMS table you would issue:

SELECT *
    FROM TEAMS

Literally translated this says, "Display all (*) columns in the TEAMS table." By default, since no further restrictions are specified, all of the records of the table are involved. The result would look exactly like the TEAMS table in Figure 8.5 (which is reasonable since the result of a relational query is a relation itself):

TEAMNUM	TEAMNAME	TEAMCITY	TEAMMGR
12	Dodgers	Los Angeles	Wilson
15	Giants	San Francisco	Johnson
20	Yankees	New York	Simpson
24	Tigers	Detroit	Corbin

To select a single record by identifying a value of a unique column, for example, "Find the record for team number 12," you would issue:

SELECT *
    FROM TEAMS
    WHERE TEAMNUM = 12

The WHERE clause is used to limit the horizontal slice through the table, causing a subset of the records to be retrieved. In this case, the column whose value is specified is a unique column, and so only one record will be retrieved:

TEAMNUM	TEAMNAME	TEAMCITY	TEAMMGR
12	Dodgers	Los Angeles	Wilson

For example, a simple project operation, "List the team number and team name of all teams," would look like this:

```
SELECT TEAMNUM, TEAMNAME
    FROM TEAMS
```

The column names immediately after the SELECT key word are the columns that are to be retrieved:

TEAMNUM	TEAMNAME
12	Dodgers
15	Giants
20	Yankees
24	Tigers

For example, to combine a simple select and project, "Find the player number and player name of all players who are over 30 years of age," you would issue:

```
SELECT PLAYNUM, PLAYNAME
    FROM PLAYERS
    WHERE AGE>30
```

Notice that the WHERE clause is quite flexible, allowing the full range of comparison operators. Incidentally if this statement was embedded in a program, we could replace the constant "30" with a variable whose value would have been set earlier in the program. The result in this case is:

PLAYNUM	PLAYNAME
523	Doe
8366	Gomez

Multiple conditions can be combined in a SELECT statement. If you want a list of the coaches who have been college coaches for more than five years, you would issue:

```
SELECT TEAMNUM, COACHNAM
   FROM WORKEXP
   WHERE EXPTYPE = 'College Coach'
     AND EXPYRS > 5
```

The result is:

TEAMNUM	COACHNAM
12	Adams
15	Taylor

Projecting over a nonunique column may yield duplicate entries in the result. For example, if you want a list of the teams, by team number, who use bats manufactured by the Acme Company you would issue:

```
SELECT TEAMNUM
   FROM BATS
   WHERE MANUF = 'Acme'
```

and the result would be:

TEAMNUM
12
12
15

In a case like this you are clearly not interested in duplicates so you add the word "distinct":

```
SELECT DISTINCT TEAMNUM
   FROM BATS
   WHERE MANUF = 'Acme'
```

and get:

TEAMNUM
12
15

Next is an example which demonstrates that the records selected can be limited by a range of column values and can be ordered by the values of any column. To get the player records of those players between the ages of 25 and 29 and order those records by age, you would issue:

```
SELECT *
    FROM PLAYERS
    WHERE AGE BETWEEN 25 AND 29
    ORDER BY AGE
```

The result is:

PLAYNUM	PLAYNAME	AGE
1779	Jones	25
4280	Cohen	25
2007	Dobbs	27
5410	Smith	27
1131	Johnson	28

Records can be selected based on the value of one of their columns being in a specified set. If you want a list of the bats that were manufactured by either the General Company or the United Company, and the teams which use them, you would issue:

```
SELECT *
    FROM BATS
    WHERE MANUF IN ('General', 'United')
```

and get as a result:

TEAMNUM	BATNUM	MANUF
12	B09	General
20	B03	United
24	B18	General
24	B21	United

And records can be retrieved based on the commonality of only a part of the values of a column. For instance to satisfy the query, "Find the records for all of the players whose last names begin with the letter "S," you would issue:

SELECT *
FROM PLAYERS
WHERE PLAYNAME LIKE 'S%'

The result:

PLAYNUM	PLAYNAME	AGE
358	Stevens	21
5410	Smith	27
8093	Smith	21

is based on the percent sign substituting for anything beyond the leading "S."

A number of built in functions give the SQL language additional capabilities. To get a count of the number of records in a table, for example to find the number of teams in the league, you would issue:

SELECT COUNT(*)
FROM TEAMS

The result is shown as:

COUNT(EXPRESSION 1)
4

Another variation on that theme is to count the number of distinct values in a particular column in a table. For example, if you want to find the number of different manufacturers of bats who supply the league, you would issue:

SELECT COUNT(DISTINCT MANUF)
FROM BATS

which produces:

COUNT(DISTINCT MANUF)
4

And a count can be guided by a WHERE clause too. To satisfy the query, "Find the number of players over age 30," you would issue:

SELECT COUNT(*)
    FROM PLAYERS
    WHERE AGE>30

which produces:

COUNT(EXPRESSION 1)
_____

2

Other special features of the same general type as COUNT include finding the sum of several numbers, their average, and the maximum and minimum values among them. For example, to find the total number of years of experience that coach Adams of the Dodgers (team number 12) has you would issue:

SELECT SUM(EXPYRS)
    FROM WORKEXP
    WHERE TEAMNUM = 12
        AND COACHNAM = 'Adams'

The system would reply:

SUM(EXPYRS)
_____

15

You might want to perform one of these operations on several subsets of the records of a table independently. For example, you might want to know the total number of years of prior experience of each of the coaches in the league. To find that, you would use the "group by" feature and issue:

SELECT TEAMNUM, COACHNAM, SUM(EXPYRS)
    FROM WORKEXP
    GROUP BY TEAMNUM, COACHNAM

The result would be:

TEAMNUM	COACHNAM	SUM(EXPYRS)
12	Adams	15
12	Baker	9
15	Taylor	15
24	Victor	12

SQL Multiple Table Retrievals (Joins)

Let's present a join command and then discuss it. The command for a join between the COACHES and TEAMS tables would be written as:

    SELECT COACHES.*, TEAMS.*
       FROM COACHES, TEAMS
       WHERE TEAMS.TEAMNUM = COACHES.TEAMNUM

and would produce:

TEAMNUM	COACHNAM	COACHPH	TEAMNUM	TEAMNAME	TEAMCITY	TEAMMGR
12	Adams	555-1524	12	Dodgers	Los Angeles	Wilson
12	Baker	555-3690	12	Dodgers	Los Angeles	Wilson
15	Taylor	555-4820	15	Giants	San Francisco	Johnson
20	Jackson	555-2444	20	Yankees	New York	Simpson
24	Victor	555-9327	24	Tigers	Detroit	Corbin
24	Dooley	555-7321	24	Tigers	Detroit	Corbin

Notice the following points about the command: the expression FROM COACHES, TEAMS indicates that there are two tables involved in this command. The expression WHERE TEAMS.TEAMNUM = COACHES.TEAMNUM defines the join column to be the team number column in each of the two tables. The use of the syntax "table.column" distinguishes exactly which column is being referred to in the case where columns in different tables have the same column name. The expression SELECT COACHES.*, TEAMS.* indicates that the join will be an equijoin: all of the columns from both tables (the join column twice) will appear in the result. In fact, we could simply have written SELECT *.

As another variation, a join can involve all of the columns of both tables, but only a subset of the records. For example, you can join the COACHES and TEAMS tables for just those records that involve the DODGERS:

    SELECT COACHES.*, TEAMS.*
       FROM COACHES, TEAMS
       WHERE TEAMS.TEAMNUM = COACHES.TEAMNUM
          AND TEAMNAME = 'Dodgers'

The result of this command is:

TEAMNUM	COACHNAM	COACHPH	TEAMNUM	TEAMNAME	TEAMCITY	TEAMMG
12	Adams	555-1524	12	Dodgers	Los Angeles	Wilso
12	Baker	555-3690	12	Dodgers	Los Angeles	Wilso

Let's begin to look at some practical examples of the use of the join facility. The query, "Find the names of the coaches on the Dodgers," is similar to the earlier, "Find the name of the salesperson on a particular account". The difference is that there was just one salesperson, but there may be several coaches. In this example, the coach names appear in a different table from the one with the "Dodgers" reference, which is the same sort of situation that we had in the salespersons and customers files. Your command would be:

```
SELECT COACHNAM
   FROM COACHES, TEAMS
   WHERE TEAMS.TEAMNUM = COACHES.TEAMNUM
      AND TEAMNAME = 'Dodgers'
```

which would result in:

COACHNAM
Adams
Baker

How about, "List the league's coaches, their telephone numbers, and the *names* of the teams that they're on"?

```
SELECT COACHNAM, COACHPH, TEAMNAME
   FROM COACHES, TEAMS
   WHERE TEAMS.TEAMNUM = COACHES.TEAMNUM
```

The result is:

COACHNAM	COACHPH	TEAMNAME
Adams	555-1524	Dodgers
Baker	555-3690	Dodgers
Taylor	555-4820	Giants
Jackson	555-2444	Yankees
Victor	555-9327	Tigers
Dooley	555-7321	Tigers

Here's one that involves the join of three tables. Suppose you are asked to list the player numbers and names of the players who have played on the Dodgers, and include the number of years that they played on the Dodgers and the batting average they compiled. The information about which players have historically played on which teams exists only in the AFFILIATION table. This is reasonable, since it involves a many-to-many relationship and would introduce redundancy if there was an attempt to combine it into either the TEAMS or PLAYERS tables. The years and batting average data, describing the relationship between a particular player and a particular team, also belongs in the AFFILIATION table. But the player names only appear in the PLAYER table and the team name, Dodgers, only appears in the TEAMS table. What you have to do in this situation is join the TEAMS and AFFILIATION tables using the TEAMNUM column as the join column, and join the PLAYERS and AFFILIATION tables using the PLAYNUM column as the join column. Your command would look like this:

```
SELECT PLAYERS.PLAYNUM, PLAYNAME, YEARS, BATAVG
    FROM PLAYERS, AFFILIATION, TEAMS
    WHERE PLAYERS.PLAYNUM = AFFILIATION.PLAYNUM
    AND AFFILIATION.TEAMNUM = TEAMS.TEAMNUM
    AND TEAMNAME = 'Dodgers'
```

and the result would be:

PLAYNUM	PLAYNAME	YEARS	BATAVG
523	Doe	10	0.257
1779	Jones	1	0.223
5410	Smith	6	0.307
8093	Smith	5	0.250

As a final example of a join, suppose you were asked to find the age of the oldest player on the Dodgers. Again, this request requires a three table join to satisfy it. The name "Dodgers" appears only in the TEAMS table, the age data appears only in the PLAYERS table, and the connection between those two is maintained in the AFFILIATION table. You would issue:

```
SELECT MAX(AGE)
    FROM PLAYERS, AFFILIATION, TEAMS
    WHERE PLAYERS.PLAYNUM = AFFILIATION.PLAYNUM
    AND AFFILIATION.TEAMNUM = TEAMS.TEAMNUM
    AND TEAMNAME = 'Dodgers'
```

which produces:

MAX(AGE)

32

Another syntax variation is known as a "subquery." It allows the nesting of SQL commands so that the table which results from one SQL command can then be queried by another SQL command. For example, take the query, "Find the names and telephone numbers of the coaches on the Dodgers." As you are now aware, this could be accomplished by issuing a join type command. But it could also be answered with a subquery type command. In the following subquery type command, the second SELECT statement will be executed first, because it is within the innermost set of parentheses. It will find the team number for Dodgers. This result will then be operated on by the first SELECT statement, which will find the name and telephone number of the coaches on that team (the Dodgers).

```
SELECT COACHNAM, COACHPH
    FROM COACHES
    WHERE TEAMNUM IN
    (SELECT TEAMNUM
        FROM TEAMS
        WHERE TEAMNAME = 'Dodgers')
```

The result of this query is:

COACHNAM	COACHPH
Adams	555-1524
Baker	555-3690

SQL Update, Delete, and Insert Operations

The three data manipulation operations are straightforward, except for the question of data integrity. For example, remember that the system will not stop you from entering a record in the COACHES table with a team number for which there is no record in the TEAMS table. It is up to the users of the system to maintain their own data integrity in this sense.

The first of the data manipulation commands is UPDATE. If the Dodgers move back to Brooklyn and change their manager to Malloy, you would issue the following to update the TEAMS table.

```
UPDATE TEAMS
   SET TEAMCITY = 'Brooklyn',
      TEAMMGR = 'Malloy'
   WHERE TEAMNAME = 'Dodgers'
```

The TEAMS table would then look like:

TEAMNUM	TEAMNAME	TEAMCITY	TEAMMGR
12	Dodgers	Brooklyn	Malloy
15	Giants	San Francisco	Johnson
20	Yankees	New York	Simpson
24	Tigers	Detroit	Corbin

Several records can be changed at once through such an operation too. If the Acme Company changes its name to the Royal Company and you want to reflect this change in the BATS table, you would issue:

```
UPDATE BATS
   SET MANUF = 'Royal',
   WHERE MANUF = 'Acme'
```

The BATS table would then look like this:

TEAMNUM	BATNUM	MANUF
12	B01	Royal
12	B09	General
12	B13	Royal
15	B01	Royal
20	B03	United
20	B04	Modern
24	B18	General
24	B21	United

Suppose the Dodgers dissolve and you want to delete them from the TEAMS table (here again, you have to manage yourself what happens to references to them in other tables). You would issue:

```
DELETE
   FROM TEAMS
   WHERE TEAMNAME = 'Dodgers'
```

The remainder of the TEAMS table would be:

TEAMNUM	TEAMNAME	TEAMCITY	TEAMMGR
15	Giants	San Francisco	Johnson
20	Yankees	New York	Simpson
24	Tigers	Detroit	Corbin

If the WHERE clause specified a nonunique value, then several records would have been deleted.

To insert the Cardinals into the TEAMS table you would issue:

```
INSERT
    INTO TEAMS
    VALUES (17, 'Cardinals', 'St. Louis', 'Gregory')
```

The TEAMS table (assuming that it appeared as in Figure 8.5 at the time you issued this command) would look like:

TEAMNUM	TEAMNAME	TEAMCITY	TEAMMGR
12	Dodgers	Los Angeles	Wilson
15	Giants	San Francisco	Johnson
20	Yankees	New York	Simpson
24	Tigers	Detroit	Corbin
17	Cardinals	St. Louis	Gregory

While this table is no longer in sorted order, remember that if (as would probably be the case) there was an index over the TEAMNUM column in existence, the system would automatically insert the value 17 (with a pointer to the Cardinals record in the TEAMS table) into that index in the proper position to maintain the sorted order in the index.

Query-by-Example (QBE)

Introduction

Another relational database language is IBM's Query-by-Example (QBE). This was IBM's first commercially offered relational language and one of the first in the industry. Additionally its highly innovative user interface sets it apart from other relational systems.

The user interface, designed for technical and nontechnical people alike, is a two-dimensional, on-line, video display terminal oriented query facility. In fact, as you begin to look at the QBE format, you will note the difference between its pictorial approach and SQL's linear more textual approach. (In practice, it has been found that some people prefer one and some the other style.) The user begins by specifying which table(s) is needed for a particular query. If he or she is not sure about that, then the system can provide him or her with a list of the available tables and their descriptions. Once a table(s) is chosen, the system displays an outline of that table, showing the table name and the names of it fields. To issue a query, the user gives an *example* of the required information, which amounts to specifying a variable name in the column of the desired information. The user also specifies any limiting factors in that and other columns, either in the same table or in certain circumstances, in a special "condition box." To execute a join operation, the user brings the required tables onto the screen simultaneously, and identifies the join fields by specifying the same variable name under the appropriate join field columns. The query results can either be displayed and scrolled if necessary or can be printed.

The two-dimensional nature of QBE makes it particularly extendable to forms-oriented processing. Other novel features of QBE include the following. Output (display) files can be manipulated by the user on-line, for example records in an output display can be selectively deleted before that output is put to further use; table names and column headings can be multiword in form; column headings in the stored files can be changed as they are moved to output tables; and new headings can be created for calculated fields in the output.

We will describe QBE further in the context of our familiar baseball example. In fact, we will follow the same sequence of queries that we used in discussing SQL. As you read through this section, you might want to refer back to the SQL section to see the comparison of how the same queries are handled in QBE and SQL.

QBE Single File Retrievals

To begin, let's retrieve the entire Teams table. To do this in QBE, you must have a skeleton of the Teams table on the screen. You can accomplish this by simply typing the name of the table into a blank skeleton. If you didn't know the name of the table you were interested in, QBE would present you with a list of the tables that you have access to and you could peruse them as necessary. The skeleton of the Teams table looks like this:

TEAMS	TEAMNUM	TEAMNAME	TEAMCITY	TEAMMGR

Notice that the first "column" heading is not a field but indicates the name of the table, TEAMS.

To display the contents of the entire table you enter "P." under the table name (all of the QBE commands begin with a command letter followed by a period):

TEAMS	TEAMNUM	TEAMNAME	TEAMCITY	TEAMMGR
P.				

The result is shown as:

TEAMS	TEAMNUM	TEAMNAME	TEAMCITY	TEAMMGR
	12	Dodgers	Los Angeles	Wilson
	15	Giants	San Francisco	Johnson
	20	Yankees	New York	Simpson
	24	Tigers	Detroit	Corbin

To find just the record for team number 12, you would limit the search in the table quite literally by specifying that you are interested only in that team number:

TEAMS	TEAMNUM	TEAMNAME	TEAMCITY	TEAMMGR
P.	12			

The result would then be:

TEAMS	TEAMNUM	TEAMNAME	TEAMCITY	TEAMMGR
	12	Dodgers	Los Angeles	Wilson

To project out only the team numbers and names, you specify the P. command under just those fields that you're interested in, instead of under the table name:

TEAMS	TEAMNUM	TEAMNAME	TEAMCITY	TEAMMGR
	P.	P.		

Then you get:

TEAMS	TEAMNUM	TEAMNAME
	12	Dodgers
	15	Giants
	20	Yankees
	24	Tigers

To find the numbers and names of the players who are over 30 years of age you would specify in the skeleton for the Players table:

PLAYERS	PLAYNUM	PLAYNAME	AGE
	P.	P.	>30

This yields:

PLAYERS	PLAYNUM	PLAYNAME
	523	Doe
	8366	Gomez

Switching to the work experience (WORKEXP) table, you can get a list of the coaches who have been college coaches for more than five years by specifying:

WORKEXP	TEAMNUM	COACHNAM	EXPTYPE	EXPYRS
	P.	P.	College Coach	>5

This yields:

WORKEXP	TEAMNUM	COACHNAM
	12	Adams
	15	Taylor

To find the teams that use bats manufactured by the Acme Company, you would specify:

BATS	TEAMNUM	BATNUM	MANUF
	P.		Acme

Since QBE automatically eliminates duplicate tuples in a result, this query yields:

BATS	TEAMNUM
	12
	15

If you did want to get all of the records involving the Acme Company, again with only the team number in the output (although that doesn't make all that much sense in this example) you would have specified:

BATS	TEAMNUM	BATNUM	MANUF
	P.ALL.		Acme

and gotten:

BATS	TEAMNUM
	12
	12
	15

Remember the query in the SQL section of this chapter that involved finding the players between the ages of 25 and 29 and ordering the results by age? Since both of these specifications involve age, and writing them under the

AGE column in the Players skeleton would be too complex for QBE to handle, you must form part of the query in a special "Conditions Box":

PLAYERS	PLAYNUM	PLAYNAME	AGE
P.			AO.__OLD

CONDITIONS
25 <= __OLD <= 29

Notice that the "P." command has returned to a position under the table name because the result must include all of the columns in the table. The "AO." indicates ascending order of the resulting tuples by age. The specification in the CONDITIONS box is connected to the AGE column by the common and arbitrary variable "__OLD". The result is:

PLAYERS	PLAYNUM	PLAYNAME	AGE
	1779	Jones	25
	4280	Cohen	25
	2007	Dobbs	27
	5410	Smith	27
	1131	Johnson	28

To produce a list of the bats manufactured by either the General Company or the United Company you would specify:

BATS	TEAMNUM	BATNUM	MANUF
P.			__M

CONDITIONS
__M = ('General' | 'United')

which results in:

BATS	TEAMNUM	BATNUM	MANUF
	12	B09	General
	20	B03	United
	24	B18	General
	24	B21	United

The QBE form for retrieving all occurrences of a field which have a common portion requires showing the common portion as a constant and the unknown portion as an arbitrary variable. To find the records of all of those players whose last names begin with the letter "S," you would specify:

PLAYERS	PLAYNUM	PLAYNAME	AGE
P.		S_NAME	

The result is:

PLAYERS	PLAYNUM	PLAYNAME	AGE
	358	Stevens	21
	5410	Smith	27
	8093	Smith	21

QBE has commands equivalent to the built-in functions that we discussed in SQL. For example, to find the number of records in the Teams table, you would specify:

TEAMS	TEAMNUM	TEAMNAME	TEAMCITY	TEAMMGR
	P.CNT.ALL.			

The result is presented as:

TEAMS	TEAMNUM CNT
	4

To find the number of different manufacturers who supply bats to the league, you would use the "UNQ" (unique) key word, which is the QBE equivalent of the SQL "DISTINCT" key word:

BATS	TEAMNUM	BATNUM	MANUF
			P.CNT.UNQ.ALL.

which yields:

BATS	MANUF CNT
	4

Bringing back the condition box, you can get a count of the number of players over age 30 by specifying:

PLAYERS	PLAYNUM	PLAYNAME	AGE
			P.CNT.ALL._X

CONDITIONS
_X > 30

Remember that the variable "_X" is arbitrary. The result is:

PLAYERS	AGE CNT
	2

To find the total number of years of experience coach Adams of the Dodgers (team number 12) has, you would use the Work Experience table and specify:

WORKEXP	TEAMNUM	COACHNAM	EXPTYPE	EXPYRS
	12	Adams		P.SUM.ALL.

The result is:

WORKEXP	EXPYRS SUM
	15

The equivalent of the "Group By" specification in SQL is the "G." key word in QBE. To find the total number of years of experience of each coach in the league, you would issue:

WORKEXP	TEAMNUM	COACHNAM	EXPTYPE	EXPYRS
	P.G.	P.G.		P.SUM.ALL.

which would yield:

WORKEXP	TEAMNUM	COACHNAM	EXPYRS SUM
	12	Adams	15
	12	Baker	9
	15	Taylor	15
	24	Victor	12

QBE Multiple File Retrievals (Joins)

To specify a command that requires a join in QBE, you must display all of the involved tables simultaneously. The join fields are indicated by placing the same (arbitrary) variable name under the matching join columns in the different tables. If the output involves fields from more than one table, then an additional skeleton must be created which describes the form of the output. As a first example, as it was in the SQL section, here is the join between the COACHES and TEAMS tables:

COACHES	TEAMNUM	COACHNAM	COACHPH
	_TEAM	_COACH	_PHONE

TEAMS	TEAMNUM	TEAMNAME	TEAMCITY	TEAMMGR
	_TEAM	_TEAMNAM	_CITY	_MGR

TEAMNUM	COACHNAM	COACHPH	TEAMNUM	TEAMNAME	TEAMCITY	TEAMMGR
P._TEAM	_COACH	_PHONE	_TEAM	_TEAMNAM	_CITY	_MGR

Notice the way that the (arbitrary) variable names specified in the COACHES and TEAMS tables guide the system in constructing the output by their placement in the output skeleton. The variable _TEAM sets up the two join fields and carries their result to the output table as well. The result is:

TEAMNUM	COACHNAM	COACHPH	TEAMNUM	TEAMNAME	TEAMCITY	TEAMMGR
12	Adams	555-1524	12	Dodgers	Los Angeles	Wilson
12	Baker	555-3690	12	Dodgers	Los Angeles	Wilson
15	Taylor	555-4820	15	Giants	San Francisco	Johnson
20	Jackson	555-2444	20	Yankees	New York	Simpson
24	Victor	555-9327	24	Tigers	Detroit	Corbin
24	Dooley	555-7321	24	Tigers	Detroit	Corbin

To find the coach and team data for only those coaches on the Dodgers you would specify:

COACHES	TEAMNUM	COACHNAM	COACHPH
	_TEAM	_COACH	_PHONE

TEAMS	TEAMNUM	TEAMNAME	TEAMCITY	TEAMMGR
	_TEAM	_TEAMNAM	_CITY	_MGR

	TEAMNUM	COACHNAM	COACHPH	TEAMNUM	TEAMNAME	TEAMCITY	TEAMMGR
P.	_TEAM	_COACH	_PHONE	_TEAM	_TEAMNAM	_CITY	_MGR

CONDITIONS
_TEAMNAM = Dodgers

The result is:

TEAMNUM	COACHNAM	COACHPH	TEAMNUM	TEAMNAME	TEAMCITY	TEAMMGR
12	Adams	555-1524	12	Dodgers	Los Angeles	Wilson
12	Baker	555-3690	12	Dodgers	Los Angeles	Wilson

Continuing to follow the pattern of queries from the SQL section, the next query is, "Find the names of the coaches on the Dodgers." Remember this requires a join because the coach names appear in a different table from the one with the "Dodgers" reference. You specify:

COACHES	TEAMNUM	COACHNAM	COACHPH
	_TEAM	P.	

TEAMS	TEAMNUM	TEAMNAME	TEAMCITY	TEAMMGR
	_TEAM	Dodgers		

Since the output, the coach name, comes from only one of the involved tables, we dispense with the additional output skeleton which we needed before. Again the __TEAM variable sets up the join fields, and the constant Dodgers satisfies the query limitation. The result is:

COACHES	COACHNAM
	Adams
	Baker

Next "List the league's coaches, their telephone numbers, and the *names* of the teams that they're on" is specified as:

COACHES	TEAMNUM	COACHNAM	COACHPH
	__TEAM	__COACH	__PHONE

TEAMS	TEAMNUM	TEAMNAME	TEAMCITY	TEAMMGR
	__TEAM	__TNAME		

	COACHNAM	COACHPH	TEAMNAME
P.	__COACH	__PHONE	__TNAME

Notice the return to the output skeleton form because fields from both tables are included in the output, which looks like:

COACHNAM	COACHPH	TEAMNAME
Taylor	555-4820	Giants
Adams	555-1524	Dodgers
Baker	555-3690	Dodgers
Victor	555-9327	Tigers
Dooley	555-7321	Tigers
Jackson	555-2444	Yankees

Now for the three table join. The query directs you to list the player numbers and names of the players who have played on the Dodgers, and include the number of years that they played on the Dodgers and the batting average they compiled. The tables needed are PLAYERS, TEAMS, and AF-FILIATION. The player information appears in the PLAYERS table, the "Dodgers" reference is in the TEAMS table, and the connection between them is in the AFFILIATION table:

PLAYERS	PLAYNUM	PLAYNAME	AGE
	_PLAYN	_PNAME	

AFFILIATION	PLAYNUM	TEAMNUM	YEARS	BATAVG
	_PLAYN	_TNUM	_YRS	_BAVG

TEAMS	TEAMNUM	TEAMNAME	TEAMCITY	TEAMMGR
	_TNUM	Dodgers		

	PLAYNUM	PLAYNAME	YEARS	BATAVG
P.	_PLAYN	_PNAME	_YRS	_BAVG

_PLAYN ties the PLAYERS and AFFILIATION tables together; _TNUM ties the AFFILIATION and TEAMS tables together. The result is:

PLAYNUM	PLAYNAME	YEARS	BATAVG
523	Doe	10	0.257
1779	Jones	1	0.223
5410	Smith	6	0.307
8093	Smith	5	0.250

The final join example called for the age of the oldest player on the Dodgers. Here again, the age information is in the PLAYERS table, the "Dodgers" reference is in the TEAMS table, and the connection between them is in the AFFILIATION table:

PLAYERS	PLAYNUM	PLAYNAME	AGE
	_PLAYN		P.MAX.ALL.

AFFILIATION	PLAYNUM	TEAMNUM	YEARS	BATAVG
	_PLAYN	_TNUM		

TEAMS	TEAMNUM	TEAMNAME	TEAMCITY	TEAMMGR
	_TNUM	Dodgers		

Since the result consists of the age only, the result skeleton is not needed. The result is:

PLAYERS	AGE MAX
	32

QBE Update, Delete, and Insert Operations

The QBE data manipulation operations are straightforward and follow the same general syntax that we've been working with. To update the TEAMS table to reflect their moving back to Brooklyn and hiring Malloy as their manager, you specify:

TEAMS	TEAMNUM	TEAMNAME	TEAMCITY	TEAMMGR
		Dodgers	U. Brooklyn	U.Malloy

Obviously, "U." is the update command. If we now specify a P. command in the TEAMS skeleton, we would see that it looks like:

TEAMS	TEAMNUM	TEAMNAME	TEAMCITY	TEAMMGR
	12	Dodgers	Brooklyn	Malloy
	15	Giants	San Francisco	Johnson
	20	Yankees	New York	Simpson
	24	Tigers	Detroit	Corbin

To change the name of the Acme Company to the Royal Company in all of Acme's records in the BATS table, there are two equivalent command forms. One form is:

BATS	TEAMNUM	BATNUM	MANUF
			Acme U. Royal

The other form is:

BATS	TEAMNUM	BATNUM	MANUF
	_T	_B	Acme
U.	_T	_B	Royal

In the second form, the variables _T and _B are used because TEAMNUM and BATNUM together constitute the unique table key. The first line finds the records with Acme in them, and the second line with _T and _B transferring the key field values resets them to Royal. In either case, a P. command would show the BATS table to show:

BATS	TEAMNUM	BATNUM	MANUF
	12	B01	Royal
	12	B09	General
	12	B13	Royal
	15	B01	Royal
	20	B03	United
	20	B04	Modern
	24	B18	General
	24	B21	United

To delete the Dodgers record, you specify:

TEAMS	TEAMNUM	TEAMNAME	TEAMCITY	TEAMMGR
D.		Dodgers		

Of course, D. is the delete command. TEAMS now shows:

TEAMS	TEAMNUM	TEAMNAME	TEAMCITY	TEAMMGR
	15	Giants	San Francisco	Johnson
	20	Yankees	New York	Simpson
	24	Tigers	Detroit	Corbin

Finally, you use the I. command to insert a record for the Cardinals into the original TEAMS table:

TEAMS	TEAMNUM	TEAMNAME	TEAMCITY	TEAMMGR
I.	17	Cardinals	St. Louis	Gregory

Displaying the TEAMS table yields:

TEAMS	TEAMNUM	TEAMNAME	TEAMCITY	TEAMMGR
	12	Dodgers	Brooklyn	Malloy
	15	Giants	San Francisco	Johnson
	20	Yankees	New York	Simpson
	24	Tigers	Detroit	Corbin
	17	Cardinals	St. Louis	Gregory

While the placement at the end of the table reflects the physical position, any future output can be ordered by any field with the proper ascending and descending sequence commands.

References

Cheng, J. M., Loosley, C. R., Shibamiya, A., and Worthington, P. S., "IBM Database 2 Performance: Design, Implementation, and Tuning," *IBM Systems Journal*, vol. 23, no. 2, 1984, pp. 189–210.

Date, C. J., *A Guide to DB2*, Addison-Wesley, Reading, MA, 1984.

Date, C. J., *An Introduction to Database Systems*, 3rd ed., vol. 1, Addison-Wesley, Reading, MA, 1981.

Haderle, D. J., and Jackson, R. D., "IBM Database 2 Overview," *IBM Systems Journal*, vol. 23, no. 2, 1984, pp. 112–125.

IBM Corporation, *IBM DATABASE 2 Data Base Planning and Administration Guide*, IBM Form No. SC26-4077, 1983.

IBM Corporation, *IBM DATABASE 2 Relational Concepts*, IBM Form No. GG24-1581, 1983.

IBM Corporation, *IBM DATABASE 2 SQL Usage Guide*, IBM Form No. GG24-1583, 1983.

IBM Corporation, *Query-by-Example Program Description/Operations Manual*, IBM Form No. SH20-2077, 1980.

IBM Corporation, *Query-by-Example Terminal User's Guide*, IBM Form No. SH20-2078, 1983.

IBM Corporation, *SQL/Data System Planning and Administration—VM/SP*, IBM Form No. SH24-5043, 1983.

IBM Corporation, *SQL/Data System Terminal User's Guide—VM/SP*, IBM Form No. SH24-5045, 1983.

Kim, W., "Relational Database Systems," *ACM Computing Surveys*, Vol. 11, no. 3, September, 1979, pp. 185–212.

King, J. M., *Evaluating Data Base Management Systems*, Van Nostrand Reinhold, New York, 1981.

Kroenke, D., *Database Processing*, 2nd ed., Science Research Associates, Chicago, IL, 1983.

Questions and Exercises

8.1.   What is a relation? What are primary, candidate, and foreign keys?

8.2.   What is the distinction between a relational database and an ordinary set of independent linear files?

8.3.   How would you compare a relational database management system with a set of application programs that process a set of independent linear files?

8.4.   How would you compare a set of application programs which process data within a relational database management system environment with a set of application programs which process a set of independent linear files?

8.5. In your own words, describe the essence of how a relational database management system works.

8.6. Describe the Select operation. What does it accomplish?

8.7. Describe the Project operation. What does it accomplish?

8.8. Refer to the Customer relation in Figure 8.3b, and using the relational command style shown early in the chapter, indicate the results of the following commands:

    a. Select tuples from the Customer relation in which CUSTOMER NUMBER = 1047.

    b. Select tuples from the Customer relation in which SALESPERSON NUMBER = 361.

    c. Project the CUSTOMER NUMBER and CITY over the Customer relation.

    d. Project the CITY over the Customer relation.

    e. Select tuples from the Customer relation in which SALESPERSON NUMBER = 137. Project the CUSTOMER NUMBER and CITY over that result.

8.9. Describe the join operation. What does it accomplish?

8.10. Consider *only the first three rows of both* the Salesperson relation and the Customer relation of Figure 8.3. Using the relational command style shown early in the chapter, indicate the results of the following command sequences.

    a. Join the Salesperson relation and the Customer relation, using the SALESPERSON NUMBER of each as the join field. Select tuples from that result in which SALESPERSON NUMBER = 137. Project the SALESPERSON NUMBER, SALESPERSON NAME, CUSTOMER NUMBER, and CITY over that result.

    b. Join the Salesperson relation and the Customer relation, using the SALESPERSON NUMBER of each as the join field. Select tuples from that result in which CITY = Hartford. Project SALESPERSON NAME over that result.

8.11. Consider the Salesperson relation and the Customer relation of Figure 8.3. Using the relational command style shown early in the chapter, write relational statements to answer the following questions.

    a. Find the Salesperson record for Carlyle.

    b. Find the Customer records for all customers in Boston.

    c.   Produce a list of all of the customers (by customer number) with the city each is in.

    d.   Produce a list of the customers (by customer number and city) which salesperson 186 is responsible for.

    e.   Produce a list of the customers (by customer number and city) that salesperson Adams is responsible for.

    f.   What are the names of the salespersons who have accounts in New York?

8.12.   In your own words, describe the comparison between the ways that data integration (the join concept) are accomplished in the relational vs. the hierarchical and network database management systems.

8.13.   In your own words, describe the comparison between the flexibility in design and modification afforded by the relational vs. the hierarchical and network database management systems.

8.14.   What are the major factors that influence the performance of relational vs. hierarchical and network database management systems.

8.15.   What is referential integrity? Discuss it in terms of relational and hierarchical and network database management systems.

8.16.   Outline the concepts behind the optimizer in the IBM SQL system. Are there other ways you can think of to improve relational database performance?

The following four relations, which constitute an appliance repair company's database, will be used in all of the following questions about both SQL and QBE. The company maintains data on its technicians (employee number, name, title), the types of appliances that it services along with the hourly billing rate to repair each, the specific appliances (by serial number) for which it has sold repair contracts, and which technicians are qualified to service which types of appliances (including the number of years that a technician has been qualified on a particular appliance type).

TECHNUM	TECHNAME	TITLE
062	Regan	Senior
297	Mercer	Trainee
553	Hewitt	Senior
718	Stein	Staff

TECHNICIANS Relation

APPLTYPE	CATEGORY	RATE
Washer	Major	20
Dryer	Major	20
Toaster	Minor	10
Blender	Minor	8
Freezer	Major	25

TYPES Relation

APPLNUM	APPLTYPE	AGE	OWNER
00730	Toaster	5	M. Peters
08331	Freezer	7	R. Carr
16365	Freezer	3	S. Small
22770	Blender	1	C. Ramos
40034	Washer	10	S. Small
47222	Dryer	12	S. Small
49371	Freezer	9	N. Rice
58449	Toaster	7	L. Shaw
60558	Washer	3	M. Peters
72598	Washer	7	S. Bauer

APPLIANCES Relation

TECHNUM	APPLTYPE	YRSQUAL
553	Dryer	15
062	Washer	18
297	Toaster	1
297	Dryer	1
718	Washer	5
553	Freezer	12
062	Blender	14
062	Freezer	10
062	Dryer	12

QUALIFICATION Relation

8.17.   Using the appliance repair company database, translate the following SQL commands to English (or your national language) and indicate their results with the data shown.

a.   SELECT *
      FROM TECHNICIANS
      WHERE TITLE = 'Senior'

b.   SELECT APPLNUM, OWNER, AGE
        FROM APPLIANCES
        WHERE APPLTYPE = 'Freezer'
        ORDER BY AGE

c.   SELECT APPLTYPE, OWNER
        FROM APPLIANCES
        WHERE AGE BETWEEN 5 AND 10

d.   SELECT COUNT(*)
        FROM TECHNICIANS

e.   SELECT AVG(RATE)
        FROM TYPES
        WHERE CATEGORY = 'Major'

f.   SELECT CATEGORY, AVG(RATE)
        FROM TYPES
        GROUP BY CATEGORY

g. SELECT APPLNUM, OWNER
    FROM TYPES, APPLIANCES
    WHERE TYPES.APPLTYPE = APPLIANCES.APPLTYPE
    AND CATEGORY = 'Minor'

h. SELECT APPLTYPE, MAX(YRSQUAL)
    FROM TECHNICIANS, QUALIFICATION
    WHERE TECHNICIANS.TECHNUM = QUALIFICA-
    TION.TECHNUM
    AND TECHNAME = 'Regan'

i. SELECT APPLNUM, OWNER
    FROM TECHNICIANS, QUALIFICATION, APPLIANCES
    WHERE TECHNICIANS.TECHNUM = QUALIFICA-
    TION.TECHNUM
    AND QUALIFICATION.APPLTYPE = APPLIANCES.
    APPLTYPE
    AND TECHNAME = 'Hewitt'

8.18. Formulate SQL commands to answer the following requests for data from the appliance repair company database. (Some of the queries may be somewhat ambiguous in terms of exactly which fields are required in the response—use your judgment.)

a. Which are the major appliances?

b. Who owns freezers?

c. What are the serial numbers and ages of the toasters on service contracts?

d. What is the name of the technician who is most qualified to fix freezers?

e. What is the average age of the washers on service contracts?

f. Whose homes might Stein have to visit?

g. How many different job titles are represented?

h. What is the average age of each owner's major appliances?

i. Whose freezers are over six years old?

j. What are the different billing rates and which appliances do they apply to for owner S. Small?

k. What is the average billing rate for the major appliances that Regan is qualified to fix?

8.19. How do you feel about the difference between the two-dimensional QBE interface in comparison with the SQL interface?

8.20. Using the appliance repair company database, translate the following QBE commands to English (or your national language) and indicate their results with the data shown.

a.

TYPES	APPLTYPE	CATEGORY	RATE
	P.		>18

b.

APPLIANCES	APPLNUM	APPLTYPE	AGE	OWNER
P.		Freezer	<6	

c.

APPLIANCES	APPLNUM	APPLTYPE	AGE	OWNER
	P.	_APPL		P.

CONDITIONS
_APPL = ('Washer' | 'Dryer')

d.

TECHNICIANS	TECHNUM	TECHNAME	TITLE
			P.CNT.ALL._QQ

CONDITIONS
_QQ = 'Senior'

e.

APPLIANCES	APPLNUM	APPLTYPE	AGE	OWNER
			P.AVG.ALL.	P.G.

f.

TECHNICIANS	TECHNUM	TECHNAME	TITLE
	_NUM	P.	

QUALIFICATION	TECHNUM	APPLTYPE	YRSQUAL
	_NUM	Dryer	>10

g.

TYPES	APPLTYPE	CATEGORY	RATE
	_APPL	_CAT	

APPLIANCES	APPLNUM	APPLTYPE	AGE	OWNER
	_NUM	_APPL	>9	_OWN

	TYPE	CATEGORY	OWNER	NUMBER
P.	_APPL	_CAT	_OWN	_NUM

h.

TECHNICIANS	TECHNUM	TECHNAME	TITLE
	_NUM	P.	

QUALIFICATION	TECHNUM	APPLTYPE	YRSQUAL
	_NUM	_APPL	

TYPES	APPLTYPE	CATEGORY	RATE
	_APPL		>19

8.21. Formulate QBE commands to answer the following requests for data from the appliance repair company database. (Some of the queries may be somewhat ambiguous in terms of exactly which fields are required in the response—use your judgment.)

a. Which are the major appliances?

b. Who owns freezers?

c. What are the serial numbers and ages of the toasters on service contracts?

d. What is the name of the technician who is most qualified to fix freezers?

e. What is the average age of the washers on service contracts?

f. Whose homes might Stein have to visit?

g. How many different job titles are represented?

h. What is the average age of each owner's major appliances?

i. Whose freezers are over six years old?

j. What are the different billing rates, and what appliances do they apply to for owner S. Small?

k. What is the average billing rate for the major appliances that Regan is qualified to fix?

9

The Pseudo-Relational Approach to Database

Introduction

Many of those who work in the field of database consider the hierarchical, network, and relational "models" of database system design to be the only ones in existence today. In this book we will speak of a fourth "approach" to database, which has been labeled in the literature as the "pseudo-relational," "flat-file integrated," "semi-relational," or "relational-like" approach.

The pseudo-relational approach is really a hybrid, composed of several of the features of the database approaches that we have already looked at. The fundamental data structure is that of simple linear files, a feature it shares with the relational approach. But as a general rule, pseudo-relational database systems are not geared towards performing execution-time joins the way relational systems are. Like the hierarchical and network approaches, they require that some form of linkage between related records of different files must have been constructed in advance of the on-line query and been stored with the database.

There is no formal definition for the pseudo-relational approach to database management system construction. A description of the pseudo-relational approach is really a statement of the basic concept, such as we have given, coupled with the variations in the implementation of the concept that various database system developers have actually incorporated into their designs—and there are several such variations. We will make more comparisons between the pseudo-relational approach and the other approaches as this chapter progresses. As an aside, one occasionally sees the term "inverted file structure" used to describe a data storage form consisting of simple linear files which have indexes built over all or many of their fields. Whether systems based on such structures qualify as database systems or not depends, fundamentally, as should be evident to you by now, on whether or not they have some kind of join capability.

Pseudo-Relational Database Concepts

Figure 9.1 is a repetition of Figure 8.3, the Salesperson and Customer files (we will drop the term "relation" in this chapter) that we used in the last chapter. Note that on the left we have added relative record numbers which simply indicate which record is the first, the second, the third, and so forth record of the file.

And once again, we are faced with the now familiar dilemma of wanting

	SALESPERSON NUMBER	SALESPERSON NAME	COMMISSION PERCENTAGE	YEAR OF HIRE
1	137	Baker	10	1975
2	186	Adams	15	1971
3	204	Dickens	10	1963
4	361	Carlyle	20	1963

(a)

	CUSTOMER NUMBER	SALESPERSON NUMBER	CITY
1	0121	137	New York
2	0839	186	Hartford
3	0933	137	Boston
4	1047	137	Boston
5	1525	361	Newark
6	1700	361	Washington
7	1826	137	New York
8	2198	204	New York
9	2267	186	New York

(b)

Figure 9.1. (a) Salesperson file and (b) Customer file.

to maintain the nonredundant nature of the data, while at the same time integrating the data between the two files. We've seen how the hierarchical and network approaches structure the data and develop integration with physical pointers within those structures. We've also seen how the relational approach integrates data, stored in relations, on-the-fly, at execution time through the join fields. Let's try something else for the pseudo-relational approach.

Figure 9.2 shows a "link file" that indicates which records of the Salesperson and Customer files are related to each other. Of course, the way that the records are related is in the spirit of the join concept. For example, record 1 of the Salesperson file has a SALESPERSON NUMBER field value of 137. Record 1 of the Customer file also has a SALESPERSON NUMBER value of 137. Thus appropriate to the join concept, a record is created in the link file in Figure 9.2 (the first record in that link file) which indicates that record 1 of the Salesperson file and record 1 of the Customer file are related. In fact, this link file contains a record for every combination of

SALESPERSON RECORD	CUSTOMER RECORD
1	1
1	3
1	4
1	7
2	2
2	9
3	8
4	5
4	6

Figure 9.2.   Link file between the Salesperson and Customer files.

records of the Salesperson and Customer files that have identical SALES-PERSON NUMBER field values. Isn't that a sense of what we have described as a join? Sure it is!

So in the pseudo-relational approach, the data remains in independent simple linear files, but additional link files are created normally well in advance of any queries being posed to the data, which indicate how the records of the different files relate to each other in the sense of the join concept.

The advantages and disadvantages of the pseudo-relational approach parallel those aspects of the other database approaches from which it is derived. The pseudo-relational approach has what many would consider to be the relative simplicity of simple linear files. It also has the performance boost of joins being done in advance with the results of those joins being stored for future use by queries. On the other hand it has the disadvantage of not having the true relational on-the-fly join capability. Also at the time that data values are changed in a file, the system must take the time to update any affected indexes. If those index updates are postponed, then the system must go through extra processing to do an indexed search for records based on those changed values. Another negative is that as with the hierarchical and network approaches, decisions must be made at the time the database is designed as to which files must be prejoined and the results stored in link files.

But as we said at the outset of this chapter, there is no hard and fast definition of the pseudo-relational approach. For example, some such systems may allow link files to be created dynamically at the time that a query which requires one is posed. What the performance implications of such an action would be clearly depends on the intricacies of the particular system involved. Another variation would be a system which permits precreated link files to exist *and* has a true, on-the-fly join capability. Such systems would more likely be classed as relational rather than pseudo-relational, but at this point the labels that we give to the systems become unimportant; there is no harm in the boundaries between the different approaches blurring. Nevertheless, there are enough database systems that are linear file oriented and have only the link file type of join capability that we feel they deserve to be considered in a class by themselves, with the label "pseudo-relational."

IBM System/38 Database

Introduction

The IBM System/38 is a medium-scale computer system which is architecturally novel in a number of ways. One such aspect of the System/38 is of concern to us here: as an integral part of its design philosophy it is designed to create a legitimate user-friendly database environment for all of its users. As we shall demonstrate, the approach to database that the System/38 takes is a form of the pseudo-relational approach.

Moving quickly over already familiar territory, let's begin with some basic concepts. Data in the System/38 is stored in what we have been referring to as simple linear files. In keeping with standard database terminology, these files are called "physical files." Indexes can be built over any field or combination of fields of the physical files. (The indexes are built in the form of structures called "binary trees," about which we shall defer a discussion until the end of this chapter.) New records are added to a file at the end of the file, an arrangement known as "arrival sequence." When a record is added to a file, the system automatically adds corresponding index records to all indexes that reference that file, and naturally places those new index records in their proper sorted positions in the indexes. So while the file itself may not be in order by any set of field values, the indexes effectively provide such orderings.

Records can be retrieved from the files in the physical sequence in which they are stored, directly (the System/38 people say "randomly" here) using an appropriate index built over the file, in field-value sequence via any of the indexes built over the file or directly by relative record number. Notice

	PLAYNUM	PLAYNAME	AGE
1	358	Stevens	21
2	523	Doe	32
3	1131	Johnson	28
4	1779	Jones	25
5	2007	Dobbs	27
6	4280	Cohen	25
7	4319	Ross	24
8	5410	Smith	27
9	6564	Linton	24
10	8093	Smith	21
11	8366	Gomez	33

Figure 9.3. Players physical file.

that retrieving a record by its relative record number implies that on an earlier retrieval of the record we noted and somewhere maintained its relative record number for future use.

Physical and Logical Files

Just as the System/38 term "physical file" follows standard database usage, so does the System/38 term "logical file." A logical file is a programmer's view of the data; a mapping onto one or more of the physical files.

Logical File Based on One Physical File. A logical file based on a single physical file can present the programmer with a view of the data that differs significantly from the original physical file. It may contain only a subset of the fields of the physical file, a subset of the records, or both. It may present the file with the order of the fields rearranged. It may present the records of the file in a different sequence, based on an index existing over the field which is to provide that sequence.

Figure 9.3 shows the original Players file from Figure 8.5. Let's assume that file is the System/38 physical file for the players in the league. Figure 9.4*a* shows a logical file based on that physical file, in which the records appear in ascending order by age and within age by the players' last names. This implies that there is a binary index tree which is based on the concatenation of the Age and Playname fields. Figure 9.4*b* shows a logical file in which the AGE field has been left out and the order of the PLAYNUM and PLAYNAME fields has been reversed. Figure 9.4*c* shows a logical file

PLAYNUM	PLAYNAME	AGE
8093	Smith	21
358	Stevens	21
6564	Linton	24
4319	Ross	24
4280	Cohen	25
1779	Jones	25
2007	Dobbs	27
5410	Smith	27
1131	Johnson	28
523	Doe	32
8366	Gomez	33

(a)

PLAYNAME	PLAYNUM
Stevens	358
Doe	523
Johnson	1131
Jones	1779
Dobbs	2007
Cohen	4280
Ross	4319
Smith	5410
Linton	6564
Smith	8093
Gomez	8366

(b)

AGE	PLAYNUM
21	358
25	1779
27	2007
25	4280
24	4319
27	5410
24	6564
21	8093

(c)

Figure 9.4. Three logical files based on the physical file in Figure 9.3. (a) A Players logical file with the Age field missing and the other fields reordered, and (c) A Players logical file sorted on Age and Playname, (b) A Players logical file consisting of only those records in which the Age value is 27 or less, and with one field left out and other fields reordered.

245

in which only the records for those players 27 years of age or younger appear. In addition, the PLAYNAME field does not appear and the other two fields are in reversed order.

Descriptions of the physical and logical files are specified in the Data Description Specifications (DDS). In addition to the usual specifications of characteristics of the fields, the DDS can contain column headings and other textual information, range bounds for numeric fields, and validity checking specifications. When a programmer wants to write code to access a field or file from his program, he can just reference the DDS entry for the appropriate (logical or physical) file, instead of coding the field or file description from scratch. At program compile time, the system will copy the pertinent information about the fields and files from the DDS into the program and compile it with the rest of the program. Other data in the DDS, such as the range checking and validity checking information, is kept with the files.

Another feature of the System/38 is the Field Reference File (FRF), which is a form of a control block. This facility maintains information about the domain of values of the fields in the System/38 files. An important data feature of the System/38 is that through the FRF, different fields with different names can be controlled by the same domain definition. The domain information is taken from the FRF and used to control the validity of the data entered into the files and displayed from the files. The result is a high level of data integrity.

Logical File Based on More Than One Physical File: The Join. A limited form of a join takes place when a logical file is created over more than one physical file. Normally a join operation combines the fields of the records of two different files into records of a new resultant file based on like values in the join fields. In System/38, a logical file based on two physical files logically interleaves the records of these two physical files with an ordering based on what, in effect, are the values of the join fields. Let's look at an example.

Figure 9.5 shows the Teams and Coaches files from Figure 8.5. The join fields, the fields of those two files that relate the records of one to the other, are, clearly, the two TEAMNUM fields. The TEAMNUM field in the Coaches table indicates which team a particular coach works for. Figure 9.6 shows a System/38 logical file based on the Teams and Coaches physical files. The records are arranged (with the indentation of the Coaches records for emphasis in that figure) so that the records of the coaches for a particular team follow that team's record. All of the teams records can be retrieved in order, all of the coaches records can be retrieved in order, or the teams and coaches records, even though they represent two different record types, can be

	TEAMNUM	TEAMNAME	TEAMCITY	TEAMMGR
1	12	Dodgers	Los Angeles	Wilson
2	15	Giants	San Francisco	Johnson
3	20	Yankees	New York	Simpson
4	24	Tigers	Detroit	Corbin

(a)

	TEAMNUM	COACHNAM	COACHPH
1	12	Adams	555-1524
2	12	Baker	555-3690
3	15	Taylor	555-4820
4	20	Jackson	555-2444
5	24	Victor	555-9327
6	24	Dooley	555-7321

(b)

Figure 9.5. *(a)* Teams and *(b)* Coaches physical file.

retrieved in the order shown in Figure 9.6, with the records for the coaches on a team following that team's record.

Data Retrieval and Manipulation

There are several modes of retrieving and manipulating data in the System/38 environment. One is with what we referred to earlier in this book as embedded commands. In fact, System/38 logical and physical files can be

12		Dodgers		Los Angeles		Wilson
	12		Adams		555-1524	
	12		Baker		555-3690	
15		Giants		San Francisco		Johnson
	15		Taylor		555-4820	
20		Yankees		New York		Simpson
	20		Jackson		555-2444	
24		Tigers		Detroit		Corbin
	24		Dooley		555-7321	
	24		Victor		555-9327	

Figure 9.6. Logical file based on the Teams and Coaches physical files.

	PLAYNUM	PLAYNAME	AGE
1	1779	Jones	25
2	1732	Blake	22
3	4319	Ross	24
4	6564	Linton	24
5	4802	Turner	33
6	4809	Norton	28

Figure 9.7. A portion of the Players file.

accessed and modified with data retrieval, insert, delete, and update operations in the RPG III, COBOL, PL/I, and BASIC languages. Again we note that the descriptions of the files can be taken in directly from the DDS at program compile time.

Another data access tool is called the Data File Utility (DFU), which, as its name implies, is a special purpose program for inquiring into and modifying the data in System/38 files. Applications Made Easy (AME) is an application generator, capable of producing structured RPG III code from application specifications. Thus it too is a means for working with System/38 files.

Finally the System/38 milieu includes a Query Facility, which is designed for real-time ad hoc queries. It is a menu-driven tool, which leads the user through a series of display screen formats. In addition to simply retrieving data, it is capable of higher level functions, such as producing totals of a set of numeric fields. And this Query Facility includes the capability to access records in one file based on data retrieved in another file which is a form of a join.

The Binary Index Tree

Introduction. The indexes in System/38 are constructed in the form of binary trees (or, more precisely full binary trees). A (full) binary tree is a tree in which every node either has two branches emanating downwards from it or is a terminal node with no branches emanating downwards from it. As the System/38 binary index tree is an interesting idea and is quite different from the indexing structures that we described in Chapter 3, we will digress and describe it in the context of an example.

Figure 9.7 is a portion of the Players file of our baseball league. For illustrative purposes it includes some of the records from the Players table

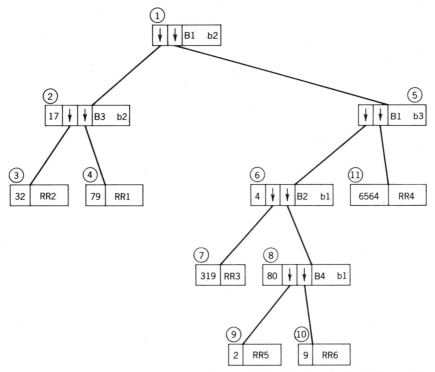

Figure 9.8. Binary index tree over the Playnum field of the Players file in Figure 9.7.

in Figure 8.5 as well as some others. Also notice that it is not in sequence by the PLAYNUM (or any other) field, which makes the point that a file in System/38 need not be in any physical sequence.

Figure 9.8 is a binary index tree that is built over the PLAYNUM field of the Players file in Figure 9.7. First we will describe the strange looking data in that tree, then we will discuss how to conduct a search through it, and finally we will explain how to construct it.

Structure of the Tree. First of all, the circled numbers that label the nodes in Figure 9.8 are simply there for our convenience in this explanation. The downward pointing arrows are pointers to other nodes in the tree. Since the structure is a full binary tree, there must be exactly two such arrows in every nonterminal node. The numbers at the left end of some of the nodes are either partial or full values of the data field(s) (also referred to as the "key field") being indexed, in this case the PLAYNUM field of the Players file. A partial value, which may only appear in a nonterminal node, is known as "common data" and as we will explain, forms part of the value of all of the keys represented below it in the tree. The RR values refer to the relative record numbers of the records of the Players file. For example, notice that node 11 indicates that the record with PLAYNUM value 6564 exists at relative record number position 4 in the Players file. Refer back to Figure 9.7 to confirm this. Remember that this means that Linton's record was the fourth to be added to that file and is physically the fourth record in the linear file. Some of the field values are built up progressively, starting from the root of the index tree downwards. For example, moving from node 1 to node 2 to node 3, you construct field value 1732 and, in the terminal node find that the record with that PLAYNUM value is the second in the Players file. RR pointers to the physical file may only appear in terminal nodes. The capital and small "b"s represent bits within bytes of the field values to be tested in guiding the traversal through the tree (which is our notation and is not found in the System/38 literature). The capital "B" stands for "byte," counting from the left and starting with 1. The small "b" stands for "bit," counting from the left and for simplicity starting with 1 as the leftmost bit of the four bits that represent the digits 0-9 in binary. Of course, these represent only the four righthand bits of the byte, but the four lefthand bits are identical for all of the digits and so do not affect the outcome as we shall see.

Searching the Tree. Remember that the purposes of an index are to allow direct access to a record in a file through the value of one of its fields, and to permit the sequential retrieval of the records of a file according to the values of one of its fields. Let's demonstrate a direct access through the binary index tree with an example. Suppose we are searching for the record in the Players file with PLAYNUM value 4802. We enter the index at the root node (node 1). This node tells us to test byte 1, bit 2. (We will discuss how we established this test in the next section.) On such a bit test, the general rule is that a 0 sends us to the left, while a 1 sends us to the right. Since byte 1 of 4802 is a 4, and bit 2 of a 4 (0100) is a 1, we move down to the right. There we encounter node 5. The test on byte 1 (the same 4), bit 3, yields a 0 and we move down and to the left. This brings us to node 6 where, for the first time, we find common data: a 4. This means that all of the nodes from that point downwards in the tree involve PLAYNUM values with a 4 in their leftmost byte position. Why the leftmost byte position? Because that 4 is the first common data that we've come upon in tracing down from the root. If the common data does not correspond to the data in the same byte position(s) in the field value that we are searching for then we are not permitted to make the specified bit test, we declare a "not found" condition for that field value, and we end the search through the index. But in fact, the first byte of 4802 is a 4, and so we test byte 2 (an 8), bit 1, find a 1, and move down and to the right. At node 8 we find 80 as common data and note that it corresponds to the 80 in the second and third byte positions of the search field value 4802. The test on byte 4 (a 2), bit 1, yields a 0 which sends us down and to the left to terminal node 9. The 2 that we find there completes the value 4802. Since node 9 is a terminal node, if the 2 was not there then we would have registered a not found condition. At node 9 we are told that the record with PLAYNUM value 4802 is at relative record position 5 in the Players file, and so it is. This process may sound rather complex, for what is supposed to be a fast indexed direct search, but remember that at each nonterminal node the test made is a single bit test, and the stored instructions on which bit to test were put there at the time that the binary index tree was created.

To use the binary index tree to retrieve all of the records in sequence we merely traverse it in a top-to-bottom, left-to-right fashion, which happens to be the order in which the nodes were numbered. Convince yourself that such a traversal will find the PLAYNUM field values (and the corresponding records in the Players file through the relative record numbers) in ascending sequence.

Constructing the Tree. Finally there's the question of how the binary index tree was built in the first place. Constructing a System/38 binary index tree is really a matter of performing multiple inserts of new key field values into new nodes. Basically to perform an insert, the system starts at the root and searches through the tree as if assuming that a node with that value is already in the tree and it is trying to retrieve it. When it reaches a terminal node, it replaces that terminal with a nonterminal node which has the old terminal value and the new value to be inserted at the two terminals emanating downwards from it. As we shall see, there's a bit more to it than that.

Let's assume that we are going to start building the Players file, in Figure 9.7, and the binary index tree on the PLAYNUM field from scratch. First the record for player Jones is added to the (new) Players file, and the binary index tree looks like the simple structure in Figure 9.9a. It is a single node which indicates that the record with PLAYNUM value 1779 (the record for Jones) is at relative record position 1 in the Players file. Next the record for Blake is added to the file. Its PLAYNUM value, 1732, is compared to the single index record of Figure 9.9a. Starting from the left, 1732 shares two byte values in common with the value 1779 in the tree. So Figure 9.9b shows that a new root is created with 17 as common data. The first byte from the left that is different between 1732 and 1779 is byte 3. Comparing the bit representations for the 3 of 1732 (0011) and the 7 of 1779 (0111) the

Figure 9.9a. Development of the binary index tree: The first record.

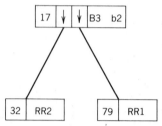

Figure 9.9b. Development of the binary index tree: After adding the second record.

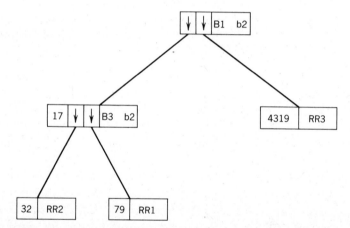

Figure 9.9c. Development of the binary index tree: After adding the third record.

first bit from the left that is different is bit 2. So the value that has the 0 bit is sent off to the left, and the value that has the 1 bit is sent off to the right. That's why the partial key 32, which completes the value 1732 with the relative record 2 indication is down and to the left, and 79 for 1779 is down and to the right, in Figure 9.9*b*. The B3b2 test information and the common data are stored in the nonterminal node that separates them. Next the record for Ross, with PLAYNUM value 4319, is added to the Players file. To find the proper place to add it in the tree in Figure 9.9*b*, we would do what we did, in a somewhat trivial way, in the construction of Figure 9.9*b*. That is, we would trace through the tree as if conducting a search for the value that we have to add, and then actually add it when we reach a terminal node, as we described earlier (the single node in Figure 9.9*a* was a terminal node, in a trivial sense). So we try to do the same thing with the value 4319 and the tree of Figure 9.9*b*. But we can't move down from the root node because the common data specified in it (17) does not correspond to the first two byte positions of the value 4319 that we are trying to add to the tree. When that happens on an insert attempt, the tree is built *upwards* from that point. Thus the tree of Figure 9.9*c* shows a new root that differentiates between the 1 of the common data 17 of the old root, and the 4 of the new value 4319. And so on through the rest of the records to be added.

There's more to it than that, but that's the basic idea. It turns out that the algorithm just described may place some values out of sequential order in the top-to-bottom, left-to-right traversal sense. When this happens, the System/38 invokes other instructions that force a change in the ordering so that the proper sequence is preserved. Also you might wonder how efficient the index search process is if the entire tree is not in main memory during the search, which is a good bet for a large file. The answer lies in a clever method of paging portions of the tree into main memory as needed.

Implementing a Join with the Tree. Figure 9.10 shows a simplified view of the binary index tree that makes the logical file in Figure 9.6 possible. Once again, the circled node labels are just for our own reference purposes. We have left out the bit test information at the nonterminal nodes for simplicity. In the terminal nodes, the "T" and "C" adjuncts to the RR numbers refer to the Teams and Coaches files, respectively. The fields involved in this tree are the TEAMNUM fields of both the Teams and Coaches physical files and the COACHNAM field of the Coaches file. Let's trace through part of this tree. Node 2 shows common data of 1, indicating that all of the nodes below it will eventually lead to teams and coaches records involving teams whose team numbers begin with the value 1. Node 3 shows common data of 2 in the second of the team number byte positions. Combining the information in nodes 2 and 3 we realize that all of the nodes below node 3 have something to do with team 12, the Dodgers. Node 4 is a terminal node and shows a null (the hyphen here) where a whole or partial coach name might be. This means that node 4 refers to the record for team 12 itself, and sure enough that node has a pointer to relative record position 1 of the Teams file (TRR1), which is where the record for team 12 resides. Backing up from terminal node 4 and continuing in the usual top-to-bottom, left-to-right order of node traversal, we find that node 5 leads to nodes 6 and 7, which do indeed represent and contain pointers to the coach records for Adams and Baker, the two Dodger coaches. The next node in order is node 8, which leads to the specific nodes for team number 15 and its coach, and so on.

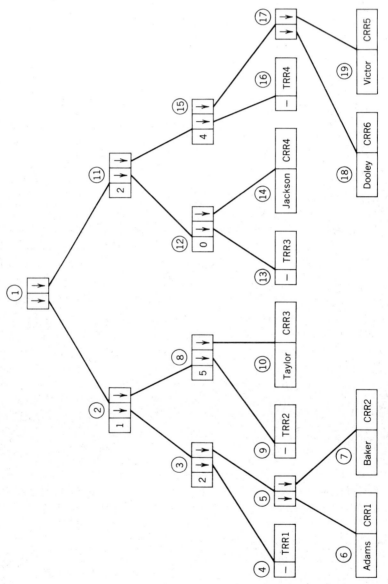

Figure 9.10. Binary index tree for the logical file in Figure 9.6.

Note: At the time of publication IBM announced a new, more general join facility for the System/38, which will be added to the existing facilities.

References

IBM Corporation, *IBM System/38 Control Program Facility Concepts Manual*, IBM Form No. GC21-7729, 1981.

IBM Corporation, *IBM System/38 Control Program Facility Programmer's Guide*, IBM Form No. SC21-7730, 1981.

IBM Corporation, *IBM System/38 Introduction*, IBM Form No. GC21-7728, 1983.

Questions and Exercises

9.1. Explain the statement, "The pseudo-relational approach to database is a hybrid between the relational and the hierarchical and network approaches."

9.2. What is a link file in the pseudo-relational approach? What are the advantages and disadvantages associated with them?

9.3. How does the System/38 distinguish between stored files and programmer views of those files? What is the significance of that distinction?

9.4. Construct a logical view of the System/38 physical file in Figure 9.3 in which the player name comes first, the player age comes second, the player number is left out, the records are in alphabetic order by player name, and only those players older than 27 are included.

9.5. Describe the limited form of the join in System/38 database.

9.6. In your own words, describe how a System/38 binary index tree is constructed.

9.7. What are the advantages of the binary index tree approach?

9.8. Build a System/38 binary index tree with the following key values in the order shown.

    a. 5527
    b. 8326
    c. 5528
    d. 1274
    e. 1500
    f. 5524
    g. 7231

9.9.   How is the System/38 binary index tree used to accomplish a join in System/38 database?

9.10.   Describe how the System/38 would find the record for Dooley in the binary index tree of Figure 9.10.

10
Database Design

The Concept of Database Design

Introduction

Database design refers to the process of organizing the data fields needed by one or more applications into an organized structure. This structure must foster the required relationships among the fields while conforming to the physical constraints of the particular database management system in use. There are two parts to the process that people usually associate with the term "database design." One is "logical database design" which has two components. The first involves organizing the data fields into non-redundant groupings based on the data relationships. The second involves an initial organizing of those logical groupings into structures based on the nature of the DBMS and of the applications that will use the data. There are several techniques for performing logical database design, each with its own emphasis and approach. The second part of database design is "physical database design," which refers to refitting the previously de-scribed derived structures to conform to the performance and operational idiosyncracies of the DBMS, again guided by the application's processing requirements.

But the preparation for database design really begins at a much earlier stage of the data processing life cycle. Or put another way, how did we know what the fields and relationships to be incorporated in the database by the database design process were in the first place? The story begins at a stage called "Information Systems Strategic Planning."

Information Systems Strategic Planning

The history of data processing has been such that applications have usually been developed quite independently of each other. We've already discussed one result of this: large scale redundancy of data in scattered files, instead of data sharing where applicable. There should come a stage in every company's data processing growing process when it recognizes that the helter-skelter mode of application development must yield to a well planned approach. As a first step, the company must make a serious study of its current data processing environment, its future data processing needs, and the ways that its various corporate components interact in terms of passing data back and forth.

One available methodology designed to accomplish those purposes is IBM's Business Systems Planning (BSP) technique. Figure 10.1 shows the flow of steps in a BSP study. The scope of the study might be an entire

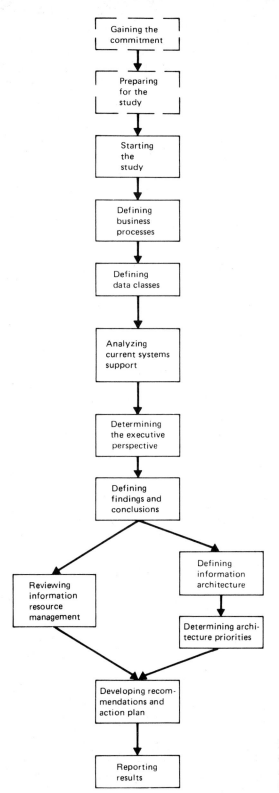

Figure 10.1. Steps in the BSP process. (Reprinted by permission from *Information Systems Planning Guide* (GE20-0527-3) by IBM Corp.)

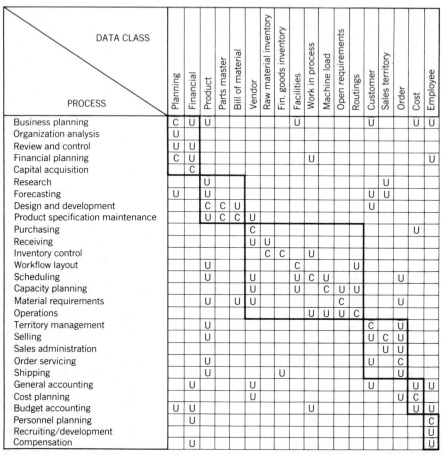

PROCESS \ DATA CLASS	Planning	Financial	Product	Parts master	Bill of material	Vendor	Raw material inventory	Fin. goods inventory	Facilities	Work in process	Machine load	Open requirements	Routings	Customer	Sales territory	Order	Cost	Employee
Business planning	C	U	U						U					U			U	U
Organization analysis	U																	
Review and control	U	U																
Financial planning	C	U							U									U
Capital acquisition		C																
Research			U											U				
Forecasting	U		U											U	U			
Design and development			C	C	U									U				
Product specification maintenance			U	C	C	U												
Purchasing						C											U	
Receiving						U	U											
Inventory control							C	C		U								
Workflow layout			U						C				U					
Scheduling			U				U		U	C	U				U			
Capacity planning			U						U	C	U	U						
Material requirements			U	U	U								C			U		
Operations										U	U	U	C					
Territory management			U											C		U		
Selling			U											U	C	U		
Sales administration														U	U			
Order servicing			U											U		C		
Shipping			U					U								U		
General accounting		U				U								U			U	U
Cost planning		U				U										U	C	
Budget accounting	U	U							U								U	U
Personnel planning		U																C
Recruiting/development																		U
Compensation		U																U

Figure 10.2. Sample data class vs. business process matrix in BSP. (Reprinted by permission from *Information Systems Planning Guide* (GE20-0527-3) by IBM Corp.)

company, a division, or some other well defined operating unit depending on size. The study, which ideally takes about six weeks to complete, should be conducted by a group of 8-12 people representing the major functional areas of the company, as well as key systems analysts and, very importantly, one major corporate executive. In terms of the eventual database design, the key parts of the BSP process are the steps in Figure 10.1 labeled, "Defining business processes," "Defining data classes," and "Defining Information Architecture."

Defining business processes refers to a thorough study of the company which determines its component operations. Defining data classes refers to a study which defines the major types of data (*not* down to the field level) required by the company and thus by the company's business processes. Figure 10.2 shows a sample matrix which relates a company's busi-

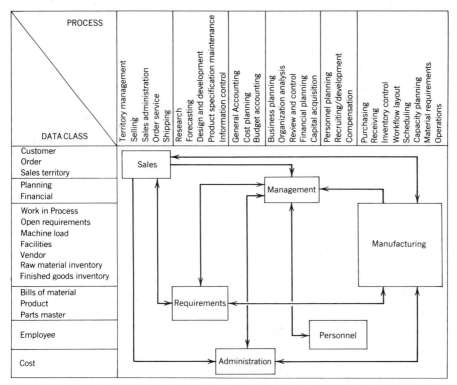

Figure 10.3. Sample BSP information architecture. (Reprinted by permission from *Information Systems Planning Guide* (GE20-0527-3) by IBM Corp.)

ness processes, shown on the left, to its data classes, shown across the top. At the individual intersection points the "C" label indicates the process responsible for "creating" the data in that data class while the "U" label indicates that the process "uses" the data in the data class. The groupings delineated by the dark-edged rectangles are based on processes that are related to each other (e.g., the third group down is composed of manufacturing processes).

From the "U" boxes that fall outside of the dark-edged rectangles in Figure 10.2, it is evident that in a large number of instances, processes belonging to one of the major groupings use data created by processes belonging to another one of the major groupings. For example, the material requirements process of the manufacturing grouping uses product data created by the design and development process of the requirements (research and development) grouping. Such cross involvements of data among the different business process groupings is natural and their discovery is a crucial result of the BSP work. Figure 10.3 (with the business process and data class axes switched) continues the development of the matrix in Figure

10.2 through the "Defining information architecture" stage. At this point we have a good idea of the organization's data classes and business processes, and the data oriented relationships among them.

With this strategic level information architecture defined, we can now turn our attention to individual application development efforts. We will divide the processes into smaller subprocesses and arrange them on a priority basis for computer implementation. The information architecture will serve as a permanent record of how all of the computer applications relate to each other in the strategic plan.

Systems Analysis

Deciding to implement one of the subprocesses that we identified in the BSP study, we move into the application development cycle. The application development cycle begins with the all important systems analysis phase. Systems analysis is the detailed study of how the business process (really what we were calling "subprocess" in the last section) being considered for computer implementation works. Systems analysis is an implementation independent exercise and does not involve the mention of tapes, disks, CPUs, or any other computer components. It is truly foolhardy to proceed with a computer implementation of a process that is not thoroughly understood. Any misconceptions of how the process works are sure to become embedded in the application code. The later on in the application development cycle that these errors are discovered, the more expensive it will be to fix them.

The systems analyst serves as an interface between the people responsible for carrying out the business process (the users) and the people responsible for the computer implementation of it (the programmers). The systems analyst will interview the users and study documentation about the business process, reformulate this information in an appropriate form, and pass it on to the programmers. A systems analysis methodology should support the systems analyst in performing this task. The methodology and its forms for recording the business process information must be detailed enough for the programmers to work with. But at the same time it must be unintimidating enough for the nonanalytically oriented users to be able to read and understand for the purpose of providing feedback on its accuracy. One such methodology is called "Structured Systems Analysis".

Structured systems analysis is a data-directed, engineering oriented approach to systems analysis which was developed in the mid-to-late 1970s. Since the term "structured" has become one of the most overutilized words in data processing, one is immediately drawn to wonder about the use of

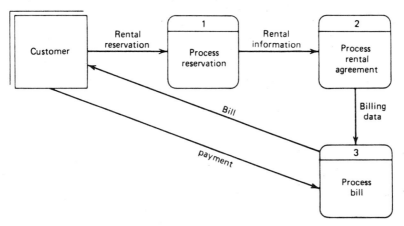

Figure 10.4. Structured systems analysis: data flow diagram for the car rental reservation system.

the term here. In fact this approach, as will be shown, is "structured" in the sense that it is top-down in nature, is designed to be integrated with structured program design techniques, and is a unified approach to solving the systems analysis problem.

In reality, structured systems analysis is the marriage of several techniques, some fairly new and some relatively old. The central vehicle is the Data Flow Diagram (DFD), which is intended to graphically show the movement of data through a system. Other tools used include Data Structure Diagrams, decision trees, decision tables, structured English, tight English, data normalization, and data dictionaries.

A DFD is a two-dimensional structure composed of four basic element types: process boxes (represented by vertically oriented, rounded edge rectangles), data stores (open-ended, horizontally oriented rectangles), external entities (squares), and data flow arrows. Process boxes transform data, data stores hold data, data flow arrows facilitate the movement of data, and external entities are the data interfaces with people or systems outside of the present system. Figure 10.4 is an example of a DFD for a car rental company's reservation and billing system.

Data Flow Diagrams are intended to be nonphysical, showing only the flow of information among processes, stores, and external entities, and not showing disks, tapes, CPUs, or any other potential physical implementation vehicles. They are designed to be understandable not only to programmers, but to users as well, in order to facilitate the user feedback process. To that end, one feature of the DFD concept is that the diagrams are drawn in a top-down fashion. Admittedly the diagram in Figure 10.4 is a high-level

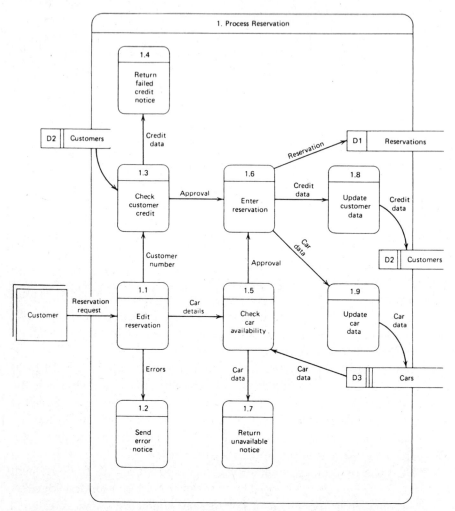

Figure 10.5. Structured systems analysis: detail of the "Process Reservation" box.

view of the system. But it does fulfill two needs. For one thing it outlines the entire system, and for another, it provides an easy to understand entry vehicle for a nonanalytically oriented user.

The diagram in Figure 10.5 is an "explosion" of the "Process Reservation" process box in Figure 10.4. The process boxes in Figure 10.5, when taken together, describe in further detail the function outlined in the process box in Figure 10.4. The intention is that the process boxes be repeatedly exploded down, creating a hierarchy of process box levels, until each lowest level process box represents an amount of function implementable by a module of code (about 50 to 100 lines in a higher level language) in a structured design sense. Thus, all of the DFDs taken together describe the application in a top-down, comprehensive, and yet easy to understand manner.

The DFDs will eventually be used by program designers and programmers for the implementation of the application. Therefore it follows that there must be yet another level of logic detail to describe the details of the functions in the lowest level process boxes. For that need, structured systems analysis turns to several well known, detail level techniques: decision trees, decision tables, structured English, and tight English. One problem that arises from the choice of any one of these techniques is that the more formal tools—decision tables and structured English—can more readily be converted to code by programmers, but are more difficult for uninitiated users to comment on for feedback. Conversely, the less formal tools—decision trees and tight English—make user feedback more of a real possibility, but require more work on the part of the programmers. An attempt by the systems analyst to use two methods for a single lowest level process box to solve that problem, opens the question, unfortunately, of a possible integrity problem.

The data stores are collections of fields of information. Exactly what fields belong in a given store can be discerned from a study of the data flows into and out of the data store. A further question about the fields in a data store is the manner in which they should be passed on to the file or data base designers after the systems analysis phase. The stated philosophy of structured systems analysis is that the fields in a data store should be passed in a form in which they are grouped into simplified sets (which would contain nonredundant data if implemented directly as physical files). It is felt that this is the clearest form for the designers to use in the eventual design phase. The suggested technique for accomplishing this is data normalization. Data normalization has usually been associated with data base design as opposed to with systems analysis (and will be discussed in detail shortly). There are two arguments for data normalization being performed as part of structured systems analysis. For one thing, data normalization requires a thorough understanding of the true semantic meaning of the fields and the relationships of the fields to each other in the application, and it is the systems analyst who has the earliest and deepest understanding of that. In addition, one of the standard techniques for data base design requires data normalization as its first step regardless of the eventual physical structure used. Thus, if it has to be performed unconditionally, it might as well be done at this stage, even if the eventual physical vehicle has not been selected yet.

Since all of the DFDs and associated information must be recorded and maintained, a suggestion is made for a recording method. This method is the use of a data dictionary (discussed in detail in the Chapter 11). The method dictates that the systems analysts be the originators of the items in the dictionary. These would include the process boxes, data flows, data stores, and external entities, as well as field descriptions. The latter would presumably be used and enhanced by the physical design people at a later time.

Another aspect of structured systems analysis is its potential interface to structured system design techniques. As stated earlier, each lowest level process box is intended to become a module of code in a structured design sense. Thus, the program designer is expected to convert the DFD lowest level process boxes (and overall logic) into a top-down modular design. Clearly the program designer's job is not eliminated. Not only does the program designer have to do the stated conversion, but in addition the function in some process boxes may have to be combined into a single program module, or alternately, the function in a single process box may have to be divided among several program modules, all to accommodate the realities of the physical system.

Several items can be noted in terms of the usage of the structured systems analysis techniques relative to standard systems development phases. The most significant of these is that the systems analysts should first develop a DFD of the existing system (if one does not already exist from when that system was created) and then later, as the analysis phase progresses and further management approvals are obtained, should develop a DFD of the proposed system. Another point is that a DFD can be subdivided to reflect that a particular physical implementation may only encompass part of the studied application, for economic or other reasons. A third item is that further information can be put into the DFDs even after the analysis phase is over, in the form of notes in the process boxes which indicate where or how the function was eventually implemented.

The Need for Database Design

A variety of reasons make careful database design essential. These include data redundancy, application performance, data independence, data security, and ease of programming. All are important factors in the data processing environment, and all can be adversely affected by a poor database design.

Intrafile and Multifile Redundancy

Proper database design is essential in avoiding both the intrafile and multifile redundancies that were discussed earlier. Strictly speaking, the amount of apparent redundancy (key and nonkey fields) varies with the type of DBMS for which the files are being designed. In all cases at least in the early stages of design, the goal is to eliminate all redundancy among the nonkey fields. In the later stages of design, as the data takes on the form of structures of the particular DBMS there may or may not be overt redundancy among the key fields. Specifically, the relational approach requires certain fields to appear as attributes of different relations, while in the navigational cases, this field duplication is replaced by pointers.

Performance

Performance, the operational speed of applications and systems, can be affected or influenced by a number of factors in the database environment. Several of these factors are common data processing issues which are beyond the control of database design. The latter items include CPU processing speed, disk data transfer rate, channel speed, the contention of different applications sharing the same hardware system, and of course, the efficiency of the techniques embodied in the DBMS itself.

However, there are many elements of the database environment which affect performance, and which are under the control of the database designer. Many of them are product specific; that is they depend on quirks of the particular DBMS. But others are general enough in nature to deserve mention here and further discussion later. Most of these are directly or indirectly related to the scourge of database performance: the number and nature of accesses to the data on the direct access, secondary storage devices, commonly known as "disk I/Os."

One common example of a performance related choice is which access method to use and exactly how to implement it for the application at hand. The designer may have to decide whether to use a hashed access method or an indexed method, how many fields to index, which data placement or "hashing" method to use (in the hashed case), and so on. There may be a variety of types of pointers to link various records together, each with different performance ramifications for different types of applications. There may be a variety of ways to design the juxtaposition of various record types in a hierarchy or network, and in addition, options for grouping occurrences on the same direct access device. Further comments on specific systems will be made later.

Data Independence

Data independence, the ability to modify data structures without affecting existing programs, is fundamentally a function of the data model used by a particular DBMS. All such systems provide an enhanced degree of data independence when compared to ordinary file processing. Nevertheless, there are database design choices that can be made, particularly when dealing with hierarchical and network DBMSs, which can affect the degree of independence achieved. The intricacy of the matter does not even end there, because beyond the specifics of the data structure and of the database design, the way that a program is written can affect data independence.

Data Security

Database management systems generally have a variety of built-in data security safeguards. These range from passwords associated with a given user, to passwords associated with particular data, to various ways of prohibiting all but certain users to perform certain operations on certain data. Data security becomes an issue in database design when the minimum amount of data that the system is capable of returning from the database on a program call is greater than the amount that the person who executed the program has the right to see. In that case, the structure may have to be designed so that data, which otherwise would have been placed together into a retrievable unit, is split over several units.

Ease of Programming

While the use of database management systems requires programmers to learn new concepts and protocols, the overall effect of the use of DBMSs is to decrease programming complexity and the attendant programming error rates. One reason for this is the standardization that results from using the same protocol for data manipulations in all programs. Another reason involves the integrated nature of the data structures, which allows a programmer to obtain data from physically separate files or distinct record types (depending on the data model used) with one call from the high level programming interface. Without the use of a DBMS, and assuming the avoidance of unacceptable levels of data redundancy, the alternative would be accessing data in one file, using it to access data in another file, and so on through as many files as necessary to satisfy the query. This latter method is clearly much more error prone, not to mention more time consuming to write.

Within the improved level of programming that the use of DBMSs affords, certain decisions in database design can make the programmer's job somewhat harder or easier. Unfortunately the decisions which can simplify programming specifications usually have an adverse affect on data redundancy, system performance, or both. For example, combining fields together within one data structure unit may allow a programmer to simplify the specifications needed to retrieve that data, but will usually result in an increase in data redundancy. Adding additional indexes into the data structure creates more flexibility in on-line retrieval and simplifies program retrieval specifications, at the expense of performance when the data must be updated. A highly volatile file with a large number of indexes connected to it may degrade the performance of the entire system.

Database Design Methodologies

This section will present two of the most common database design techniques. In both cases, we will begin with the data oriented information generated as output from systems analysis, and proceed to relational, pseudo-relational, hierarchical, and network database models. The method of explanation will be by example with appropriate commentary along the way.

The first method, "data normalization and data structuring", is representative of the class of methods which takes as input a list of fields and the associations among those fields. The second method, the, "entity-relationship" method is representative of the class of methods which takes entities and relationships as input.

Data Normalization and Data Structuring

The Example. This first method of database design requires one major step for the relational approach and two major steps for the other three approaches. Fortunately for convenience of explanation, the one major step for the relational approach is, in fact, the first of the two steps for the other three approaches.

Figure 10.6 shows an example set of fields which concern the personnel information system of a nationwide chain of automobile repair shops. It is clear from this list of fields that the goal of the system is to keep track of

MECHANIC NUMBER (MECH NO)
SKILL NUMBER (SKLL NO)
SKILL CATEGORY (SKLL CAT)
MECHANIC NAME (MECH NAME)
MECHANIC AGE (MECH AGE)
SHOP NUMBER (SHOP NO)
SHOP CITY
SHOP SUPERVISOR (SUPV)
MECHANIC'S SKILL PROFICIENCY LEVEL (PROF)

Figure 10.6.   Example Set of Fields.

the company's mechanics, their skills, their locations, and other associated information. The MECHANIC'S SKILL PROFICIENCY LEVEL field is intended to store a particular mechanic's proficiency level in a particular skill. (It is worth taking an aside here to note that this set of fields was chosen for this example to make certain database design points. As we shall see, a much higher percentage of the fields in this collection will participate as key fields than would be the case in most actual situations.) Figure 10.7 shows the associations among our example fields. The single-headed arrows indicate unique identifications. Thus Association number 2 indicates that for a given mechanic number, there is exactly one name associated with it (mechanic numbers are unique), and Association number 10 indicates that for a given shop number there is exactly one city associated with it. If I give you mechanic number 81, you can uniquely give me back John Smith. If I give you shop number 12, you can uniquely give me back Chicago. Note that unless explicitly stated, the inverse cannot be assumed to hold true. Thus there may be several John Smiths in the company, and there may be several shops in Chicago. The double-headed arrows in Figure 10.7 indicate multiple associations: an instance of the item on the left may be associated with several instances of the item on the right. Association number 1 says that a mechanic may have several skills. Association number 8 says that a shop may have several mechanics working in it.

Potential Database Problems.   Before beginning the database design process, it is instructive to revisit the problems that poor database design can cause in the context of this example. Figure 10.8 shows seven sample records of a file made up of all of the fields listed in Figure 10.6. It assumes that no database design effort was made and thus all of the fields were just lumped together in one file. MECHANIC NUMBER and SKILL NUMBER were chosen as a compound (multifield) key, since the two taken together can uniquely identify a record in the file. Note that it follows that since a key value can uniquely identify a record in a file, the key value

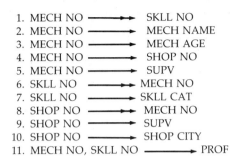

1. MECH NO ⟶ SKLL NO
2. MECH NO ⟶ MECH NAME
3. MECH NO ⟶ MECH AGE
4. MECH NO ⟶ SHOP NO
5. MECH NO ⟶ SUPV
6. SKLL NO ⟶ MECH NO
7. SKLL NO ⟶ SKLL CAT
8. SHOP NO ⟶ MECH NO
9. SHOP NO ⟶ SUPV
10. SHOP NO ⟶ SHOP CITY
11. MECH NO, SKLL NO ⟶ PROF

Figure 10.7. Associations between the fields.

uniquely determines the values of the nonkey fields of that record (conversely the nonkey values are "dependent" on the key value).

It is evident that there is a great deal of redundancy in the file in Figure 10.8. Mechanic number 35 has three skills. To represent this requires three records, since MECHANIC NUMBER and SKILL NUMBER must be taken together to form a legitimate key. In fact, each MECHANIC NUMBER— SKILL NUMBER pair must appear in a separate record in order to be associated with a PROFICIENCY LEVEL number, which is dependent on the combination of who the mechanic is and what skill is under discussion. As a result of that situation, one example of redundancy is that the mechanic's age, name, shop number, shop city, and supervisor must be carried in the file as many times as the number of skills the mechanic has. Another example is the information about who the supervisor is at a particular shop must be carried at least once for each mechanic who works at that shop. These facts bring with them all of the standard problems of redundancy: extra storage space, extra time spent on update, and potential integrity problems.

Another potential problem with the file involves the deletion and addition of data. Suppose Adams and Doe are the only two mechanics in shop number 52. If they quit, and as might reasonably be expected, we delete the records concerning them, then we have also deleted the fact that Brown is the supervisor of shop number 52 from the file. These two fundamentally different pieces of information cannot exist separately in the current design. A similar, but reversed, situation exists in adding data to the file. Ordinarily if we add a new mechanic to the file we would expect to find the shop city and supervisor information from records already in the file which involve that shop. But if the new mechanic is the first one in the shop, then the shop city and supervisor data does not currently exist in the file and must be sought elsewhere. Adding a mechanic who does not yet possess any skills could have serious implications in terms of the key. Thus it is clear

Key {								
MECH NO	SKLL NO	SKLL CAT	MECH NAME	MECH AGE	SHOP NO	SHOP CITY	SUPV	PROF
21	113	Body	Adams	55	52	NYC	Brown	3
35	113	Body	Baker	32	44	LA	Green	5
35	179	Engn	Baker	32	44	LA	Green	1
35	204	Tran	Baker	32	44	LA	Green	6
50	179	Engn	Cody	40	44	LA	Green	2
77	148	Tire	Doe	47	52	NYC	Brown	6
77	361	Engn	Doe	47	52	NYC	Brown	6
. . .								

Figure 10.8. Sample records.

272

272

that simply putting all of the fields into one file leaves a great deal to be desired.

Data Normalization.   Data normalization is a methodology for arranging fields into tables (or files or relations) so that redundancy among the nonkey fields is eliminated. Each of the resultant tables deals with a single area of knowledge, as opposed to the mixture seen in Figure 10.8. The input required by the normalization process is a list of the set of data fields and the associations among them, as for instance in Figures 10.6 and 10.7. Nevertheless it is easier to explain the process in the context of an example which includes sample records, and so we shall continue with the example which we have been using. We stress again that the lists of data fields and associations, which are the required inputs here, are parts of the output of the systems analysis phase.

Unnormalized Data.   Figure 10.9 shows the example data in a somewhat loosely structured arrangement called "unnormalized" form. Unnormalized data may include such situations as a multivalued field. For instance, the second record in Figure 10.9 refers to mechanic number 35, and notes, within that single record, that he has three skills. This form of data has certain distinct disadvantages, including the need for some form of variable length records, and additional complexity for the programmer which would invariably lead to increased programming errors. Furthermore in the case of mechanic number 35's record, we happen to know that skill number 113 matches up with skill category "body," and so on through all of the listed pairs of skill numbers and categories, but such matches may not always exist in all similar situations causing incredible confusion.

First Normal Form.   First normal form data has the property that every data entry, or field value, must be nondecomposable. Figure 10.10 is the first normal form representation of the data in Figure 10.8. Every field entry of every record consists of only one piece of nonsubdividable data. Essentially the unnormalized records with multivalued fields were cloned to produce several records with some data repeated, as necessary. Except for the fact that the data shown in Figure 10.8 is meant to represent only part of a file, while the data in Figure 10.10 is meant to represent an entire file (for illustrative purposes), the two are identical. Clearly the first normal form representation of data is not, in and of itself, helpful as a redundancy controlling arrangement but is merely a jumping off point for further work.

Second Normal Form.   We have already established that the data in Figure 10.10 (like Figure 10.8) is highly redundant. At this point the methodology

MECH NO	SKLL NO	SKLL CAT	MECH NAME	MECH AGE	SHOP NO	SHOP CITY	SUPV	PROF
21	113	Body	Adams	55	52	NYC	Brown	3
35	113 179 204	Body Engn Tran	Baker	32	44	LA	Green	5 1 6
50	179	Engn	Cody	40	44	LA	Green	2
77	148 361	Tire Engn	Doe	47	52	NYC	Brown	6 6

Figure 10.9. Unnormalized data.

MECH NO	SKLL NO	SKLL CAT	MECH NAME	MECH AGE	SHOP NO	SHOP CITY	SUPV	PROF
21	113	Body	Adams	55	52	NYC	Brown	3
35	113	Body	Baker	32	44	LA	Green	5
35	179	Engn	Baker	32	44	LA	Green	1
35	204	Tran	Baker	32	44	LA	Green	6
50	179	Engn	Cody	40	44	LA	Green	2
77	148	Tire	Doe	47	52	NYC	Brown	6
77	361	Engn	Doe	47	52	NYC	Brown	6

Key: { MECH NO, SKLL NO }

Figure 10.10. First normal form.

275

turns to the question of what to look for and change in the data structure to begin to alleviate the redundancy.

The fact that the MECHANIC NUMBER - SKILL NUMBER combination of fields is a valid key for this file has already been established. Again this means, among other things, that every nonkey field in the file is dependent on the key, which can be verified by the single-arrow associations in Figure 10.7. While both parts of the compound key are necessary to define the PROFICIENCY FIELD (association number 11 in Figure 10.7), only one or the other of the two parts of the key are needed to define each of the other nonkey fields. This fact is a clue to the redundancy and its, at least partial, elimination.

Figure 10.11 shows the same data in second normal form. It has been divided into three tables, each of which has the property that its entire key is needed to define each of its nonkey fields. Within a given table, no nonkey field is defined by part of the key alone. Several fields were duplicated in this process. MECHANIC NUMBER, which of course, appeared only once as a field in first normal form, now appears both in the Mechanic Table and in the Proficiency Table. As we shall see, this kind of field duplication is necessary, at this stage (and for the relational case in general) among those fields participating as key fields. In fact, the total number of field value occurrences has decreased from 63 in Figure 10.10 to 55 in Figure 10.11, indicating a net decrease in redundancy. Also notice that individually identifiable areas of knowledge are represented in each of the tables (although not to the final degree, as we shall soon see).

Third Normal Form.   The Skill Table and the Proficiency Table in Figure 10.11 are both completely free of nonkey redundancy at this point. In fact, they are both already in third normal form. But a glance at the Mechanic Table will reveal some residual redundancy. For example, Both records 1 and 4 indicate that shop number 52 is in New York City and is supervised by Brown; likewise for records 2 and 3 and shop number 44. Yet according to the list of relationships, the key of that table, MECHANIC NUMBER, identifies each of its other fields, and since the key consists of only one field, the second normal form rule of nonkey dependence on the entire key is, of course, met.

The problem has to do with the associations between SHOP NUMBER and SHOP CITY, and between SHOP NUMBER and SUPERVISOR (Associations number 9 and number 10 in Figure 10.7). SHOP NUMBER defines SHOP CITY and SUPERVISOR, but is clearly not a valid key of the entire table (it does not define MECHANIC NUMBER, MECHANIC NAME, or MECHANIC AGE). Thus the situation is one of a nonkey field defining

Key

MECH NO	MECH NAME	MECH AGE	SHOP NO	SHOP CITY	SUPV
21	Adams	55	52	NYC	Brown
35	Baker	32	44	LA	Green
50	Cody	40	44	LA	Green
77	Doe	47	52	NYC	Brown

Mechanic table

Key

SKLL NO	SKLL CAT
113	Body
148	Tire
179	Engn
204	Tran
361	Engn

Skill table

Key

MECH NO	SKLL NO	PROF
21	113	3
35	113	5
35	179	1
35	204	6
50	179	2
77	148	6
77	361	6

Proficiency table

Figure 10.11. Second normal form.

other nonkey fields. This kind of incestuous relationship, which is another kind of indication of fundamentally different kinds of information being mixed together in the same table, is what is causing the remaining redundancy.

Figure 10.12 shows the third normal form representation of the data. Notice that a new table, the Shop Table has been created to separate out the shop-related data. Also notice that in splitting off the Shop Table, a copy of the SHOP NUMBER column was left behind in the Mechanic Table.

Key

MECH NO	MECH NAME	MECH AGE	SHOP NO
21	Adams	55	52
35	Baker	32	44
50	Cody	40	44
77	Doe	47	52

Mechanic table

Key

SKLL NO	SKLL CAT
113	Body
148	Tire
179	Engn
204	Tran
361	Engn

Skill table

Key

SHOP NO	SHOP CITY	SUPV
44	LA	Green
52	NYC	Brown

Shop table

Key

MECH NO	SKLL NO	PROF
21	113	3
35	113	5
35	179	1
35	204	6
50	179	2
77	148	6
77	361	6

Proficiency table

Figure 10.12. Third normal form.

This is done because it was the only way to continue to indicate which shop a mechanic was associated with.

So in third normal form we can say that in each table, no situation exists where a nonkey field defines another nonkey field. There is a fairly common exception to this when there are two fields that *could* be the key, such as an employee identification number and a social security number. The one of the two that is not chosen as the key would seem to be a nonkey field which then defines other nonkey fields, but in this specific case it is not a violation of the stated rule. The third normal form data in Figure 10.12 contains no redundancy among the nonkey fields. This is the goal that we sought.

Other Normal Forms. As further research continues to be done in this field, new problems and solutions arise. Two exceptions have been identified which involve third normal form data, which still contain redundancy. Both involve combinations of multiple associations. They have been named fourth and fifth normal forms, are encountered infrequently in practice, and are beyond the scope of this book.

The Value of Normalized Tables. Two major statements can be made about normalized data. One is that this form of data, free of redundancy among the nonkey fields, is an intermediate plateau in the design of data structures for hierarchical and network databases.

The other point is that normalized data, subject to possible structural modifications for performance reasons, *is* the final design for relational databases. In fact, the normalization process assures that join fields will appear in all of the tables that they should appear in based on the given relationships among the fields. That is a very strong statement and a fact which is central to the use of normalization for the design of all of the types of databases.

The same remarks about normalization producing the database design, subject to performance modifications, applies to pseudo-relational databases, subject to the addition of tables or indexes, which prejoin the normalized tables based on the data relationships and application needs. In fact, the same basic remark also applies to ordinary, nondatabase, flat files, for which normalization is also an ideal design technique.

Data Structuring—Hierarchical Databases. Generally in converting from a set of normalized tables to a hierarchical data structure, the normalized tables are transformed into nodes in the hierarchy. Occurrences

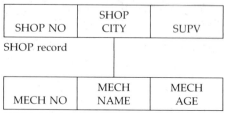

SHOP NO	SHOP CITY	SUPV

SHOP record

MECH NO	MECH NAME	MECH AGE

MECHANIC record

Figure 10.13. Hierarchy representing the one-to many relationship.

of the same and different record types are connected by a variety of types of pointers. In effect, certain of the normalized tables are chosen to have their records prejoined to each other, to physically realize a selected set of relationships. The primary advantage of this technique is superior performance during execution of accesses based on those relationships.

The procedure for designing a hierarchical database, such as for a DL/I system, begins with a set of normalized tables. We will continue following the example we have been using and resume with the normalized tables in Figure 10.12.

The Structuring Process. The process begins by noting the multiple associations in Figure 10.7, the original list of associations among the fields. A multiple association whose inverse multiple association does not appear on the list is recorded as a one-to-many relationship. There is one such relationship in Figure 10.7

$$\text{SHOP NO} \longrightarrow \gg \text{MECH NO}$$

which is association number 8. A multiple association whose inverse does appear on the list is recorded as a many-to-many relationship. There is one such relationship in Figure 10.7

$$\text{MECH NO} \ll \longrightarrow \gg \text{SKLL NO}$$

which is formed by the combination of associations number 1 and number 6.

Next form hierarchies from the one-to-many relationships. Since every branch of a hierarchical data structure represents a one-to-many relationship, this step is quite straightforward. Figure 10.13 shows a hierarchy built out of the one one-to-many relationship in the example. The MECHANIC

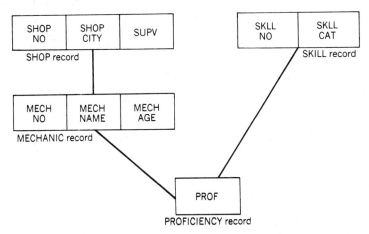

Figure 10.14. Two hierarchies connected to represent the many-to-many relationship.

and SHOP nodes in the hierarchy are directly derived from the normalized Mechanic and Shop tables of Figure 10.12. Note that the SHOP NO field in the Mechanic table in Figure 10.12, does not appear in the MECHANIC record in Figure 10.13. In the normalized tables, the only way to indicate which shop a mechanic works at is to include SHOP NO as a field in the Mechanic table. In a sense, the fact that SHOP NO also appears as a field in the Shop table seems to be a form of redundancy involving a field which serves, as least in one table, as the key. But when these tables are converted into records in a hierarchy, which represents the one-to-many relationship between shops and mechanics, the SHOP NO field is not included in the Mechanic record. The point is that the knowledge of which shop a mechanic works at is now stored by means of the pointers which connect a particular shop to all of the mechanics who work there.

A many-to-many relationship cannot be built directly in a hierarchical data structure. It must be simulated by two one-to-many relationships, each of whose target, or "many" side record type is the same specially created new record. When the data is eventually loaded using this structure, there will be one occurrence of this new special record *for every occurrence of the relationship* (for every connection between two entities in the relationship). Figure 10.14 shows the hierarchy of Figure 10.13 on the left, with a new (single record type) hierarchy on the right, consisting of just the SKILL record type. Mechanic and skill, which have a many-to-many relationship to each other, are both in a one-to-many relationship with a specially created record type labeled PROFICIENCY. The skill node, forming the new hierarchy on the righthand side, is derived from the Skill table in Figure 10.12. The proficiency node is derived from the Proficiency table in Figure

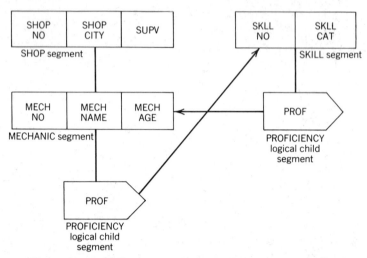

Figure 10.15. DL/I representation including logical relationship.

10.12. Remember that the many-to-many relationship being implemented links MECHANIC occurrences to SKILL occurrences. The Proficiency table in Figure 10.12 not only indicates these linkages, but gives additional information, (the proficiency of a particular mechanic in a particular skill) about them.

DL/I. Figure 10.15 shows substantially the same hierarchical structure as shown in Figure 10.14, except that it has been modified to conform to DL/I conventions. The term "record" is replaced by "segment." The special record type serving as the connector for the many-to-many relationship is called a "logical child" segment. The fact that it appears in both hierarchies (with the proficiency data duplicated in both places in one variation) indicates that the many-to-many relationship can in fact be exercised in both directions. That is, for a given skill, we can find all of the mechanics who have that skill, and for a given mechanic, we can find all of the skills which he has. If the logical child appeared in only one of the hierarchies, then the relationship could only be traversed from that side.

Access and Performance Modifications. Substantial work remains after normalization and structuring. The tentative hierarchical structure has to be adjusted for access, performance, and occasionally, security reasons. This process is what we referred to earlier as physical design.

In terms of access, the designer must make an accounting of which fields of which segments must be directly accessible. This will be based on the systems analysis results for the set of applications slated to use the database. Ordinarily, only the root segments can be directly accessed and only by their key fields at that (and even the provision of that capability is a decision that has to be made). But suppose that an application requires direct access to a field in a nonroot segment. For instance, say that in the current example there is a need to find mechanics directly by mechanic number. Or, suppose that an application requires direct access to a nonkey field in a root segment, for example a need to find shops directly by city. Then either secondary indexes must be employed or the structure must be rearranged so certain non-root segments become roots of new hierarchies, with logical relationships employed to connect the new and the old hierarchies together to maintain the appropriate relationships.

Another example of an application dependent decision is the choice of access methods. Access to the root segments can be either sequential, both direct (specifically indexed) and sequential, or direct via hashing methods. Of course, such a decision is based on the needs of the applications which will use the data.

A wide variety of factors must be taken into account in DL/I in terms of performance, many of which are interrelated: a change in one may require a balancing or compensating change in another. For example, long twin chains (e.g., a large number of mechanics working in one shop) can have a deleterious effect on performance because the system does not permit direct access into the middle of such a chain when access is being made from the superior segment. Starting from the beginning of the chain, access can only be made by sequentially traversing the pointer-connected segment occurrences. Depending on the length of the chain and the number of segment occurrences that can be brought into main memory from disk at one time, traversing such a chain can mean an unacceptable number of time consuming disk accesses. Among the solutions to this problem are inserting a new dummy level segment type above the one with the long twin chains, and obviously increasing the number of occurrences which can be read into main memory at one time.

Another example of a performance consideration which should affect the design concerns the number of occurrences of a hierarchy's root segment. Again using the structure in Figure 10.15, assume that there is a fairly small number of shops but that there are a substantial number of mechanics in each shop. Also assume that most program references will be to MECHANIC and will presume the knowledge of the mechanic's name or number and shop location. Under these circumstances it makes little sense to have a SHOP segment root. The capability provided by the IMS access methods of being able to access a root segment directly, and particularly the speed of such access using the hashed organization facility, is extremely powerful and is wasted on a root which has few occurrences. In the case described, the MECHANIC segment should be made the root, with the SHOP NUMBER field appended to the MECHANIC NUMBER field to form a two-field key. This would create some redundancy in the SHOP NUMBER field, but that kind of key field redundancy has to be considered acceptable under the circumstances. The SHOP CITY and SU-PERVISOR information can be held, still nonredundantly, in a separate small file.

Other performance considerations, which become more or less important depending on the particular case, include the number of levels (depth) of the hierarchy, the distance from the root of particular segments, relative segment sizes, the use of variable length segments, and so on.

Data Structuring—Network Databases. The basic principles of database design, using the normalization and structuring approach, are the same in the design of CODASYL network databases as they are in the design of DL/I hierarchies. The set of normalized relations together with a list of the one-to-many and the many-to-many relationships among the entities is the starting point.

Figure 10.16 shows a network constructed from the third normal form relations of Figure 10.12 and the one-to-many relationship

(SHOP NO ———>> MECH NO)

and the many-to-many relationship

(MECH NO <<———>> SKLL NO)

of Figure 10.7. Notice the specification of the three "sets" involved. Also notice the "link" record connecting the MECHANIC and SKILL records which realizes the many-to-many relationship. Just as in the construction of the DL/I database in Figure 10.15, the one-to-many relationship was drawn first followed by the many-to-many relationship. In the network case when the time came to draw the many-to-many relationship, the SKILL record was added to the network structure that had already been started with the one-to-many relationship between the SHOP and the MECHANIC records. That is as opposed, technically, to the DL/I case in which a second hierarchy had to be created when the SKILL record (or segment) had to be added to the picture.

As for further modifications based on performance issues, the same re-marks, in principle, which applied to DL/I, apply here. Factors such as chain lengths, access method types, pointer options, network complexity, and so on must be considered in the atmosphere of the particular application

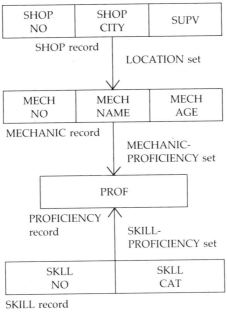

Figure 10.16. CODASYL network representation.

requirements and the specific DBMS being used. Modifications in the network must then be made based on these factors.

Data Structuring—Pseudo-Relational Databases. Again in the pseudo-relational case, the normalized relations and the one-to-many and many-to-many relationships comprise the jumping off point to structuring. Structuring consists of basically three steps.

First a decision has to be made concerning the viability of creating files in the exact form of the normalized relations (since the fundamental data structure in such systems is simple linear files). There is no question that keeping the files in the same form as the normalized relations is the optimum in terms of minimizing data redundancy. However, in specific instances, the normalization process may produce a large number of relations each containing a relatively small number of fields. This situation could have an important negative impact on performance and/or on application programming complexity. In this case it may be necessary to tolerate a certain amount of redundancy in combining the fields from some of the normalized relations to create larger files.

Second data structures logically linking (actually "joining") various files

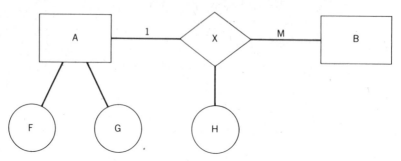

Figure 10.17.   Entity-relationship diagram.

to each other must be designed. Such structures may take the form of matched linear lists or binary index trees based on concatenated file keys as in IBM's System/38.

Third the designer must study the data requirements of the set of applications and determine which fields of each particular file must be accessible on a direct basis. Such systems have the ability to have some kind of an index built for each field that has such a requirement.

The Entity-Relationship Model

Introduction.   Another major method of database design involves the entity-relationship model. Database design using the entity-relationship model begins with a list of the entity types involved and the relationships among them. The philosophy of assuming that the designer knows what the entity types are at the outset is significantly different from the philosophy behind the normalization based approach. Both methods assume that a thorough systems analysis has been done. However the entity-relationship approach asserts that one of the results of systems analysis is a clear understanding of what the entities involved are. The normalization based approach takes the view that systems analysis produces a list of the applications' data fields and the relationships among them and that it is then the responsibility of the normalization process to separate the fields which identify entities from those which merely further describe entities, as we have seen.

The entity-relationship approach uses "entity-relationship" diagrams, a hypothetical example of which is shown in Figure 10.17. The rectangular boxes represent entity types, the diamond shaped box represents a relationship between entities, and the circular figures represent attributes. Thus Figure 10.17 shows two entities, A and B, which have a one-to-many relationship X to each other (note the "1" and "M" on either side of X). Entity

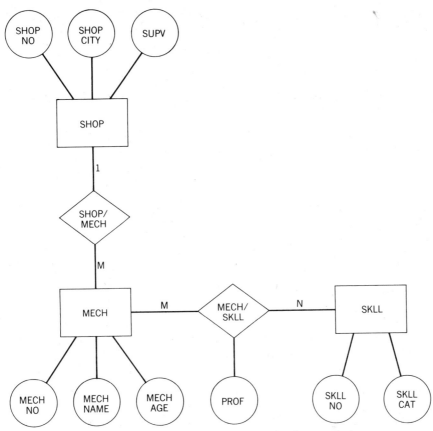

Figure 10.18. Entity-relationship diagram for the sample data.

A has two attributes (fields describing it) F and G. The relationship X has further descriptive information about it, H. H represents information about the relationship X, that is about pairs of As and Bs, which does not apply to either an A occurrence by itself or a B occurrence by itself.

Figure 10.18 is an entity-relationship diagram for the fields and relationships shown in Figures 10.6 and 10.7 (the same example used in the normalization-structuring discussion). Shop, mechanic, and skill have been recognized as the three entities in the application. The one-to-many relationship between SHOP and MECHANIC and the many-to-many relationship between MECHANIC and SKILL are both clearly displayed. Notice the fields (including the key fields) which describe the entities and the PROFICIENCY data which further describes the relationship between ME-CHANICS and SKILLS.

Other embellishments can be added to entity-relationship diagrams. One such device is a notation to show that occurrences of a particular entity cannot exist with the presence of an occurrence of another entity. Another is an indication that an entity does not have a unique key associated with it and must depend on another entity for proper identification.

From Entity-Relationship Diagrams to CODASYL Network Structures. Finally the entity-relationship diagram must be converted to a form that corresponds to the data structure of the particular DBMS in use. To convert from an entity-relationship diagram to a CODASYL network representation is straightforward: the entity-relationship diagram is, in fact, a network itself. Compare the entity-relationship diagram of Figure 10.18 with the CODASYL network of Figure 10.16. The two figures are virtually identical, with the recognition that the connector in the middle of the many-to-many relationship must be converted into a record type and serve as the target of the two one-to-many relationships which replace the many-to-many relationship.

From Entity-Relationship Diagrams to Hierarchical Structures. Converting from an entity-relationship diagram to a set of DL/I hierarchies requires a bit more effort, but is still basically direct. The one-to-many relationships shown in the entity-relationship diagram simply become parent-child segment combinations in the DL/I hierarchies. The many-to-many relationships form the basis for DL/I logical relationships. The diamond shaped box in between the two entities in the many-to-many relationship becomes the logical child in the DL/I logical relationship, and any fields attached to the diamond shaped box become intersection data. Thus the entity-relationship diagram of Figure 10.18 can be converted to the DL/I hierarchies of Figure 10.15.

From Entity-Relationship Diagrams to Relational and Pseudo-Relational Structures. To convert from an entity-relationship diagram to a set of relational structures or ordinary flat files for that matter is, in a manner of speaking, a reversal of the design effort using the normalization based approach. The set of attributes of each entity in the entity-relationship diagram becomes a relation or file, with the unique identifying attribute becoming the key. But, in addition, the identifying attribute of the entity on the "one side" of the one-to-many relationship must be duplicated and made one of the attributes of the relation based on the entity on the "many side" of that relationship. Once the network-like diagram is dismantled, that is the only way of keeping track of which occurrence of the entity on the "one"

	Normalization Approach	Entity-Relationship Approach
Relational	Normalization	Entity-relationship diagram "dismantled" into a set of relations
Pseudo-Relational	Normalization plus join tables or indices	Entity-relationship diagram "dismantled" into a set of relations plus join tables or indices
Hierarchical	Normalization followed by hierarchical structuring	Entity-relationship diagram converted to a hierarchical structure
Network	Normalization followed by network structuring	Entity-relationship diagram converted to a network structure

Figure 10.19. Database design summary chart (all results are subject to modifications for performance reasons).

side is related to an occurrence on the "many" side. If there is a multilevel hierarchy of entities, then such duplication must be propagated throughout the hierarchy when converting it to relations or files. In addition, relations or files must be created from the many-to-many relationships found in the entity-relationship diagram. The key of such a relation will consist of the identifying or key fields of the two entities involved, and the nonkey fields will be the relationship modifiers (the fields attached to the diamond shaped box).

Consider a conversion of the entity-relationship diagram in Figure 10.18 back to the third normal form relations in Figure 10.12. Notice that the shop, mechanic, and skill entities each form the basis for a relation. The Mechanic relation must contain a copy of the key (SHOP NO) of the Shop relation because it was the target in the one-to-many relationship. The Proficiency relation in Figure 10.12 is derived from the many-to-many relationship between MECHANIC and SKILL in Figure 10.18. Note that the key, MECH NO - SKLL NO, is formed from the identifying fields of the mechanic and skill entities, and the nonkey field, PROFICIENCY, was formerly the field connected to the diamond shaped relationship connector.

Figure 10.19 is a summary chart of the four DBMS approaches and the two discussed database design techniques. It is interesting to note that in practice the data normalization and entity-relationship based approaches to database design are sometimes used in tandem for the construction of a single database. For example, the designer might make initial assumptions about entities, attributes, and relationships in the style of the entity-relationship approach, and then test those assumptions using data normalization.

Other Tools for Database Design

There are several kinds of software tools which can aid in the database design process.

Automated Database Design Aids

Within the last few years, several automated database design software products have been introduced. Typically, they require a list of the fields that will comprise the database and the relationships among those fields. In general they are capable of performing logical database design, and, in some cases with partial human intervention, physical database design for specific DBMSs. As part of their operation they can perform editing on the input data and in so doing find errors and inconsistencies.

Database design programs have met with mixed success in the field. The biggest complaint from their users is that specifying the fields and relationships in the depth and precision required (of any computer program) is too time consuming. This, however, is an unfortunate attitude, since the set of fields and relationships *must* be specified precisely for database design, whether or not an automated tool is to be used. The result of doing otherwise is inevitably a poor database design.

Performance Prediction and Monitoring Aids

Once the logical and physical database designs are complete, there are various methodologies available to predict the eventual performance of the system. In order to be accurate enough to be of any real use, these methodologies must consider a substantial amount of information beyond the structure of the database. For example, they must also consider the relative frequency of occurrence of the different record types, the application program calling patterns, and the resource competition from other applications using the same or different databases. Some of the methodologies have been partially automated as simulation routines.

Conclusion

Once the database design process is completed, the focus of the application development process turns to the programmers. Presumably, program design was taking place simultaneously with database design. Thus the programmers can be presented at once with their coding assignments and with the necessary data structures to use.

Beyond coding are the remaining steps in the sequence. These include various levels of program testing, installation, and ongoing maintenance. All of the steps from programming through maintenance will be greatly benefited by the careful and continuous flowing work that was done from the earliest stages of the application development process through database design.

References

Chen, P. P., "Applications of the Entity-Relationship Model", *Proceedings of the NYU Symposium on Database Design,* May 18–19, 1978, pp. 25–33.

Chen, P. P., and Yao, S. B., "Design and Performance Tools for Data Base Systems," *Proceedings of the Third International Conference on Very Large Data Bases,* October 6–8, 1977, pp. 3–15.

Curtice, R. M., "Data Base Design Using a CODASYL System," *Proceedings of the ACM Annual Conference,* November, 1974, pp. 473–480.

Curtice, R. M., and Jones, P. E., *Logical Data Base Design,* Van Nostrand Reinhold, New York, 1982.

Date, C. J., *An Introduction to Database Systems,* 3rd ed., vol. 1, Addison-Wesley, Reading, MA, 1981.

DeMarco, T., *Structured Analysis and System Specification,* Yourdon, New York, 1978.

Gane, G., and Sarson, T., *Structured Systems Analysis: Tools and Techniques,* Prentice-Hall, Englewood Cliffs, NJ, 1979.

Gerritsen, R., "A Preliminary System for the Design of DBTG Data Structures," *Communications of the ACM,* vol. 18, no. 10, October, 1975, pp. 551–557

Gillenson, M. L., and Goldberg, R., *Strategic Planning, Systems Analysis, and Database Design,* Wiley, New York, 1984.

Hawryszkiewycz, I. T., *Database Analysis and Design,* Science Research Associates, Chicago, 1984.

Hubbard, G. U., *Computer-Assisted Data Base Design,* Van Nostrand Reinhold, 1981.

IBM Corporation, "Business Systems Planning—Information Systems Planning Guide", 3rd ed., IBM Form No. GE20-0527-3, 1981.

Inmon, W. H., *Effective Data Base Design,* Prentice-Hall, Englewood Cliffs, NJ, 1981.

Navathe, S. B., and Schkolnick, M., "View Representation in Logical Database Design," *Proceedings of the SIGMOD International Conference on Management of Data,* May 31, June 1–2, 1978, pp. 144–156.

Ng, P. A., "Further Analysis of the Entity-Relationship Approach to Database Design," *IEEE Transactions on Software Engineering*, vol. SE-7, no. 1, January, 1981, pp. 85–99.

Novak, D. O., and Fry, J. P., "The State of the Art of Logical Database Design," *Proceedings of the Fifth Texas Conference on Computing Systems*, October 18–19, 1976, pp. 30–38.

Perkinson, R. C., *Data Analysis: The Key to Data Base Design*, QED Information Sciences, Wellesley, MA, 1984.

Perron, R., *Design Guide for CODASYL Data Base Management Systems*, QED Information Sciences, Wellesley, MA, 1981.

Teorey, T. J., and Fry, J. P., "The Logical Record Access Approach to Database Design," *Computing Surveys*, vol. 12, no. 2, June, 1980, pp. 179–211.

Teorey, T. J., and Fry, J. P., *Design of Database Structures*, Prentice-Hall, Englewood Cliffs, NJ, 1982.

Vetter, M., and Maddison, R. N., *Database Design Methodology*, Prentice/Hall International, Englewood Cliffs, NJ, 1981.

Weinberg, V., *Structured Analysis*, Yourdon Press, New York, 1979.

Questions and Exercises

10.1.   What is database design?

10.2.   Why should we be concerned about information systems strategic planning and systems analysis in conjunction with database design?

10.3.   What is information systems strategic planning? What are its goals?

10.4.   Explain how analyzing business processes and data classes can help to accomplish the goals of information systems strategic planning.

10.5.   What is systems analysis? Where does it fit into the application development cycle?

10.6.   Describe the structured systems analysis approach. Do you think that it would work well in a practical application situation?

10.7.   How do you feel about the structured systems analysis concepts of keeping systems analysis diagrams free of physical computer component references and in a form that nontechnical users can understand?

10.8.   Describe the flow of how data is considered in information systems strategic planning, in systems analysis, and in database design.

10.9.   Discuss the issues that make a careful job of database design imperative.

10.10.   In your own words, describe the data normalization process. What does it accomplish?

10.11.   Discuss the data normalization process in terms of relational database. How does the end product of data normalization relate to a useable relational database design? What about the placement of join fields?

10.12.   Describe the process for converting from normalized tables to hierarchical and network database designs.

10.13.   What is the difference between logical and physical database design? Explain.

10.14.   Describe the entity-relationship approach to database design.

10.15.   Compare and contrast the data normalization based approach to database design with the entity-relationship based approach. What are the comparative advantages and disadvantages of the two?

10.16.   Wing-N-Prayer Airlines is developing a historical aircraft maintenance system to help it satisfy government safety regulations. In addition to producing information about individual airplanes, the system will also be expected to provide fast response to queries about individual mechanics and maintenance locations. Design a

    a.   Relational database

    b.   Hierarchical database

    c.   Network database

    d.   Pseudo-relational database

for this application. The fields and some dependencies and restrictions follow. Note that some of the fields may indicate information that can be represented in ways other than as fields. Also state any additional assumptions that you make about the data in places where you feel the problem description is ambiguous.

Fields

    a.   Aircraft serial number

    b.   Aircraft type

    c.   Aircraft passenger capacity

    d.   Maintenance location

    e.   Location manager

    f.   Location building number

    g.   Maintenance procedure

    h.   Procedure length (time)

    i.   Procedure frequency

    j.   Date procedure performed on a particular aircraft

    k.   Date aircraft next scheduled for procedure

l.   Location capable of performing a procedure

m.   Mechanic name

n.   Mechanic qualified to perform a procedure

o.   Mechanic education

p.   Tool (identification number) signed out to a mechanic

Dependencies and Restrictions

a.   A given location may perform several procedures

b.   A given procedure may only be performed at one location (for all aircraft)

c.   A location may have several buildings

d.   The database must maintain historical records on all maintenance procedure performances for the entire lives of all aircraft

e.   A mechanic may be qualified to perform several procedures, but may obviously only perform those which are feasible at the location he or she is currently working at

f.   A mechanic may have several units of education and several tools signed out to him

10.17.   The Federal Bureaucracy Administration (FBA) has decided to implement a new information system designed to maintain data about states, cities, and certain of their elected officials. Design a

a.   Relational database

b.   Hierarchical database

c.   Network database

d.   Pseudo-relational database

for this application. The fields and some dependencies and restrictions follow. Note that some of the fields may indicate information that can be represented in ways other than as fields. Also state any additional assumptions that you make about the data in places where you feel the problem description is ambiguous.

Fields

a.   City

b.   City council member name

c.   City council member occupation

d.   City population

e. Mayor name

f. Mayor spouse

g. Mayor social security number

h. Senate committee

i. Senate committee location

j. Senate committee staff member

k. Senate committee year formed

l. Senator name

m. Senator social security number

n. Senator committee membership

o. Senator rank on committee

p. Senator spouse

q. State

r. State flower

s. State motto

t. State population

Dependencies and Restrictions

a. The senators are federal, rather than state senators

b. Access to the data will generally be by state but may occasionally be by city or senator

c. Senators generally serve on several committees at once

d. Senate committee staff members are not senators and may only serve on one senate committee

e. Each city has several city council members

f. Each city council member holds one full-time job

g. Mayor names are not unique

h. City names are only unique within a state

10.18. The Football Players Association wants to design a database to support an information system which will maintain historical data about players and teams. Typical queries will involve getting all or some of the team related information about a player, or all or some of the player related information about a team. Also there will be ownership oriented queries. Design a

a. Relational database

b. Hierarchical database

    c.   Network database

    d.   Pseudo-relational database

for this application. The fields and some dependencies and restrictions follow. Note that some of the fields may indicate information that can be represented in ways other than as fields. Also state any additional assumptions that you make about the data in places where you feel the problem description is ambiguous.

Fields

    a.   Team name

    b.   Player identification number

    c.   Player name

    d.   Team owner name

    e.   Player's current team

    f.   Player's past teams

    g.   Years player has been on a team

    h.   Average annual salary of a player on a team (one player on one team for all of the years he has played on that team)

    i.   Player position

    j.   Player home city

    k.   Player home state

    l.   Team city

    m.   Team state

    n.   Team mascot

    o.   Years an owner has owned a team

    p.   Head coach

    q.   Player's annual quality rating (over all teams played for in that year)

    r.   Dates of ownership

Dependencies and Restrictions

    a.   Data must be kept for the lifetime of each player

    b.   A player may be temporarily unemployed

    c.   Data must be kept on every previous team owner as well as on the current one

    d.   A team may only have one owner at a time

11

Data Dictionaries

Introduction

Like any other part of a business, a data processing installation consists of a number of generic components that have to be managed. It has an inventory: data. It has inputs: new data and requests about the data. It has products: reports, responses to requests about the data, and so on. It has equipment: the computers and all of the associated devices. It has a set of people who do the work. In the early days of data processing, and even today in small data processing installations, a bright data processing manager, with some rudimentary notes written here or there, could remember enough of the details about all of the components of his or her shop to manage them, and therefore the shop, effectively. Actually the fact of the matter is that the typical DP manager of the past never thought much about managing in the textbook sense. The DP manager tended to be so harried and pressured from all sides that "managing" became a matter of barely (and hopefully) meeting deadline after deadline for specific jobs, rather than thinking of the broader implications.

Today data processing departments are huge affairs, involving thousands of employees in the largest companies and hundreds in many others. Increasingly DP managers have corporate vice president titles; many are generalists, not having come up through the ranks of data processing. They are being held accountable for running the data processing shop as a business within a business. The pressures have become enormous, as more and more of most companies' businesses have become dependent on data processing for their day-to-day functioning. At the same time, DP managers are responsible for the security of the data, controlling costs, alerting the rest of the company to the data that's available to them, and so on. Is there any help for the DP manager in running the data processing environment? The answer begins with a look at the kinds of help that the other functional heads of the corporation have available to them.

Remember that the purpose of data processing is to help all of the functional areas of a company perform more efficiently and effectively. The financial manager has a tremendous amount of accounting and modeling support from the firm's computers. The personnel manager has everything from home address to skills inventories at his or her fingertips for every employee. The manufacturing head has constantly updated raw materials inventories. The list goes on to include virtually every nook and cranny of the company.

But what about help for the data processing manager? Historically DP managers were always so busy applying data processing to everyone else's needs, that they neglected their own needs. One is reminded of the famous

Figure 11.1. The shoemaker's children are the last to get shoes.

old parable of the shoemaker's children being the last ones to get shoes, Figure 11.1. It has only been recently that data processing has seriously considered applying its techniques to itself. From that effort has come a set of computer files that the data processing department uses to help manage its own affairs. This set of files is called a *data dictionary*.

Definition and Characteristics

Let's explore data dictionaries in two steps. In this section, we will take a look at the concept of data dictionaries at an overview level. In succeeding sections, we will go into more detail.

Figure 11.2 shows two rather common files found in the data processing installation of a typical manufacturing company. The personnel department is concerned with keeping track of the firm's employees, which we refer to as an entity set (each person is an entity). The kinds of facts that they have to store for each person include the person's employee number, last name, first name, and so on (each fact is an attribute of that entity). Similarly one of the entity sets that the manufacturing department is concerned with is the set of items in its manufacturing inventory. For each item, it must store the part number, part name, and so on.

So the personnel department and the manufacturing department each have computer files (one of each department's files is shown in Figure 11.2) to help them manage their responsibilities. What equivalent support might the data processing department have for itself?

Figure 11.3 shows two files of what might be a 5 to 10 (or more) file *data dictionary*, a set of files designed to help the data processing department manage its own responsibilities. If personnel wants to keep track of people and manufacturing wants to keep track of its inventory items, among other things, what does data processing want to keep track of? Two of those "things," entities that data processing must manage, are fields and files. Thus Figure 11.3 shows a Fields File and a Files File.

If personnel has decided that employee number, last name, first name, and so on are attributes that it must store for each employee, and manufacturing has decided on part number and part name, and so on, what are the attributes for fields and files that data processing feels that it must store for each of them in the data dictionary? Figure 11.3 shows that for fields some of the attributes are field name (FIELDNM), field type (FIELDTYP), and field length (FIELDLEN), and for files, file name (FILENM) and file length (FILELEN).

In the personnel file, each row represents one of the entities: an employee. In the inventory file each row represents a part. The equivalent in the data dictionary is that each row of the Fields File represents one of the fields in one of the application data files processed by the data processing department, and each row of the Files File represents one of the application files processed by the data processing department. Thus in this example, we see that each row of the Fields File in Figure 11.3 represents one of the fields of one of the files in Figure 11.2. Also each row of the the Files File in Figure 11.3 represents one of the files in Figure 11.2.

What we have described thus far, the storage of data about data processing entities, is one of the two major dimensions in a data dictionary. The other major dimension is the storage of information about *relationships* among the entities. It's not enough to keep track of the items of importance in the data processing environment by themselves; it is equally important to maintain information on how they interrelate. The informal links between the two files in Figure 11.4 (which is Figure 11.3 with those links added) illustrate the relationships between the files and the fields shown. The facts that the fields EMPNO, EMPLAST, and EMPFIRST are in the file Personnel, and PARTNO and PARTNM are in Inventory, are clearly very important for a DP manager to know. For example, it may be that the same field is used in several files and there must be some coordination of that multiple usage.

Because the data dictionary contains descriptive information about personnel's files, manufacturing's files, and so on, we might refer to the data dictionary as storing "data about data" or "metadata."

EMPNO	EMPLAST	EMPFIRST	· · ·
06337	Jones	Fred	· · ·
09155	Smith	Susan	· · ·
16840	Adams	John	· · ·
· · ·			

Personnel File

PARTNO	PARTNM	· · ·
115248	Nut	· · ·
124770	Bolt	· · ·
173771	Screw	· · ·
· · ·		

Inventory File

Figure 11.2. Two typical DP files.

FIELDNM	FIELDTYP	FIELDLEN	· · ·
EMPNO	Num	5	· · ·
EMPLAST	Alpha	20	· · ·
EMPFIRST	Alpha	10	· · ·
PARTNO	Num	6	· · ·
PARTNM	Alpha	20	· · ·
· · ·			

Fields File

FILENM	FILELEN	· · ·
Personnel	1000	· · ·
Inventory	15000	· · ·
·		
·		
·		

Files File

Figure 11.3. Part of a data dictionary for the files in Figure 11.2.

Dictionary Contents

Let's take a more detailed look at the kinds of entities, attributes, and relationships which may be found in a data dictionary.

Entities

There are a number of generally agreed upon data processing environment entities for inclusion in a data dictionary. Depending on the installation's needs, a subset of them may suffice or additional entities may be required.

The most obvious kind of entity to be considered in a data dictionary is the type that was used in the foregoing example: the directly data related

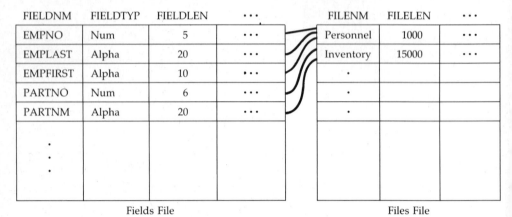

FIELDNM	FIELDTYP	FIELDLEN	•••		FILENM	FILELEN	•••
EMPNO	Num	5	•••		Personnel	1000	•••
EMPLAST	Alpha	20	•••		Inventory	15000	•••
EMPFIRST	Alpha	10	•••		.		
PARTNO	Num	6	•••		.		
PARTNM	Alpha	20	•••		.		
. . .							

Fields File   Files File

Figure 11.4.   Part of a data dictionary showing relationships.

entity. As we have seen, fields and files are representative of this class. What about records as an entity? One could argue that a Records File should contain such information as record length and a set of pointers to the Fields File indicating which fields are in which records. Then the Files File would include such information as file length and a set of pointers to the Records File indicating which record types are in the file. But if there is only one record type in a file, which is the usual case (for linear files), then all of this information—record length, file length, pointers to fields in the records of the file—can be combined in the Files File. If a company uses a DBMS which uses hierarchical structures, network structures, file linking structures, or any other special structures, then it is appropriate to have entities for them set up in the data dictionary too.

Another category of data processing environment entities is the set of software components that are involved in processing the previously named data entities. The most obvious such entity type is the program. Depending on the data processing systems in use, others include: transactions, operating systems, jobs, database management systems, and so on. A related type of entity is the set of control blocks needed by the DBMSs or other systems to describe and process the data. And if it is important to keep track of the software that processes the data, it is also important to know the hardware that the data is processed on. This might include the various computer systems that an organization has as well as the specific disk packs that a file resides on.

Another common data processing environment entity type is people. Clearly, from a responsibility, as well as a security, standpoint, it will be necessary to maintain information about the people who are involved in data processing. Also various output vehicles, such as reports would be dictionary entities.

In addition to these rather common data dictionary entity types, the experimentation with and customization of data dictionaries have produced a wide variety of other dictionary entity types. These include entities involving data communications, information systems strategic planning (e.g., IBM's BSP methodology), and systems analysis.

Attributes

There are two classes of attributes for data dictionary entities: those that are of a general nature and are likely to be found with any of the entities and those that are specific to particular dictionary entities.

The most obvious of the general attributes is name. Clearly any dictionary entity must have a name or some other identifier. Often dictionaries permit the specification of aliases of entity names. In addition, many dictionaries accept a free form textual description of the entity.

By far though, the most prevalent dictionary attributes are those that are specific to particular entities. Some examples of this category include: the value range of a field, the length of a record, the home address of a person, the capacity of a unit of storage hardware, the language that a program is written in, and so forth.

Relationships

The relationship between virtually any pair of data dictionary entities can have value to some part of the data processing organization. Some data dictionaries specify a limited set of relationships among their entities that they are designed to handle. Others allow the relationship between every pair of entities to be used.

Some examples of common dictionary relationships, including the entities that they tie together, are:

Record Construction: Which fields appear in which records
Security: Which people have access to which files
Impact of Change: Which programs might be affected by changes to which files
Physical Residence: Which files are on which disk packs
Program Data Requirements: Which programs use which files
Responsibility: Which people are responsible for updating which files

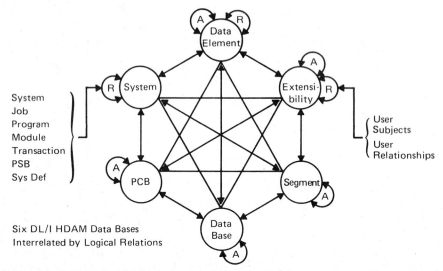

Figure 11.5. Entities and relationships in the IBM DB/DC Data Dictionary. (Reprinted by permission from *DB/DC Data Dictionary Guide* by IBM Corp.)

As an example, Figure 11.5 shows the entities and relationships in the IBM DB/DC Data Dictionary. Four of the entity types have their own DL/I databases assigned to them: Database (DL/I hierarchies or non-DL/I data sets), Segment (including non-DL/I records), Element (field), and PCB (a DL/I control block). Another group share a DL/I database. That group includes such entity types as Program, System, Job, Transaction, Module (part of a program), and PSB (another kind of DL/I control block). A sixth database is called the "extensibility" database. Using this database the user can define new entity types and attributes of those entity types, and can create relationships between those newly defined entity types and any of the standard or other user defined entity types. The connecting lines in Figure 11.5 illustrate the relationships.

Characteristics and Features

So far we've discussed the basic components of a data dictionary: data files which describe the data processing environment and relationships among the data processing entities in those files. In this section we will look at some of the variations to be found among data dictionaries.

Some data dictionaries are what might be called "free standing," meaning that they are an independent set of linear files which can coexist with a variety of DBMS and other systems. Other data dictionaries are designed to be applications of a particular DBMS and their files conform to the file structure of that DBMS. Even in this latter case though, the dictionary is usually capable of storing data about data processing entities that are not involved with that DBMS. Whether free standing or not, the files of a data dictionary need the same protections that any other files need: security, integrity, backup and recovery. If the files are based on a DBMS, then generally the DBMS file protection mechanisms will apply to it. If not (the free standing case) then the data dictionary system must provide its own.

A data dictionary, or more specifically the applications that use it, can be of either a batch or on-line nature. Obviously certain applications, requiring fast direct response, cannot be performed in a batch environment. Others, such as report generation applications, can. Taking this one step further, the data dictionary need not exist as a set of computer files at all. It could consist of a bunch of 3″ x 5″ cards in a filing cabinet, but in practice it is always implemented as a computer application. In this book we are assuming that data dictionaries involve computer files and applications, and generally have online access capabilities.

As we began saying earlier, some data dictionaries have a facility for adding additional entity types beyond the standard ones supplied. Such facilities vary in the number of entity types that can be added, in the attributes that can be associated with the entities (in some cases the attributes must be chosen from a supplied list, in others the user can describe and use any attributes), and in the degree to which relationships between new and old entities can be maintained.

Input Forms

There are four distinct ways of loading data into a dictionary: with batch forms, through individual on-line commands, on-line with full screen panels, and via extraction from existing software or commands. The following sections describe how they work:

Batch Forms

Many dictionaries have a facility which allows those performing dictionary input to fill out forms on paper which describe the given dictionary entries. The data on these forms are then entered all at once in a batch. For example, there would be a form specifically for fields, which would include space for the field name, field type, field length, and so forth. This form could be filled out for any number of fields in the data processing environment whose descriptions are due to be entered into the dictionary. Then they would all be entered in a batch mode, populating the fields file in the dictionary. While doing anything in a batch mode may seem to be old fashioned, this does have the advantages of not tying up the system at peak periods (assuming that the batch input is done during off hours) and of allowing the work to be done by employees who would otherwise not have any interaction with the dictionary.

On-Line Commands

A second way of entering data is with single line commands. For example, the command:

    A E EMPNO Type = N Bytes = 6

when entered on a terminal in an interactive environment would mean add (A) a field (or element) (E) named EMPNO to the fields file and set the type to numeric (N) and the length or bytes field to 6. Clearly it would be rather cumbersome to enter large amounts of dictionary data using this method. But for small amounts of data or for making changes to existing data, this method is quite useful.

Full Screen Panels

The third dictionary input method involves preformatted screens displayed on video terminals. Figure 11.6 shows such a screen for entering data about fields into the fields file. Notice that it includes space for the fields name, length, type, and so on. The dictionary description of a field can be entered fairly quickly by an experienced person tabbing through the different fields on the preformatted screen. Some data dictionaries have a rather extensive collection of such screens. They may, in fact, be related so that one screen can lead to another and generate relationship connections between the dictionary entries in the process. For example, a preformatted screen used for entering information into the dictionary for a record would include space for the fields that are found in that record. Entering the field names in the record definition screen would create the relationship between the record and its fields, and with the proper commands, would also allow the user to move from that screen to a field definition screen to enter more detailed information about the record's fields (as in Figure 11.6).

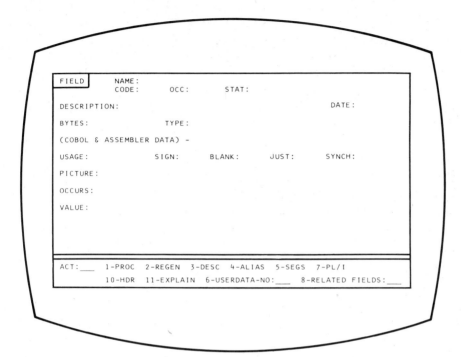

Figure 11.6. Preformatted screen for field input in the IBM DB/DC Data Dictionary. (Reprinted by permission from *DB/DC Data Dictionary Guide* by IBM Corp.)

Extraction

The fourth means of data input is also the most exotic. Various dictionary packages include programs which read database control blocks, COBOL data division specifications, or the like, extract data from them that should belong in the dictionary, and enter the data in the dictionary. When properly used, such programs can obviously be a big savings in time and energy over the three other, more manual, modes of dictionary input. Remember, though, that for *new* application development efforts, such things as control blocks and program data specifications are created *after* the dictionary has been populated with basic data about the application.

Output Forms

Data dictionaries are capable of producing several kinds of output. Some of these outputs are in the form of reports for human consumption, others are in the form of software for the system to use.

Of the output forms for people to use directly, the most obvious is the simple printed listing. Such a listing might encompass all of the instances of a particular entity type (e.g., a list of all of the fields in the data processing environment, together with their attributes). It might include only a subset of them, with all or a subset of the attributes of each. Another kind of printed report is a cross reference listing. This would take the form of a list of all of the fields in a particular record, a list of all of the programmers who have access to a particular file, and so on. As an example of a dictionary report (from the IBM DB/DC Data Dictionary), Figure 11.7 shows a DL/I hierarchy, its segments, and the fields in each segment.

A second type of human consumption output is online query. An example of this is the use of the preformatted screens that we talked about for input, for looking at the contents of the dictionary files. Instead of calling up an entity's description with a preformatted screen for the purpose of adding to it or changing it, we might want to simply look at it. Also a dictionary might provide the capability for doing a keyword search. For example, if every field in the fields file has a textual description stored with it, we might want to search for certain keywords in those descriptions to find out whether a particular field, whose name we obviously do not know, exists.

Probably the most common dictionary output which is used in the running of the system itself is the generation of control blocks required by the DBMS in use. Such control blocks are critical to the functioning of the system. The slightest error in them will generally cause major operating problems. But assume that the information about files, records, fields, and so on in the dictionary has been carefully entered and inspected, and that software exists which is capable of taking that information in the dictionary and creating DBMS control blocks from it. Then while there is still a margin for error in the instructions given to the control block generating software, the overall chance of error in control block generation will be reduced.

Another form of dictionary output is (like the control block situation) the inverse of one of the methods of dictionary input. Just as there are programs that can read the data description portions of a program and extract entries to be placed into the dictionary, there are also programs that can take entries from the dictionary and create program data description statements, such as those in a COBOL data division. Clearly such programs must, as input, be provided with directions indicating which dictionary entries must be used and how they are to be juxtaposed.

Material in the data dictionary can also be funneled into other tools. Examples are database design aids, which require fields and the relationships between them as input, and report writers.

```
REPORT DBS (D,P,DDSPDBS,0) NAME=HIER ;

* * * * * * * *         DB/DC DATA DICTIONARY REPORT        05/06/80  00:24:33
* * * * DBS => SEG => DTE REPORT * * * *                              PAGE:0001

DBSNAME: DP DDSPDBS 0
     SEGMENTS: DA DBS 0                    LEVEL:1     PARENT:
          ELEMENTS: DA DBSNAME 0              START: 1    /0    SEQ: U
                    DA DBSPFX1 0              START: 1    /0    SEQ: G
                    DA DBSPFX2 0              START: 2    /0    SEQ: G
                    DA DBSNMFL 0             START: 3    /0    SEQ: G
                    DA DBSSFX 0              START: 34   /0    SEQ: G

          DA DBSDTE 0                       LEVEL:2     PARENT:DA DBS        0
          ELEMENTS: DA DTENAME 0              START: 1    /0    SEQ: U
                    DA DTEPFX1 0              START: 1    /0    SEQ: G
                    DA DTEPFX2 0             START: 2    /0    SEQ: G
                    DA DTENMFL 0             START: 3    /0    SEQ: G
                    DA DTESFX 0              START: 34   /0    SEQ: G

          DA DBSSEG 0                       LEVEL:2     PARENT:DA DBS        0
          ELEMENTS: DA SEGNAME 0             START: 1    /0    SEQ: G
                    DA SEGPFX1 0              START: 1    /0    SEQ: G
                    DA SEGPFX2 0             START: 2    /0    SEQ: G
                    DA SEGNMFL 0             START: 3    /0    SEQ: G
                    DA SEGSFX 0              START: 34   /0    SEQ: G
                    DA PPNAME 0              START: 35   /0    SEQ: G
                    DA PPPFX1 0             START: 35   /0    SEQ: G
                    DA PPPFX2 0              START: 36   /0    SEQ: G
                    DA PPNMFL 0              START: 37   /0    SEQ: G
                    DA PPSFX 0               START: 45   /0    SEQ: G
                    DA SEGLVL 0              START: 46   /0    SEQ: G
                    DA SEGDSGN0 0            START: 47   /0    SEQ: G
                    DA PAIREDLC 0            START: 48   /0    SEQ: G
                    DA PCPNTRS 0            START: 49   /0    SEQ: G
                    DA SEGTYPE 0            START: 50   /0    SEQ: G

          DA SEGPATRB 0                     LEVEL:3     PARENT:DA DBSSEG     0
          ELEMENTS: DA FREQ 0               START: 1    /0    SEQ: G
                    DA HPNTRS 0             START: 5    /0    SEQ: G
                    DA TPNTRS 0             START: 6    /0    SEQ: G
                    DA LTPNTRS 0            START: 7    /0    SEQ: G
                    DA LPARNT 0             START: 8    /0    SEQ: G
                    DA IRULE 0              START: 9    /0    SEQ: G
                    DA DRULE 0              START: 10   /0    SEQ: G
                    DA RRULE 0              START: 11   /0    SEQ: G
                    DA WHRRULE 0            START: 12   /0    SEQ: G
                    DA COMPRTN 0            START: 13   /0    SEQ: G
                    DA CCRTNOPT 0           START: 21   /0    SEQ: G
                    DA COMPINIT 0           START: 22   /0    SEQ: G
                    DA CTR 0                START: 23   /0    SEQ: G

          DA SEGPCHLD 0                     LEVEL:3     PARENT:DA DBSSEG     0
          ELEMENTS: DA PCSGNAME 0            START: 1    /0    SEQ: G
```

Figure 11.7. A dictionary report describing a DL/I hierarchy by its segments and their fields (IBM DB/DC Data Dictionary). (Reprinted by permission from *OS/VS DB/OC Data Dictionary Applications* Guide (SH20-9190-0) by IBM Corp.)

Implementation

Benefits

Data dictionaries can be of considerable use to a variety of people in the data processing environment. In this section we will look at the dictionary from the points of view of those people in terms of their individual usage of it.

Clearly the heaviest user of the dictionary will be the data administration manager and his or her staff. As we shall explore in more detail in a later chapter, data administration is charged with managing the data in at least the database environment and possibly the data in the entire data processing milieu. As we have seen, the data dictionary is the appropriate place to document the existence of files, fields, reports, and so on, and the relationships among them, and maintaining this information falls under the purview of data administration. In addition, data administration groups are usually charged with the job of generating control blocks for the DBMS. As we have already indicated, this is a task best done using the data dictionary. Data administration personnel are usually involved, at one of several levels, with database design. The database structures, fields, and so on already stored in the dictionary from earlier applications might be needed or related to the data needed in the new design. Thus the dictionary can be a time-saver in that effort. Furthermore as the new design is being developed, the dictionary is the appropriate place to store it away, both for documentation purposes and for such purposes as future control block generation.

There are a variety of other uses of the dictionary by data administration; most are based on relationship type data. The following are merely three of many possible examples. If several programs share a file, and the owner of one of those programs proposes a change in that file, then data administration must touch base with the owners of all of the other program owners to determine whether the change in the file will affect their programs (this is called, "impact of change"). This can be accomplished using the relationship data between the file and program entities in the data dictionary; a given file is associated with a number of programs. If confidential data has leaked out of a company, the investigation might begin by having data administration retrieve the relationship information between employees and files to see who (at least through normal channels) had access to the data. If a long range planning effort is underway and a review is to be made of the data that is currently used in an application being restudied, then data administration can use the relationship between fields and database structures for this purpose.

Systems analysts and program designers can use the data dictionary in two major ways. One use is as a source of information on what fields, files, and so forth already exist in the data processing environment which might be needed in a new application development effort underway. If data needed for a new system already exists, then the new application may be able to use it. If there are existing database structures which the application can add on to, to satisfy its requirements, then that might be a large cost savings. In those and related situations, the dictionary is the repository of information to be searched.

The other dictionary use for systems analysts and designers is as a documentation device for the new information that is generated as a result of their application development effort. In a sophisticated application development environment, the systems analysts begin the process by inserting nonphysical data about the fields (at least the field name) as they arise during their work. The systems designers can later add physical information about fields, as well as information about files, database structures, and so on. Thus the application developers have a natural vehicle for documentation, and the dictionary has a natural way of being populated with data concerning new applications.

Finally there is the benefit of the data dictionary to higher level data processing management, and for that matter to high level corporate management in general. As data processing permeates increasing aspects and levels of organizations, it becomes increasingly important for management to understand the nature of the data in its systems. It is important from the viewpoint of understanding how the organization functions, as data is considered a resource which mirrors the workings of the organization. While the data administration personnel manage the data dictionary, with that kind of data in it, it is management that ultimately benefits.

Costs

There are a number of costs associated with having a data dictionary. As with any other computer application, there are the costs of the dictionary programs themselves and the costs of executing and maintaining them. There are the costs associated with teaching people how to enter data into the dictionary and with educating others on how they might benefit by using the dictionary.

The most controversial cost of the dictionary involves the initial and continuing efforts to populate it with data. When a data dictionary is introduced into a data processing environment, awaiting it are years and years of accumulated data processing entities ready for dictionary entry. Trying to enter all of that material into the dictionary overnight would be a bone-jarring task. Often the dictionary files are gradually built up with appropriate pieces of data that are generated as a result of new application development efforts. We shall have more to say about this situation shortly, but suffice it to say for now that whether a large initial effort is made, a gradual dictionary build-up is undertaken, or both, there is a significant level of expense associated with the process.

Requirements for Success

The cost/benefit trade-off for data dictionaries is a tricky one and there are a number of factors involved in having a successful dictionary installation.

It is clear that management must be supportive of the idea of installing a data dictionary. They must approve the initial outlay of money for the software, as well as the assignment of personnel to work with it. And they must be patient in allowing time to pass while the dictionary is being populated with data until it can fully live up to expectations.

There are certain uses of the dictionary that do not require a tremendous amount of data to be in the dictionary files. An example of this is the database control block generation application. The only data that must be in the dictionary is the data that must go into these specific control blocks. In order to make the dictionary productive as soon as possible, it is often suggested that control block generation be one of the first applications of a new data dictionary for the foregoing reason.

The other side of the coin is that there are other uses of the dictionary that require a large, expensive effort in data entry into the dictionary before they can be taken advantage of. For example, take the case of a systems analyst searching the dictionary to see if some data required in a new application under development already exists in the data processing environment. Unless all, or at least most, of the existing applications are reflected in the dictionary, the systems analyst is not going to have much confidence in a dictionary search that comes back with, "not found." Maybe the data does exist but has not as yet been noted in the dictionary.

So the route to a successful data dictionary installation is a gradual one. First management commitment to the idea of having a data dictionary must be obtained. Then once the dictionary has been installed, data entry must be a well planned and progressive undertaking. Often the route chosen is to begin populating the dictionary with data derived from new data processing applications under development. Immediate use of such data, such as for control block generation, is one reason for doing this. But another reason is the convenience of the dictionary for documentation of the new application, something that would have to be done one way or another in any case. A third reason is the somewhat emotional point that a new application should be associated with the newest technologies. Finally since this is the beginning of its "life," this application may be around for a long time and thus may make the longest use of the dictionary.

In addition, a schedule can be created for bringing the organization's existing applications into the world of the dictionary, over some reasonable period of time. Again, for this to work, management must believe in the long term benefit of the dictionary and supply the resources necessary while being patient about the payback.

Other requirements for a successful dictionary installation also revolve around people. These individuals, whether data administration personnel, systems analysts, or programmers, must be educated in how to enter data into the dictionary and in how to use it. They must adhere to standards and to security arrangements in executing procedures involving the dictionary. And finally, it is preferable if management believes in the value of the dictionary, as even the strongest management orders to use it often have a way of slipping with time.

Active vs. Passive Dictionaries

An increasingly important distinction in data dictionaries is the integrated or active data dictionary versus the nonintegrated or passive data dictionary. Actually there are no single accepted definitions of those terms, and there is a wide range of functions that have been connected with them.

Basically a passive dictionary is one used just for documentation purposes. Data about the fields, files, people, and so on in the data processing environment, are entered into the dictionary and cross referenced. Information in the forms of printed listings and terminal based queries about the dictionary's contents are run as needed. The passive dictionary is simply a self-contained application and set of files used for documenting the data processing environment.

But what about the wide range of other potential involvements? Since most dictionaries today are closely associated, in structure, usage, or both, with a DBMS, let us consider the dictionary in this environment. One activity that we've already looked at which brings the dictionary closer to the functioning of the database environment, is the generation of DBMS control blocks from data in the dictionary. One could add to that the programs that produce application program data definitions from data in the dictionary, and the reverse, the programs that populate the dictionary with data derived from application program source code. All such off-line dictionary activities that either put more into it or derive system products from it, form a step beyond a simple passive dictionary.

Another possibility, which makes the dictionary even a bit more active, is the *requirement* that functions like those described previously be performed. For example, a DBMS might force all application program database calls to pick up the physical details of the application data from the dictionary *at compile time.* Thus given a field name by the application program, the dictionary might, at compile time, supply information about where and how the field is stored which would be compiled into the object code.

Another step upwards in this line of reasoning, would be for a database program to get information from, or be partially controlled by (depending on how you look at it) the data dictionary *during execution time.* The dictionary might pass information about the structure of the data at execution time that wasn't compiled into the application object program, or as another example, it might supply security information about which users or programs are entitled to have access to specific files.

Without specific human intervention, very active dictionaries might be capable of surveying database application programs being installed and executed to automatically extract information about them not already in the dictionary.

Originally data dictionaries were considered to be functionally just one more application in the database environment. As we progress into the realm of increasingly active dictionaries, there are many who feel that in the future (and some vendors who claim that now) dictionaries will be at the heart of the DBMS environment. In some sense, the dictionary will be the central controller of the entire DBMS environment, managing the application files, security, backup and recovery operations, and even programming standards.

References

Allen, F. W., Loomis, M. E. S., and Mannino, M. V., "The Integrated Dictionary/Directory System," *Computing Surveys,* vol. 14, no. 2, June, 1982, pp. 245–286.

Leong-Hong, B. W., and Plagman, B. K., *Data Dictionary/Directory Systems,* Wiley, New York, 1982.

Ross, R. G., *Data Dictionaries and Data Administration,* AMACOM, New York, 1981.

Van Duyn, J., *Developing a Data Dictionary System,* Prentice-Hall, Englewood Cliffs, NJ, 1982.

Questions and Exercises

11.1.   In your own words, describe what a data dictionary is and why it is needed.

11.2.   In the same style as the dictionary files in Figure 11.3, create a dictionary file for reports. What might the meanings of the relationships be between that reports file and the files in Figure 11.3?

11.3. In the same style as the dictionary files in Figure 11.3, create a dictionary file for employees. What might the meanings of the relationships be between that employees file and the files in Figure 11.3?

11.4. In the same style as the dictionary files in Figure 11.3, create a dictionary file for programs. What might the meanings of the relationships be between that programs file and the files in Figure 11.3?

11.5. Describe possible data dictionary entities not mentioned in this chapter. What relationships might they have to the standard entities?

11.6. List a comprehensive set of attributes for the

    a. Fields file

    b. Files file

    c. Employees file

    d. Programs file

11.7. Choose five of the relationships shown in Figure 11.5 (identify them by the dictionary files they connect) and indicate a meaning for each.

11.8. What are the advantages and disadvantages of free standing vs. DBMS-specific data dictionaries?

11.9. Describe a significant advantage and a significant disadvantage of each of the four data dictionary input methods described in this chapter.

11.10. Design a full screen preformatted panel for terminal input into a data dictionary for a

    a. Report

    b. File

    c. Program

    d. Employee

11.11. Design a data dictionary report format for a report describing the information in the

    a. Fields file

    b. Files file

    c. Employees file

    d. Programs file

11.12. Design a data dictionary report for cross-reference information between

    a. The fields file and the files file

    b. The reports file and the employees file

    c. The programs file and the fields file

11.13. Convince a data processing manager that he or she should install a data dictionary.

11.14.   Describe the costs of installing and running a data dictionary.

11.15.   In your own words, describe how you might gradually introduce a data dictionary into a data processing environment.

11.16.   How would a data processing environment change with the use of a highly active data dictionary?

11.17.   Would an active data dictionary change the way programmers, systems analysts, and operators do their jobs? Explain.

11.18.   Defend or refute the following statement: "An active data dictionary is the central focus of the database environment."

12

Database Environment Issues

Introduction

As we suggested in Chapter 4, there are certain concerns about data that must be addressed regardless of whether or not the data is being stored under the control of a database management system. Those concerns include maintaining the security of the data, protecting the integrity of the data in concurrent update situations, being able to recover the data to a correct state after a data error has occurred or the entire database has been destroyed, and being able to audit the data to see who has accessed or changed it.

Again a database environment should provide solutions to all of those problems without programmers having to address them for each new application that comes along. Solutions to each can clearly be generalized for any data that fits within the framework of a given database environment. In this chapter, we shall take a brief look at each of these four database environment issues.

Security

Is it important to protect stored data from unauthorized access and unauthorized change? It certainly is and for several reasons. As more and more of our society's record keeping is computerized, an increasingly wider variety of kinds of data and a vastly increasing volume of data is being stored in computer files including, of course, in databases. Either the organizations holding the data, or the people or organizations that the data describes, have a vested interest in the security of the data. Governments must protect sensitive defense data from unauthorized intrusion. Companies must prevent their competitors from seeing their accounting data. Banks must be sure that the money they hold, now in the form of computer data, cannot be "stolen" (e.g., a field value representing the amount of money in an account cannot be tampered with). Individuals want personal information that insurance companies keep about them to remain confidential. And the list goes on and on.

Let's begin by considering the different kinds of security breaches possible in modern data processing facilities. Perhaps the most basic kind of breach is unauthorized data access, that is, someone seeing data they are not entitled to see. Another exposure is unauthorized data modification, that is, someone changing the value of stored data that they are not entitled to. And a third problem, which is a form of extension of the first two, is

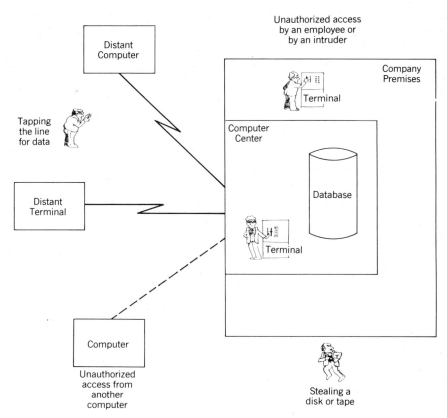

Figure 12.1. Data security exposures.

unauthorized program modification in which someone changes a program so that it retrieves or modifies data in an illegal way.

The question then becomes one of thinking about the ways in which such deliberate compromises of the data can take place, Figure 12.1. One method of breaking into a company's database is to tap its communications lines as it transfers data between two of its computers or between a terminal and one of its computers. Another method, if the computer is accessible via ordinary telephone lines, is for the intruder to make himself or herself appear to the computer as a legitimate authorized user. This will mean, as we shall discuss more fully later, finding out the computer's telephone number, producing an identification tag that the computer recognizes, and supplying the correct password to go with it (shades of the movie *War Games*). In a similar vein, the intruder might be able to surreptitiously enter the company's premises and use a terminal right on the site. Another "method" of gaining access to data is to steal the physical media on which it resides, including disk packs and printouts. Even bribes of authorized company employees have to be considered. The old adage that, "a chain is only as strong as its weakest link," really does apply here.

To make matters more complicated, there is also the case of a genuine company employee who is authorized to access some of the company's data, gaining access to other data that he or she is not authorized to see. And taking it a step even further than that, there may be a situation in which an employee attempts to modify data that he or she is authorized to look at, but that he or she is not authorized to modify.

Which brings us to the essence of this subsection: what are the kinds of security measures that can be employed to protect stored data, especially (but not only) the data in databases? First before a company considers the specific software and hardware oriented devices that are usually associated with the idea of data security, there is the issue of the physical security of the company's premises. This aspect must not be underestimated. Anyone in the computer room or in areas in which there are terminals or other input/output devices must be a recognized company member or an approved visitor. This also applies to areas which contain some of the company's data, from tape libraries to rooms with printouts. One would also hope that the company's employees are honest, but this, of course, is harder to control.

Then there is the issue of controlling access to the computer system. Here we assume that the potential intruder either has gained access to a terminal on the company's premises or has another (perhaps micro) computer with a modem and has learned the telephone number of the company's computer. Most systems today require that someone attempting to use a computer identify themselves with an identification tag of several characters and enter a secret password that goes with it. Identification tags are often publicly known (at least within the company), but passwords must be kept as secret as possible, should be changed periodically, and should not be written down to reduce the risk of someone else learning them. Passwords should not appear on the terminal screen when they are typed in, and they should be created by the user so that there is less chance of the user forgetting them.

Other forms of user identification have been suggested. One is to store personal information about the user (e.g., mother's maiden name) and have the system demand it when the user attempts to enter the system. Unfortunately since that data doesn't get updated, there is a greater risk of its being compromised over time. Other possibilities for the future are selections from physical characteristics such as the user's fingerprints, signature, or voice, as devices for recognizing them become sufficiently so-phisticated.

Now let's assume that a particular person has been recognized by the system as a legitimate user. That person might in fact be a legitimate user or might not be but has convinced the system that he or she is (perhaps by stealing someone else's identification tag and password). There are security features that can be used to protect data given that someone has passed the first hurdle as an authorized user of the system. In terms of the database environment, perhaps the most basic is that all access to the data is controlled by and must pass through the DBMS. This leads to a number of useful features. One such feature involves data kept by the system that indicates which users (by identification tag) are permitted to retrieve and to update which data files, IMS segment types, CODASYL record types, and so on. Thus if a particular person is a legitimate system user, but tries to access data that he or she is not entitled to see, the system does not permit that operation. For certain kinds of data the person might be permitted to see it but not to update it and so that distinction must be made. There are many other variations on this theme which, as with the above security features, may or may not be built into specific DBMSs. For example, some systems will allow specific users to see some, but not all, of the fields in occurrences of specific record types. Some systems will restrict users from seeing data based not only on the record types involved, but also on the values in specific occurrences of those records. Another idea is to allow a user to see two different fields in the occurrences of a particular record type, but not at the same time. For example, a user might have permission to use a personnel file to get a list of the employees' names, and to get a list of all of the salaries for statistical purposes, but he might not have permission to match specific people with specific salaries.

Another data protection feature, again pertaining to the situation in which a person has been recognized as a legitimate system user, is an additional use of passwords. We've been talking about the use of passwords to protect illegal entry to the system. But passwords can also be assigned to specific programs and to specific data files. The system would demand that the user produce the required password in order to execute a particular program or to access a particular file.

Unfortunately none of the foregoing security techniques protect against data thefts in which the intruder does not attempt to extract the data through the computer and DBMS. Examples of this situation include wiretapping as the data is being sent over communications lines and theft of a disk pack. A solution to this problem is "data encryption." The term data encryption implies that the data, bit-by-bit or character-by-character, has been changed into a form that looks totally garbled. It must be reconverted—decrypted— back to its original form to be of use. The encryption/decryption process may take place only as the data is shipped along communications lines, or the data may actually be stored in an encrypted form on the disk.

The process of encrypting data can range from simple to highly complex. Obviously the simpler the scheme, the easier it is for an intruder to figure it out and decrypt the data. Encryption generally involves an algorithm and a secret key. A very simple example of an alphabetic encryption scheme is as follows. Number the letters of the alphabet from A to Z plus blank as 1 to 27. For each letter in the data to be encrypted, add the secret key (some number in this case) and change that letter to the letter represented by the new number. Thus if the key is 4, then an A (value 1) becomes an E (since $1+4 = 5$ and E is the fifth letter of the alphabet), a B becomes an F, and so on through the alphabet to the blank which becomes a D (wrapping around from blank as the 27th "character" of the alphabet back to the beginning of the alphabet). The receiving program must be aware both of the algorithm and of the secret key so that it can work the algorithm in reverse and decrypt the data.

Generally the more complex the encryption scheme, the more time it will take to encrypt and decrypt the data, which will slow down the overall operation of the database environment. Furthermore if the stored data on the disk in encrypted, then every disk access, whether or not shipment on communications lines is involved, requires the time for decryption. Some encryption schemes, involving several levels of algorithmic transformations, and very large keys (one common scheme has a 56 bit key) have been built into hardware for performance reasons.

Concurrency

Many of today's data processing application systems, and especially those that run within the database environment, assume that many people using those systems will require access to the same data files at the same time. Modern hardware and software systems are certainly capable of providing such shared data access. One very common example of this is in airline reservations, where several different reservations clerks may have simultaneous requests from different customers for seats on the same flight. Another example is in an industrial or retail inventory application in which several clerks seek the same item in inventory simultaneously.

When concurrent access involves only simple retrieval of data there is no problem. But when concurrent access requires data modification, the

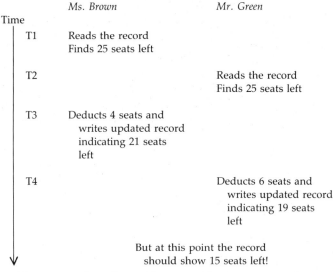

Figure 12.2. Integrity problem caused by concurrent update.

two or more users attempting to update the data simultaneously (or as simultaneously as a multiprogrammed system allows) have a rather nasty way of interfering with each other which doesn't happen if they are merely doing retrievals. This is certainly the case in the airline reservations and inventory examples, since selling seats on flights and using items in inventory requires that the number of seats or inventory items left be revised downwards.

Using the airline reservations application as an example, here is an example of what can happen. Suppose there are 25 seats left on Acme Airlines flight #345 on March 12. Two reservations clerks, Ms. Brown and Mr. Green, receive telephone calls at about the same time from two customers who are interested in this flight on that date. Brown's customer wants to book four seats on the flight while Green's customer, with a larger family, wants to book six seats on it. Brown retrieves the record for the flight on that date from the database, notes that there are 25 seats available, and begins to discuss the price and other details with her customer. At about the same time, Green retrieves the same record (really another copy of it) for his customer. Both clerks make their respective sales and indicate them through their terminals to the database. Brown's transaction dictates that four should be deducted from the number of seats available on the flight and then Green's indicates that six should be deducted.

The result in the database is shown in Figure 12.2. The record for flight #345 on March 12 now shows that there are 19 seats available. But shouldn't it be only 15, since a total of 10 seats were sold? Yes, but the point is that neither of the clerks knew that the other was in the process of selling seats on the flight at the same time that he or she was. Both Brown and Green started off with the premise that there were 25 seats left. When Brown deducted four seats, for a moment the record showed that there were 21 seats left. But then when Green deducted his six, he was deducting them from the original 25 seats that he saw when he originally retrieved the record from the database and not from the 21 seats that were left after Brown's sale.

By the way, you might question the probability of two clerks going after the same record simultaneously in a large airline reservations file. Have you ever tried to get a reservation on a flight from New York to Miami for Christmas week the week before Christmas week? Similar circumstances occur in most applications of every type imaginable. Also you might wonder if the same kind of error situation can take place in applications in which the retrieval/update operations take place in fractions of a second and not the minutes involved in Brown's and Green's telephone conversations with their customers. As should be fairly clear, the answer is very definitely: yes, as a consequence of multiprogramming in today's commercial computer systems.

The usual solution to this problem is a technique known as, "lockout". The DBMS is designed so that once one update operation has begun on a piece of data, any attempt to begin another update operation on that same piece of data will be blocked or "locked out". One way or another depending on the implementation, the bumped access request will be rescheduled. When the first query releases its lock on the data, the other one can lock it and use it for its own update operation. The level or "granularity" of lockout can vary. Lockout at a high level, for instance at the level of an entire file, unfortunately prevents much more than that one particular piece of data from being modified while the update operation is going on, but is a low overhead solution. Lockout at a low level, the field level for instance, doesn't hold up the rest of the database, but is a comparatively high overhead solution.

Unfortunately as so often happens, the introduction of this beneficial device itself causes other problems that did not previously exist. Follow the next scenario.

Let's say we have a manufacturing inventory situation in which clerks must find out if a sufficient quantity of *each of two* parts is available to satisfy an order. A program has been written which is designed to accept information from a terminal on the two parts being sought, including the quantity of each required. It then searches the database for the records for those

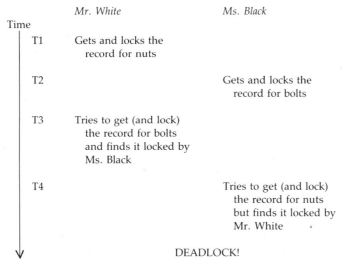

Figure 12.3. Deadlock caused by the use of locks in concurrent update.

parts, retrieves the quantity of each currently on hand, and then on approval from the clerk at the terminal, orders those parts to be shipped and has the quantity-on-hand field in the records in the database reduced accordingly. Suppose two clerks, Mr. White and Ms. Black, each request a quantity of nuts and bolts at about the same time. White happens to list the nuts before the bolts in his query, while Black happens to list the bolts before the nuts in hers. Both clerks begin their queries at about the same time. White's query grabs the nuts record and locks it, and at about the same time Blacks query grabs the bolts record and locks it. Then White's query tries to get the bolts record, but finds it locked by Black. And at about the same time, Black's query tries to get the nuts record, but finds it locked by White. Both queries then wait endlessly for each other to release what they each need to proceed. This is called "deadlock" or "the deadly embrace" and is shown in Figure 12.3. It actually bears a close relationship to the "gridlock" traffic problem that major cities worry about during rush hour.

To solve the problem of deadlock, we can consider measures that would prevent it from happening outright, or measures that would detect it when it happens and take appropriate corrective action. While prevention may sound more palatable than mere detection, it turns out that preventing deadlock is not always all that easy. Depending on the nature of the query, it may be that the program has to use information in one piece of data that it finds and locks, to determine what other piece of data it must find and lock. If that second piece of data is already locked by someone else, then the query is stuck in the middle, holding one piece of data that it needs locked, and finding the other unavailable. In addition, there are performance related issues that make deadlock prevention less than desirable.

So the usual thrust in this matter is to allow deadlock to occur, detect it when it happens, and then undo it. Deadlock can be detected either through a timeout (meaning that a query has been hung up for so long that the assumption is it must be deadlocked) or through a procedure that traces a chain of query wait situations to see if the chain begins and ends at the same query. For example, if Smith is waiting for something that Jones has locked, Jones is waiting for something that Williams has locked, and Williams is waiting for something that Smith has locked, then there is deadlock. The solution is to select one of the deadlocked queries and "roll it back" (see the following section on recovery), undoing any changes that it has made to the database up to this point of its execution, and of course, releasing all of its locks so that the other queries can now use the data that it had locked. The bumped query can then be restarted.

Backup and Recovery

No matter how sophisticated computers become, we have to assume that a variety of predicaments may, at one time or another, befall stored data. Trouble can come from something as simple as a user entering an incorrect data value into a field or as overwhelming as a fire or some other disaster destroying an entire computer center and everything in it. Thus the results can range in consequence from a single data value being rendered inaccurate, to all of the installation's files or databases being destroyed, with many other possibilities in between. In the data processing business we have to assume that from time to time something will go wrong with our data and we have to have the tools available to correct or reconstruct it. Clearly in the database environment, those tools must be general enough to handle the different kinds of data and the volume of data stored in the database. The operations involved come under the heading of *backup and recovery*.

The basic ideas in backup and recovery are fairly straightforward in concept and have been around for a long time. This is not meant to imply, however, that there is no room for variation or that the implementation of the ideas cannot get complicated. For a database to be capable of recovering

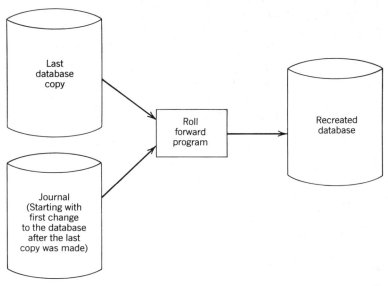

Figure 12.4. Roll forward recovery.

from a data error, a disk crash, or the like, two major actions must be taken, one on a regularly scheduled basis, and one on a constantly active basis. On a regularly scheduled basis the database files must be "backed-up," that is, a copy of each file must be made. The copy (or a copy of the copy) should be kept in a different building, or even in a different city, so that if a disaster strikes the computer center not all copies of the data will be lost. For example, disk based files are copied onto other disk packs. From that moment onward, on a constant basis, every change to the database must be recorded on a special file called a "log" or "journal". The journal can be kept on either tape or disk, although the current trend is towards keeping it on disk. While the contents of a journal entry can vary, the basic notion is to record what piece of data was changed in a given transaction, what its value was before the change, and what its value is after the change. Then the question is, how can the database copy and the journal be used to solve the various kinds of recovery problems.

First let's consider the case of a calamity that destroys a disk pack. The recovery procedure in this case is called "forward recovery" or "roll forward", Figure 12.4. To recreate the disk that was lost, you begin by readying the last copy of the lost data that was made, and the journal of the changes to it. Then a program starts reading journal entries, starting from the first one that was recorded after the copy of the database was made and continuing through to the last one that was recorded just before the disk was destroyed. For each of these journal entries, the program changes the data value concerned in the copy of the database to the "after" value shown in the journal entry. This means that whatever processing took place in the transaction that caused the journal entry to be made, the net result of the database after that transaction will be restored. Performing the operation for every transaction that caused a change in the database since the copy was taken (which is the same as saying for each entry in the journal), in the same order that these transactions were originally executed, will bring the database copy to the up-to-date level of the database that was destroyed.

There are a couple of variations on the forward recovery theme that are worth mentioning. One variation is based on the recognition that several changes may have been made to the same piece of data since the last database copy was made. If that's the case, then only the last one of those changes, which after all shows the value of this piece of data at the point that the disk was destroyed, needs to be used in updating the database copy in the roll-forward operation. If the database environment is a volatile one in which changes are made frequently and it is common for the same piece of data to be updated several times between database copy operations, then roll-forward as we have described may be needlessly inefficient. Instead it may be worthwhile to sort through the journal prior to the roll-forward operation to find the last change made to each piece of data that was updated, since the last database copy was made. Then only those final changes need be applied to the database copy in the roll-forward operation.

Another roll-forward variation is to record an indication of what the transaction itself looked like at the point of being executed, instead of recording before and after images of the data in the journal, along with other necessary supporting information. Then the roll-forward process becomes one of reexecuting all of the transactions in the order that they were originally executed. This will take a lot longer as a recovery process.

Now let's consider a different situation. Suppose that in the midst of normal operation an error is discovered that involves a piece of recently updated data. The cause might be as simple as human error in keying in a value, or as complicated as a program ending abnormally and leaving some, but not all, changes to the database that it was supposed to make. Why not just correct the incorrect data and not make a big deal out of this? Because in the interim, other programs may have read the incorrect data and made use of it thus compounding the error in other places in the database.

So the discovered error, and in fact, all other changes that were made

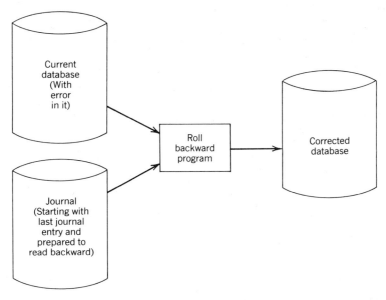

Figure 12.5. Roll backward recovery.

to the database since the error was discovered, must be "backed-out." The process is called, "backward recovery," or "roll-backward," Figure 12.5. Essentially the idea is to start with the database in its current state (note: database copies have nothing to do with this), and the journal starting with the *last* entry that was made in it. Then a program reads *backwards* through the journal, resetting each updated data value to its "before image" as recorded in the journal, until it reaches the point where the error was made. Thus the program "undoes" each transaction in the reverse order (last-in, first-out) from which it was made. If the error did, in fact, affect other transactions, then those must be rerun, which may be a manual or automatic process, depending on a number of factors, including the nature of the information kept in the journal.

A couple of other notes about recovery: Some systems are capable of automatically initiating a roll-backward operation to undo the changes made to the database by a partially completed and then halted or failed transaction. This is called "dynamic backout." There are situations in which it is helpful to restore the database to a point at which there is confidence that all changes made to the database up to that point are accurate. Some systems are capable of writing a special record to the journal, known as a "checkpoint," which specifies that kind of stable state.

Auditability

An issue which has received relatively little attention in the past, but which is gaining in importance, is that of auditability of the database. The term auditability can have several connotations and we shall just touch on a couple of them here.

One sense of database auditing is surveying the database environment to make sure that the data is properly protected. This means that adequate security procedures, backup and recovery, and concurrency procedures are in place. Depending on the depth of the audit, it may also mean that the DBMS is being used properly and that its benefits are being taken advantage of to an acceptable level.

Another sense of database auditing is being able to trace back to see who interacted with the database. This may be at the level of who made what changes to the database, or it may even be at a level of who simply retrieved what data from the database. The most obvious kind of vehicle for satisfying such a requirement is the journal. In fact, the same journal that is used for recovery operations could be used for auditing as well. If the goal in providing an "audit trail" is to be able to keep track of who made changes to the database, then the recovery journal would have to include who made the changes indicated in the journal items. If the audit trail is to keep track of simple retrievals from the database, as well as updates to it, then the journal would have to include entries for simple reads in addition to its usual entries for updates. However, note that the latter requirement, in systems with high activity rates, would generate a huge journal, and would slow down the operation of the overall system as every database access would have to be recorded in the journal.

References

Date, C. J., *An Introduction to Database Systems,* vol. 2, Addison-Wesley, Reading, MA, 1983.

Denning, D. E., and Denning, P. J., "Data Security," *Computing Surveys,* vol. 11, no. 3, September, 1979, pp. 227–250.

Fernandez, E. B., Summers, R. C., and Wood, C., *Database Security and Integrity,* Addison-Wesley, Reading, MA, 1981.

Hsiao, D. K., Kerr, D. S., and Madnick, S. E., *Computer Security,* Academic Press, New York, 1979.

King, J. M., *Evaluating Data Base Management Systems,* Van Nostrand Reinhold, New York, 1981.

Kroenke, D., *Database Processing,* 2nd ed., Science Research Associates, Chicago, IL, 1983.

Leiss, E. L., *Principles of Data Security,* Plenum Press, New York, 1982

Perry, W. E., *Ensuring Database Integrity,* Wiley, New York, 1983.

Ross, R. G., *Data Base Systems,* AMACOM, New York, 1978.

Verhofstad, J. S. M., "Recovery Techniques for Database Systems," *Computing Surveys,* vol. 10, no. 2, June, 1978, pp. 167–195.

Questions and Exercises

12.1.   In your own words, describe the different kinds of security threats to a company's data. Do you think the internal or the external (employees vs. outsiders) threats are more serious? Why?

12.2.   In your own words, describe the different kinds of security protection devices that can be employed to protect a company's data. Is any one of them more important than the others? Why?

12.3.   Make a list of the different kinds of security threats and security protection devices and indicate which devices protect against which threats.

12.4.   What are the security implications of having the computer generate random numbers as passwords (i.e., to have passwords that may be difficult for a person to remember)?

12.5.   What are the security implications of using fingerprints, signature, or voice, instead of passwords, for the system recognition scheme? What if the recognition device isn't always perfect?

12.6.   Devise a simple data encryption scheme. How long do you think it would take someone to break it?

12.7.   Devise a sample situation which demonstrates the problem of concurrent update without locks.

12.8.   Devise a sample situation which demonstrates the problem of deadlock.

12.9.   Can you envision a situation in which someone doing a simple retrieval should be locked out until an update operation has completed?

12.10.   If different queries that require multiple records from the same lock protected file always request those records in ascending order by unique key value, can deadlock ever occur? Why or why not?

12.11.   In your own words, describe the different kinds of destructive threats to a company's data.

12.12.   Of the different kinds of destructive threats to a company's data, which ones require forward recovery and which ones backward recovery?

12.13.   Consider the different items that can be written onto the journal for an update operation, including the before image of the data, the after image, and a description of the transaction itself. Which are needed for forward recovery and which for backward recovery? Explain.

12.14.   What factors do you think govern the frequency with which database copies are made for potential recovery operations? What are the pros and cons of making copies more or less frequently?

12.15.   Discuss the reasons for including auditing data in the journal. Are there disadvantages to doing so?

13

Data Administration

Introduction

Thus far in this book, we have been concerned primarily with the technical aspects of database and the database environment. But as with the components of any technology, they must be put to work by people, or they are no more than theory. Of course there are many people in the database oriented data processing milieu performing their individual jobs. Programmers write programs for specific applications with DBMS calls embedded in them. Designers design databases for individual applications. End users seek information with query languages. Systems programmers build DBMS control blocks.

But all of these people performing their individual functions for individual applications would create a chaotic environment without some sort of coordination. Some of this chaos would surface as redundant data. Some of it would cause performance problems on a shared CPU. Some of it would show up as software maintenance headaches due to a lack of standards in database design and program construction. The problem is not a matter of inability to perform on the part of the individual data processing personnel, but rather a lack of overall direction and control. It's somewhat like a symphony orchestra without a conductor. The individual musicians may be quite talented, but without someone to blend their work together, the result will be less than pleasing, Figure 13.1.

Figure 13.1. Data administration coordinates like the conductor of an orchestra.

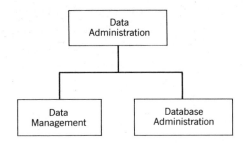

Figure 13.2. Data administration and its subfunctions.

In the late 1960s, as early DBMSs were starting to come into use, a few forward looking companies began to recognize the need for an independent group whose job it would be to manage the database environment. As the years went on, some of those groups gained some responsibility over data in nonDBMS files as well. In addition, some of them matured from a position of managing data only on an operational basis, to additionally performing strategic planning and other broader-based duties.

In this chapter we will explore this subfield of the database discipline, which is now generally called *data administration.* We will look at the advantages of managing data with a data administration group, the responsibilities that such groups have or might have, the job categories involved, the placement of the group in the data processing organization, the impact of data administration on the data processing organization, and directions for the future.

The terminology that we will follow was developed by the GUIDE International Inc. user group organization (GUIDE, 1977). The term *data administration* department refers to a group that is responsible for managing a firm's data as a valuable corporate resource. It is responsible for "developing and administering the policies, procedures, practice and plans for the definition, organization, protection, and efficient utilization of data within a corporate enterprise." As Figure 13.2 shows, data administration is comprised of two parts, which if the organization is large enough, may be arranged as two separate departments under the data administration umbrella. The two subfunctions are *data management* and *database administration.* The data management group is a planning and analysis function responsible for policy and standards setting, education, data resource control and accountability, and liaison support to systems analysts and programmers during application development. The database administration group is a more operationally oriented group responsible for the day-to-day monitoring of the database (and in some cases, of other data as well).

The database administration group carries out the policies set by the data management group at the operational level. We will explore the full range of responsibilities in more depth later. But note even at this early point, there is no hard and fast rule on what set of responsibilities a data administration organization or its component parts must perform to be considered successful or full-fledged.

Advantages of the Data Administration Approach

In Chapter 4 we made a case for the advantages of the database approach to data processing. In this section we will demonstrate the advantages of the data administration approach to managing data both in the database and nondatabase portions of the data processing environment.

Data as a Shared Corporate Resource

As we said earlier, data should be considered a critical corporate resource, together with money, plant and equipment, personnel, and so forth. Some people have suggested that data is the most important corporate resource because, by its very nature, it describes all of the others. The very existence of an organized accessible database tends to increase the amount of a company's business procedures that use data processing, leading to a more efficient company in general. And the large scale use of data and data processing can enhance a firm's competitive position by making it more responsive in the eyes of its customers and suppliers.

Data is also a shared resource. One of the basic tenets of the database approach is to reduce redundancy in the data in order to improve data integrity and reduce costs. One of the ways of reducing data redundancy is to have different users and applications that need the same data share it from one file, rather than each having their own copy in different physical files. In terms of data, another form of sharing is sharing the computer hardware that processes the data. A strain on those hardware resources caused by one application can adversely affect the performance of the other applications.

What all of this is leading to is simply this: Any shared corporate resource, including data, should be managed by an independent corporate group which, in the case of data, we call the data administration department. It makes little sense to have an important resource either not managed at all, or managed part-time and half-heartedly by some group that has other responsibilities too. It also makes little sense to have any one of the groups competing for the shared resource (say a particular application development department in this case) also managing it—the resource manager must obviously be impartial when a dispute arises.

Efficiency in Job Specialization

There are many functions involving the management of data, ranging from long range planning and standards setting to database design and database performance monitoring. (We will develop a list of them shortly.) Some of those, such as database design, for example, *must* be performed by *someone* in the data processing organization or no data processing will get done. For example, other functions, such as long-range planning, are somewhat optional depending on the degree of sophistication of the data processing environment. But one thing about all of the functions is certain: They all require a high degree of employee specialization for optimum results.

The question then becomes one of who among the data processing personnel should be responsible for performing these tasks. There are two basic possibilities. One is for the tasks to be divided among the various data processing workers whose usual responsibilities resemble most closely those needed to manage data. The lead programmers would do the database design, the systems programmers would do the database performance monitoring, and so on. The other possibility is for an independent data administration department to take the responsibility for them.

The latter choice is by far the better one because of the complexity of the tasks and because of how important a competent execution of the tasks is to the efficient running of the data processing environment. There are simply too many application developers, systems programmers, and other data processing workers, doing too many other things already, to expect that each of them can become as proficient at performing data specific tasks as people who become data administration specialists and do nothing but these tasks day in and day out. The argument is a very standard argument for job specialization in general, and it is as important in this situation as in any other.

Data Detail Lifted From Programmers

Related to the preceding section, but important enough to be treated separately, is the question of the relationship between data administration personnel and programmers. With the advent of application generators, "fourth generation" languages, and other means of circumventing or speeding up the programming process, the exact nature of the programmers' job is currently a matter of some debate. There is also an aspect of this debate that relates to data.

One of the traditional programming tasks has been writing code to describe the data structure. Perhaps the best and most well defined example of this is in the "Data Division" of COBOL programs. But who is best equipped to write COBOL Data Divisions or the equivalent in other languages, the application programmer or the data administrator? The argument here is that this is another data intensive area in which the data administrator will become a specialist, allowing the programmer to concentrate on the logic of the program, which should fundamentally be his or her area of greatest concern. Also here again, the specialization factor should produce fewer errors in the data description code.

Operational Management of Data

Earlier we looked at data as a resource from a rather high level. Another aspect of looking at data as a resource is to view it from a lower operational level. A data administration department is necessary for the proper management and control of data on an operational level.

To begin with, there isn't even a close second choice after data administration, as a place to put operational control of the data dictionary. Data administration is responsible for managing the company's data, and the data dictionary is the repository for information about what data exists, where it is, who has access to it, and so on. In addition, the independent data administration department is in the best position to see to it that the data dictionary continues to be an important and accurate source of information for all of the other data processing people who have to refer to it as well.

In the shared data environment there will always be some applications or users that depend on other applications or users to collect data and/or update the files on a regular or irregular basis. Clearly it is prudent to have an independent data administration group keep track of who is responsible for updating which files, and monitor whether they have kept to the expected schedule, for the benefit of all of the others who use these files.

There are a number of other data related tasks which should be managed by data administration specialists for the good of all who depend on the data. Data security, preventing the exposure of company data to the outside world, and data privacy, keeping sensitive data about customers, suppliers, and employees restricted, are two such issues. Also there is the question of managing (not necessarily performing all of the details of) backup and recovery when the database is damaged. And there are the related jobs of data documentation and data publicity: keeping a record of the details of the data environment (e.g., through the data dictionary), and letting the rest of the firm know what data is available for use in the shared data environment.

Data Administration Responsibilities

As we said earlier, there is no right or wrong in terms of a required set of duties that legitimizes a data administration department. Similarly there is some flexibility in dividing the duties between data management and database administration. The set of duties assigned to data administration and the breakdown between the data management and database administration subfunctions will vary with the maturity of the organization and with the technical and political atmosphere of the data processing organization and of the company as a whole.

In this section we will explore a wide range of data administration responsibilities, generally following the GUIDE International division between data management and database administration. Remember data management is the planning and analysis side of data administration, while database administration is the operational side.

Data Management Responsibilities

Data Planning. With data being treated as a critical shared resource, care must be taken in planning for its future.

The most important aspect of planning in this regard is the determination of what data will be needed for future application development, and how that data should be integrated both with its own components and with existing data. There are a number of methodologies that have been developed to do such data planning, an example of which is IBM's BSP, which we discussed previously. Such methodologies take into account the business processes that the company performs as part of its normal operations and prioritizes them for future computerization. While they generally operate at a high "strategic" level, and may not get into the details of individual fields and database design, they do provide a broad roadmap to work from.

Related to strategic data planning is the matter of what hardware and software will be needed to support the company's data processing in the future. Large data processing organizations usually have people who take this matter on as a full-time job, but clearly they should take input from the data management people regarding how much data there will be and what sort of processing will be done with it. The questions involved range from such relatively straightforward matters as how many disk packs will we need to contain the data, to broader issues of how much raw computing power will we need to support the overall data processing environment.

A third form of data management planning is the issue of how the data dictionary should be put to use. This involves what data should be stored in the dictionary, what uses the dictionary should be put to, who should interact with the dictionary and how, and on what kind of schedule all of this should take place over time.

As a company builds more and more of its data processing around the database concept, it is still faced with a large number of existing applications which predated the introduction of database. So another aspect of data management planning involves the migration of these applications into the database environment: Which applications should be migrated, on what schedule, and how should the data needed by them be accommodated by the database?

Database Standards.   In order to reduce errors, improve performance, enhance the ability of one data processing worker to understand the work done by another, and in general to provide a higher degree of coordination in the data processing environment, it is incumbent upon the data management function to set standards regarding data and its use. One example of standards is the control of the way that field names, file names, and other data related names are formed. Normally they must convey as much meaning in as few characters as possible and be approved by the data management people. Another example is insisting on consistency in the way the programs that access the database are written, especially in regard to the way that the database call instructions are written. Care here can help to prevent database call related performance problems, as well as to ease maintenance by having standard, readily understood instructions.

Liaison to Systems Analysts and Programmers.   As the liaison to application developers, the data management people (who are often called "data analysts" in this role) serve a key function. They are responsible for providing support to the systems analysts and programmers in all matters concerning the data needed by that application. During the systems analysis phase of application development that support may include help in determining what data is needed for the application, and will also include help in finding out which of the data items needed for the application already exist in the active database. Another form of assistance to application developers is helping them to construct program data descriptions, such as COBOL Data Division specifications.

Another aspect of such liaison activity, which is really a topic in itself, is the question of database design. There is no doubt that the data analysts must be involved in database design at some level, but the decision of what that precise level of involvement should be is dependent on a number of factors. In a data processing environment in which the data administration organization is very strong and in which there is a significant amount of data sharing among different applications and different functional areas of the company, the data analysts may do all of the database design work themselves. Here again, they can stand as an impartial group creating the best design for the overall good of all of the sharing users. The other choice is for the application developers to do the database design with either active consultation by the data analysts, or approval responsibility after the fact by the data analysts. In the active consultation role, the data analysts lend their expertise to the effort, as well as determine how the new data should mesh with data in the existing database, if there is to be such a merging. In the approval role, the application developers (usually the lead programmers for this activity) design the database. But since the data administration people are ultimately responsible for database performance, they must have approval capability since a poor database design can not only adversely affect the performance of the applications using that database, but can also slow the performance of other applications, using other databases, which run on the same CPU.

Training.   The data management people are responsible for training all those in the company who have a reason to understand the database concept, at a variety of levels. Management personnel have to know why database is good for the company and for their individual functions specifically. Users must understand why their previously separate data files are now being shared with others, and why the data is still secure and private. Of course, application developers must be given substantial training in how to work in the database environment, including database concepts, database standards, how to write DBMS calls in their programs, possibly how to do database design, how to use the data dictionary to their advantage, and in general, what services they can expect to be provided by the data administration department. And of course, the data management function must provide education for the data administration department's own personnel.

Arbitration of Disputes and Usage Authorization.   To introduce this heading, we should spend a moment on the question of data "ownership."

Who "owns" a piece of data or a file? To be technical about it, since data is a resource of value to the company, the data "belongs" to the company's owners or stockholders. But in practical terms, data is often controlled by the user or primary user of it. Some day we may evolve to such an advanced level of data sharing that it will no longer be clear who the owner of some individual data is, and the responsibility will fall to data administration. But for now, data is usually identified with a particular user, and the data administration group acts as "custodian" of the data in the sense of providing security, backup, performance monitoring, and other such services.

If a new application requires the use of existing data, then it is the job of data management to act as an intermediary and approach the owner of the data with the request for data sharing. The owner can authorize this sharing, and then the data management people can instruct the database administration people to allow the new application access to the data. If there is a dispute over such data sharing, then the data management group acts as an arbitrator between the disagreeing parties. Incidentally the data management group may also find itself acting as arbitrator between two database users who are sharing the same CPU and vying for better performance.

Documentation and Publicity.   Using the data dictionary as its primary tool, the data management function is responsible for documenting the nature of the data oriented environment. This includes what data exists, what files, programs, reports, and so forth there are, what people have access to these items, and so forth. Some of the information may be input by application development personnel and database administration personnel, but the data management group should be able to provide an overall picture of it.

As a related issue, the data management group should perform a publicity function, informing potential users of what data already exists in the database. Knowing what data exists might encourage people to automate more of their work and to integrate their work more directly with related business processes which are already automated.

Data Environment Management.   Again using the data dictionary, the data management function must stand ready to respond to any question about how the data oriented environment works. With the dictionary's interrelation capability, data management must always be ready to say who has access to which files, which files are used to generate which reports, which programs use which files (known as "change impact assessment" because a change in a file can affect a program that uses it), and the significance of all other meaningful combinations of data processing entities.

Database Administration Responsibilities

Usage and Security Monitoring. Database administration personnel are responsible for monitoring the database environment on an active constant basis. In doing so they will appear to act as a cross between computer operators and systems programmers, and in fact, they are often referred to as "database systems programmers."

One of the tasks involved is to keep track of who is accessing the data in the database at any moment. Usually there are software utilities that enable such personnel to perform this function. Monitoring the users of the database environment is really done from several perspectives. One is the matter of security: making sure that only authorized personnel access the data. This includes the function of instructing the system to allow new users to access the database, as ordered by data management personnel in conjunction with the data owners. Another perspective is the need to maintain records on the amount of use the various users make of the database. This can have implications in future load balancing and performance optimizing work, and may also be used in allocating system costs among the various users and applications. And a related concern is database auditing. Even assuming that only authorized users have accessed the database, there are reasons involving accounting and error correction that require a record of who has accessed and who has modified which data items. Incidentally if that function is to be performed, the tool that allows it to be accomplished is a log, similar to the one used for backup and recovery. Depending on the nature of the auditing, this log may have to record all simple data accesses, as well as all data modifications.

Performance Monitoring and Load Balancing. Another monitoring function performed by database administration is that of performance monitoring. Using utility programs, the database systems programmers can gauge the performance of the various executing database programs. This activity has a number of implications. For one thing it is important to know how fast the various applications are executing as an obvious data processing management function. This information is also pertinent to future hardware and software plans. Also, depending on the characteristics of the DBMS and the system it is running under, this information may be used to redistribute the database application load among different CPUs or among different memory regions within a system. Finally, performance information can be used to ferret out inefficient applications which may be candidates for re-design.

An additional note is that the database systems programmer must interface with the data processing organization's regular staff of systems programmers. The latter will usually still have certain DBMS related responsibilities, such as installing new releases of the DBMS as they come out. The regular systems programmers may also have performance and troubleshooting responsibilities, which may overlap with those of the database systems programmers'. The net of this is that it greatly facilitates matters if the two groups get along well with each other and can effectively work together as need be.

DBMS Troubleshooting.   Inevitably there will be a time when a DBMS application fails during execution. The reason can range from a bug in the application code to a hardware or system software failure. The question is, who do the users call when it happens? In a strongly controlled environment, the data administration personnel should be the troubleshooting interface. (Note that while some may believe that this heading belongs with the data management side of data administration, we place it here on the database administration side.) In practice depending on the complexity and the nature of the problem, a variety of data administration people may become involved.

The key to the troubleshooting operation is making an assessment of what went wrong and coordinating the appropriate personnel needed to investigate and fix it. This may include systems programmers, operators, application programmers, and the data administration people themselves.

Data Dictionary Operations.   The database administration group is responsible for the operations, as opposed to the planning aspects, of the data dictionary. This includes developing ways of interfacing with the dictionary data in terms of input and output techniques. It also means providing dictionary access to others, such as systems analysts, generating periodic dictionary reports as required by management, and providing management with answers to ad hoc questions about the data and the data processing environment.

Interface with Computer Operators.   The independent computer operations function is still very much in evidence in the data administration environment. As always, computer operators start or restart the system as needed, mount tapes and disks, perform backup and recovery operations,

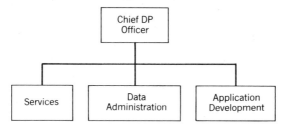

Figure 13.3. Data administration reports to chief data processing officer.

and so forth. One of the jobs of database administration is to work with the operators, giving them instruction and training on how to do their jobs in the atmosphere created by the particular DBMS in place and by the needs of the application set. For example, these tasks can range from how to start jobs in the DBMS to how to execute a recovery operation after a system failure.

Data Administration Organizational Placement

Where does the data administration organization fit in to the data processing or for that matter the entire corporate organization? We can begin to answer the question with a philosophical and somewhat futuristic thought: Are data and data processing two separate affairs or part of the same discipline? Traditionally data has been part of data processing. But if we are now thinking of data as a critical corporate resource, isn't it an independent issue, with its processing a separate concern?

Before we get too carried away, let's take a look at the realities of data and data administration in today's corporations. In the vast majority of companies today, the data administration group is part of the data processing department. There are three basic reporting paths for data administration. One is for data administration to report directly to the chief data processing officer, Figure 13.3. A second is for data administration to report to a manager of services or technical support who in turn reports either to the head of application development or to the chief data processing officer, Figure 13.4. The third choice is for data administration to report directly to the overall head of application development, Figure 13.5. The data administration to services to chief data processing officer route is the most common of the three in practice. One indisputable truth is that since the data administration function is in charge of a critical, shared resource, it must not be under the control of any of the corporate groups that are com-

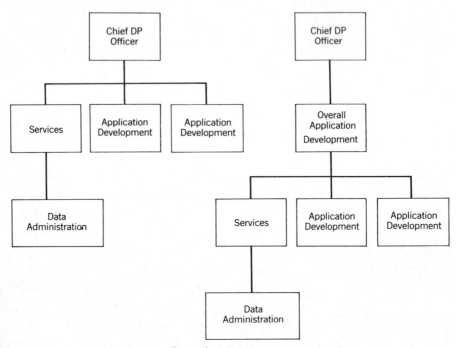

Figure 13.4. Data administration reports to services.

peting for the resource. Thus placing data administration under one of several parallel application development departments is unacceptable because data administration must be impartial in allocating resources and settling disputes among those competing for the data and for performance under the DBMS.

But there are significant variations to this theme, particularly among large firms and firms with very active data administration groups, and these variations will become more widespread as time goes on and both data administration and data processing activity increase. The most common such variation is for a company to have multiple data administration groups. This often happens when a large company has independent data processing organizations supporting either different divisions, or operations in different geographic locations, or both, and each one of these different data processing organizations develops its own data administration group. In that case, there may or may not also be a higher level data administration function reporting in at the highest levels of the data processing organization, or even outside of the data processing organization entirely. This higher level data processing group may vary from a corporate data standards setting and loose coordinating group, to a powerful group which can dic-

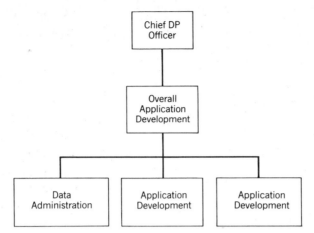

Figure 13.5. Data administration reports to application development.

tate specific procedures and even common applications to the individual sites.

Data Administration Organizational Impact

The data administration approach to the management of data cannot be implemented in full overnight. It inherently involves changes in the job responsibilities of application developers and others and changes in data processing procedures in general. New data administration departments are likely to encounter resistance from managers who do not understand the concept, from application developers who are naturally suspicious of changes in their job responsibilities and in new ways of producing pro-grams, and from users who are concerned about the concept of sharing their data with other users. Historically we have seen that there is a learning curve associated with data administration for all concerned, and that suc-cessful data administration groups develop gradually in assuming more responsibilities.

How does the data processing environment differ after the successful introduction and development of data administration? With its stress on planning, data administration creates an awareness of the interrelationship of corporate data. It causes other data processing workers to study more carefully the business processes that they are trying to automate. Systems analysis is taken more seriously than before and, hopefully, management devotes more of the application development period to it.

As more of the data intensive work is absorbed by data administration, application programmers can concentrate on the logic aspects of their programming tasks. This, plus the improved database designs and more accurate program data specifications produced by the data administration specialists, leads to a more error free application development process and a more solid final program. Also the quality and consistency of the data in the databases improves as redundancy decreases and integrity improves.

In general, the increased emphasis of data as a resource puts the company's entire data processing operation in a new light in the eyes of corporate management. Management realizes that data is an asset that can be used to further the company's competitive position in its marketplaces. More emphasis is placed on data processing and a greater focus is placed on the data processing department's ability to automate more of the corporation's business processes.

Data Administration and New Computing Technologies

Recently there have been several new developments in data processing technology that are all somewhat related to each other and to the data administration concept. One development is the personal computer. Another is the so-called "fourth generation language". These provide a higher level of application development than that of standard languages such as COBOL or PASCAL, suitable for use by programming or non-programming oriented personnel. A third development is the concept known as the "information center", which provides programmers and non-programmers alike with access to computing through fourth generation languages, assistance with the use of personal computers, and other tools which avoid the normal data processing application development process.

The relationship of the information center and its tools to data administration is clear. Fourth generation languages, personal computers, and other "user friendly" computer tools require the appropriate data to get any work done. A potential user of one of these tools who can approach the data administration department and get access to data that he or she would otherwise have to laboriously collect has a tremendous head start in getting the job done. And that should come as no surprise at this point. Data is a resource which should be managed as such and which should be made available to those in the company who have a legitimate need for it. The information center, fourth generation languages, and personal computers provide the *means* for a wider variety of people in the corporation to use the *data* managed by the data administration function to further the company's goals.

Information Resource Management

Speculating about the future of data administration is an exercise which quickly turns into speculating about the future of data processing. Once again we have to ask, "Which came first, the 'data' or the 'processing'?" Historically we have been concerned about the processing almost to the exclusion of the data. This ordering has slowly started to change with the advent of increasingly widespread use of DBMSs.

Already we can find chief data processing officers with titles like Vice President of Information Resources. The future may see this spirit trickle down from the highest level through the entire data processing organization to the point that data is recognized as the critical concern and its processing is seen as more of a mechanical necessity than an end in itself.

As part of that transformation we will see more data and applications migrated to the database environment. This data and more of the non-database data will fall under the control or influence of the data administration organization. More kinds of data, such as pictorial data, will be held in the corporate databases. There will be increased growth towards data sharing, reduced redundancy, and a well planned and integrated corporate database. We will approach and reach an environment that we can truly call *Information Resource Management*.

References

Durell, W. R., *Data Administration*, McGraw-Hill, New York, 1985.

Gillenson, M. L., "The State of Practice of Data Administration—1981," *ACM Communications*, vol. 25, no. 10, October, 1982, pp. 699–706.

Gillenson, M. L., "Trends in Data Administration: 1981–1983," IBM Systems Research Institute Technical Report #TR73-027, New York, January, 1984.

Gillenson, M. L., and Goldberg, R., *Strategic Planning, Systems Analysis, and Database Design*, Wiley, New York, 1984.

GUIDE International Corp., "Establishing the Data Administration Function," Chicago, 1977.

GUIDE International Corp., "Data Administration Methodology," Chicago, 1978.

Lyon, J. K., *The Database Administrator*, Wiley, New York, 1976.

Martin, J., *Managing the Data-Base Environment*, Prentice-Hall, Englewood Cliffs, NJ, 1983.

McCririck, I. B., and Goldstein, R. C., "What Do Data Administrators Really Do?," *Datamation*, vol. 26, no. 8, pp. 131–134, August, 1980.

Ross, R. G., *Data Dictionaries and Data Administration*, AMACOM, New York, 1981.

Weldon, J. - L., *Data Base Administration*, Plenum Press, New York, 1981.

Questions and Exercises

13.1. Choose one of the traditional corporate resources (e.g., money, plant and equipment, personnel, and so on) and outline the corporate organization in place to manage it.

13.2. Choose one of the traditional corporate resources (e.g., money, plant and equipment, personnel, and so on) and describe the effects on the corporation if there was no group responsible for managing it.

13.3. Describe the importance of sharing data from a management point of view.

13.4. How might data be shared between the

a. Personnel and equipment management departments

b. Accounting and manufacturing departments

c. Research and manufacturing departments

d. Accounting and data processing departments

13.5. Convince a company to create a data administration department.

13.6. Describe how the data administration function might change the jobs of others in the data processing department.

13.7. Outline the responsibilities of the *data management* portion of the data administration department. Which of these responsibilities do you think is the most important? Why?

13.8. How should the data planning function be coordinated with other corporate planning functions?

13.9. How would you respond to a programmer or systems analyst who considers the data management role as an intrusion into his or her profession?

13.10. Consider the distinction between data ownership and data custodianship. How comfortable would you feel as the data administration person responsible for arbitrating disputes concerning the sharing of data?

13.11. Outline the responsibilities of the *database administration* portion of the data administration department. Which of these responsibilities do you think is the most important? Why?

13.12. How would you respond to a programmer or systems analyst who considers the database administration role as an intrusion into his or her profession?

13.13. Describe the division of labor concerning the data dictionary between the data management and database administration personnel.

13.14. List a set of arguments for placing the data administration function

  a. High in the data processing organization
  b. Outside of the data processing organization
  c. Partially inside of the data processing organization and partially outside of it

13.15. Describe the impact of the introduction of the data administration group in the data processing organization.

13.16. Do you think data administration should be responsible for the data kept in a company's micro or personal computers? Why or why not?

13.17. Do you think that ultimately the rest of the data processing organization will report to the data administration organization? Why or why not?

14

Evolving Topics

Introduction

In this chapter we introduce three topics in database which are relatively new, considered relatively experimental, or both. A *database machine* is a hardware solution to improving performance in the database environment. *Distributed database* denotes the concept of a database split into parts which are stored at different nodes on a distributed computing network. *Database on personal computers* points out the special problems encountered when trying to implement the concepts of database on small computing machines.

Database Machines

The Database Machine Concept

Thus far in this book, our discussion of database has centered on software and data, as opposed to hardware. Except for the early description of disk devices, we've talked exclusively about database management systems, data dictionaries, data concepts, data structures, and so on. But there is a new branch of the field of database that is concerned with specialized hardware. This branch has come to be called *database machines*.

As we shall see in discussing the various approaches, work in database machines has proceeded in several different directions. The motivations have included:

To free the host processor of its data access responsibility

To improve performance in the database oriented environment

To permit access to data by multiple host processors

To improve data security and integrity

Let's take a look at the approaches, discuss some of their advantages and disadvantages, and then conclude with the experience to date.

Database Machine Approaches

Backend Conventional Processor.   Figure 14.1 shows a typical database environment, in which the host computer is responsible for running the DBMS. The responsibility for the host computer includes holding all or part of the DBMS in its main memory, processing requests for data stored in the database and communicating these requests to the disk devices via

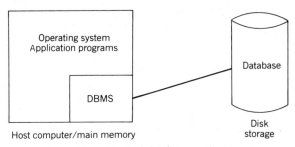

Figure 14.1. Typical database environment.

their controllers. Some people have reasoned that if these functions were moved to a separate device, the host computer could spend more of its time performing other processing duties, and the data requests could be satisfied more efficiently.

Figure 14.2 shows a database environment that employs a backend conventional processor as a database machine. A physically separate, small(er) conventional computer has been placed between the host computer and the disk storage medium. This database machine is simply a conventional computer configured to perform only one function: to run the DBMS. It takes requests for data from the host computer in the form of either calls from a program or ad hoc queries from a terminal, translates these requests into data access commands, retrieves the data from the disk storage medium, and returns the data to the host computer.

Associative Memory. A hardware solution has been proposed for the large number of compare operations that are an inherent aspect of relational DBMSs. The idea is to design special purpose data storage hardware that is capable of performing a given operation on different parts of a file in the database simultaneously. For example, the value of a given field in every record of a file may have to be compared against a specified value.

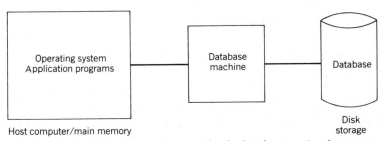

Figure 14.2. Database environment with a backend conventional processor.

This kind of operation is particularly common in the relational DBMS environment. So wouldn't it be desirable, from a performance point of view, to be able to test the field in several of these records in tandem and handle the results accordingly, rather than process them one at a time from the beginning to the end of the file?

Associative memory devices, also known as "content addressable parallel processors", can be constructed in several ways. As an example, imagine a disk drive with a fixed read/write head *on every track of every cylinder*. Also imagine a microprocessor incorporated into every one of these read/write heads. When a data access request is made involving the kind of compare operation that we just described, each of those microprocessors can simultaneously be given directions to perform the operation. Conceivably if the processing speed of those microprocessors is fast enough relative to the rotation speed of the disk, then every record in a file that's stored on the disk pack could be examined in a single, complete rotation. Other variations on the theme might have a smaller number of microprocessors covering larger portions of the stored file. For example, there might be one microprocessor per cylinder, with all of the records on the cylinder being examined by the microprocessor in several revolutions of the disk pack.

Figure 14.3 shows two possible arrangements for the incorporation of an associative memory into the database environment. Figure 14.3*a* suggests that there is not a separate database processor as such, but simply that the secondary memory is of the associative type. Figure 14.3*b* indicates that there is a separate database processor, which may or may not be part of the same physical unit as the associative memory (the reason for the dashed outline).

Other Database Machine Approaches.   There is no clear agreement among those working in the field as to exactly what does and does not constitute a database machine. It's safe to say that everyone considers the two approaches discussed previously to fall within the database machine concept. Some think that these are the only two approaches, others would add to that group from among the following devices or arrangements.

First there is the "network node". The idea here is to have a database machine serve as a node in a distributed computing network. The database that is controlled by the database machine is made available to whichever processors in the network are authorized to use it.

Second is the "storage hierarchy". A series of data storage devices is arranged so that at one end of the series is a relatively small amount of very fast and very expensive storage, while at the other end is a relatively

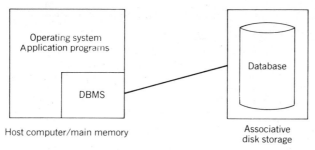

Figure 14.3a.   Database environments: associative memory without a separate database processor.

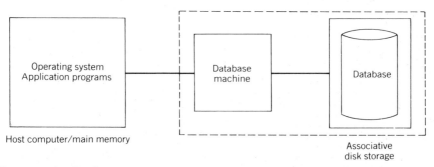

Figure 14.3.b.   Database environments: associative memory with a separate database processor.

large amount of comparatively slow, but comparatively cheap storage. Most of the data in the database is stored at the slow cheap end of the series, but the data that is active for a particular application percolates up to (is copied to) the faster end of the spectrum for rapid retrieval. Actually one could argue that the usual main memory—disk secondary memory combination is a limited kind of storage hierarchy. A bit more apropos is the main memory—disk device—mass storage system sequence.

Finally some practitioners consider a computer system such as the IBM System/38, which we discussed in Chapter 9, to be a database machine. The use of the term here refers not to the features that we've been discussing, but rather to the overall database oriented environment that such computers are designed to support.

Database Machines Analysis

Advantages.   A wide range of advantages have been suggested as justification for the use of database machines. Many of them are speculative or debatable. Some depend on the relative costs of rapidly changing hard-

while others depend on the efficiency of the implementation of the particular database machine approach.

The most prominent reason for installing a database machine is to improve system performance. Unfortunately the fact that with a database machine a new level of communication is added between the database and the host computer, will very likely slow down the response time for any one particular database query. Any improvement in performance will come from the fact that operations involving more than one query can go on simultaneously, with the host computer and database machine operating independently. Of course this brings up the point that the only way that a database machine makes sense in the first place is if the host computer is being used mostly in support of DBMSs and the queries being processed by them. Another point about performance improvement is that a sufficiently sophisticated associative processor database machine will, hopefully, speed up the kinds of search operations that we described earlier, which is after all what it is intended to do.

The fact that the database machine performs work that used to be done by the host computer frees the host in two ways. It frees the host from most or all of its database processing responsibilities, including processing queries and maintaining files, allowing it to devote that processing time to other uses. And it frees the primary memory space that contained DBMS modules during execution.

A database machine, and the data that it controls, can be shared by multiple host computers. Similarly the database machine can be the data node on a distributed processing network. In fact the host computers and their software need not be of any one particular configuration if the database machine has the capability of translating queries of different formats into a common form for processing.

The hardware in the database machine can be specialized, there being no need for items such as floating point processors. And the hardware can be of more advanced technology than that of the host, permitting an improvement in efficiency without the host having to be replaced. And conceivably, the acquisition of a new larger host computer can be postponed because of new found capacity in the existing one due to the off loading of some work to the database machine.

Additional arguments involve data security, integrity, and recovery. Since the data controlled by a database machine can only be accessed through a single interface, the security effort can be highly focused. There is no fear of someone skirting the DBMS to get to the data, as there is in the usual arrangement. Of course there still must be a way of protecting against an unauthorized person appearing to be authorized, and coming into the database machine through the standard interface. Along the same lines, the integrity of the data can be better assured. As for recovery, a failure in the host computer is better insulated from the database, although failures in the database machine must still be contended with.

Disadvantages. The counter argument to the performance advantage has already been stated as the additional level of communication necessary for a single query. In addition, there are other issues concerning the fact that two different processors (the host and the database machine) exist in this arrangement. The two-processor approach can mean increased complexity and cost in development and maintenance, increased training and support, and a possible decrease in reliability because there are two machines that can fail. And if the two machines are manufactured by different companies, the coordination between the two could be a problem. Similarly we talked about the advantages of multiple languages sending queries of different formats to the database machine, but that can be a significant problem to work out too. In fact, even the single query format from a single host can require a significant effort in conversion to a form that the database machine understands.

Some other negative arguments include: Since hardware in general is getting progressively cheaper, the emphasis in the database machine approach about saving money through a better use of hardware may be fruitless. In fact, it may be simpler and cheaper to upgrade the main computer than to introduce a database machine. The two-processor host computer—database machine approach is less flexible than a general multiprocessor approach because the specialization of the database machine restricts the capability to load balance among the different processors. Finally if several host computers are all sharing and accessing a database machine simultaneously, the flow of information into and out of the database machine could become a bottleneck that could slow the speed of all of these processors.

Conclusion. At the time of this writing there are several database machines on the market and others in various stages of experimentation, representing all of the major categories. There are those who think that they are worthwhile, those who are skeptical of their value, those who think that they work well only in certain application situations and not in others, and those who think that further breakthroughs in hardware speed and cost (particularly for the associative processor case) will be necessary before they can come into their own. Measured by amount of use, database machines are not a significant factor in commercial database practice today, but may become more so in the future.

Distributed Databases

The Distributed Database Concept

The usual centralized form of computer system design consists of a single processor together with its associated data storage devices. The system offers data processing capabilities to users who are located either at the same site or, through terminals, at geographically dispersed sites. While the management of the system and its data can be controlled in a straightforward manner in this arrangement, there are potential problems with it as well. For example, if the central site goes down, then everyone is blocked from using the computer until it comes back up again. Also the communications costs from the terminals to the central site can be expensive. One solution to such problems, and an alternative design to the centralized processing concept, is distributed processing.

In a distributed processing or distributed computing system, computers located at different geographic sites can communicate with each other to facilitate a variety of processing modes. For example, an actual application task can be shipped to a free processor, instead of having to wait for a busy processor. But many of the aspects of distributed computing directly involve the ways in which the data is stored on the network and accessed by the application programs. As a result, an entire subfield of distributed processing—and of database—has come into being and has come to be known as *distributed data* or *distributed database.*

Since distributed database is a state of the art topic, it is difficult to come up with a precise definition of it. Broadly stated, it is the arrangement in which data at different sites (or nodes) on a distributed computing system (or network) can be accessed by programs or users at other nodes on the network. And there is a wide variety of ways in which that dispersed data might be processed.

At one end of the spectrum is a distributed system which permits a program executed at one node to access data at another node. Such systems exist today as commercial realities. For example, DL/I databases at nodes in a distributed network can be accessed from other nodes through a feature called Multiple Systems Coupling (MSC) in IMS/DC environments, or through a feature called Intersystem Communication (ISC) in CICS environments. In the case of MSC, a program at one node orders the execution of a program at the node at which the required data resides and that second program performs the data access. The results are then shipped back to the original requesting node. In the case of ISC, a program at one nodes directly requests data from the DL/I database at another node on the network.

At the other end of the spectrum is a far more complex situation in which files required to satisfy a query that involves a relational join reside at different nodes on the network. In one way or another the data is brought together (or the query is split apart or both) the join is performed, and the result is sent back to the node that issued the query. Furthermore the person issuing the query does not have to be aware that the data resides at different nodes or be aware of how the join is accomplished. Work on such systems is at this point considered experimental.

Some people in the field have attempted to distinguish between the simpler and more complex cases just described by referring to the former as "distributed data" and the latter as "distributed database." While such a distinction may be useful, it is difficult to place each of the many variations into one bucket or the other, and so we shall not pursue this distinction any further here. What we will do is approach the subject of distributed database in the "traditional" fashion, by describing some of the major variations of the design options with which workers in the field have been experimenting.

Specifically we will look at some design choices for storing data on the network, some ways to handle the problem of updating data on the network if it is stored redundantly in more than one location, some choices for satisfying a query that requires data stored at two or more locations on the network, and some ideas concerning catalogs that give the systems information about which data is stored at which nodes.

The Placement of the Data

Most work on advanced concepts in distributed database has been done within the context of the relational approach to database management. So in the discussion of data placement in this section, and in the succeeding sections on this topic, this is the approach that we will assume is in use. Thus the question of data placement in the distributed network becomes one of deciding which relational files will be placed at which nodes of the

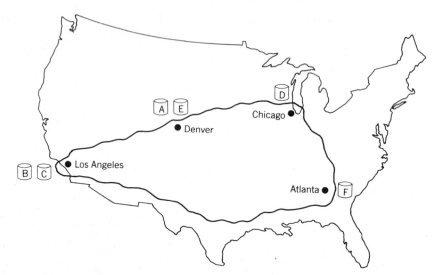

Figure 14.4.   Distributed data with no duplication.

network. As we look at the different data placement possibilities, keep in mind that a central issue involves whether files can be replicated at different nodes or not.

Perhaps the simplest way of distributing data on a network is to place specific files at specific nodes, with no data duplication. Figure 14.4 shows such an arrangement. The advantage here is that when some data must be updated, the update takes place at only one site which eases data integrity control. One disadvantage is that if a node goes down, the data at that node is inaccessible to everyone on the network. Also depending on the nature of the data and the applications, there may be a great expenditure in cost and communication time if the various nodes often require data situated at other nodes. One could argue that this arrangement defeats much of the purpose of having a distributed system in the first place.

The arrangement in Figure 14.5 goes to the other extreme. All of the files are duplicated at every node. Accessing data is certainly fast and cheap, since every data retrieval operation can be done right at the node that requested it. But the amount of storage space taken up and the problems associated with having to perform data updates at every node on the network (since every node has a copy of every file) make this scheme unrealistic for virtually all application situations.

Figure 14.6 shows a more useful variation of the data duplication concept. All of the files are stored at one of the nodes (Los Angeles), while some of the files are each also stored at *one* other node. The choice of where to

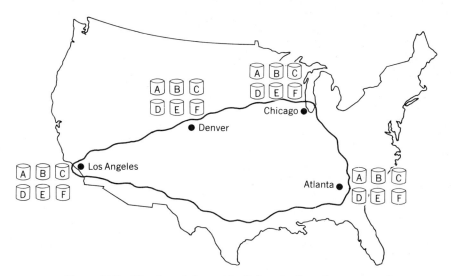

Figure 14.5. Distributed data with all data duplicated at every node.

store the files, other than at the node that contains all of them, is done on a "locality of reference" criterion. That is, they are stored at the sites that access them most frequently, which reduces the communications costs incurred by accessing data at nonlocal nodes of the network. But if the data required is not at the site requesting it, there is no doubt about which node to look at for the data. It will always be at the node that has a copy of all

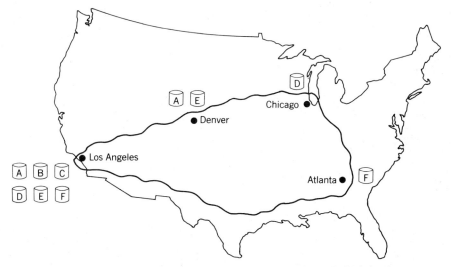

Figure 14.6. Distributed data with one node having a copy of all of the data.

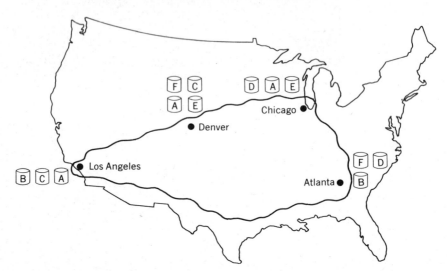

Figure 14.7.   Distributed data with files duplicated at selected nodes.

of the files. Since there is data duplication, even though it is limited, there is still the issue of updating duplicate data at more than one (in this case exactly two) nodes. Also if the node that has all of the data goes down, then much of the work on the network might grind to a halt. For example, if Chicago needs data in file C, and Los Angeles is down, it is out of luck.

The most flexible of the arrangements is shown in Figure 14.7. Files can be duplicated at as many nodes as makes sense based on the application requirements. Thus a file that is used almost exclusively at one site only might be stored only at that site. A file that is referenced frequently by programs or users at several sites, or for which there is a critical requirement that it be available at *some* site at *all* times (the problem being the possibility of sites going down) might be duplicated at several sites. The flexibility of this scheme makes it the most attractive for research of all of the possibilities. But while it has the advantages that data duplication in a distributed system brings, it also has the inherent problems. These problems, including updating duplicate data at separate sites, gathering data at separate sites needed in a single join operation, and finding data that is only stored on a few sites in a distributed network will be discussed in the succeeding sections.

As a final point in this section, note that we have been assuming that whether or not we duplicate the files at separate nodes on the network, each file or copy of a file remains whole. Another related issue is breaking files into pieces and storing different pieces at different nodes. Researchers have suggested dividing files horizontally, placing some records of a file at one node and other records at other nodes, and dividing them vertically, placing some fields of all (or some) of the records at one node and other fields of all (or some) of the records at other nodes. Clearly this is an even more complex proposition.

Integrity: Updating and Controlling Duplicate Data

In the last section, we made the point that having data duplicated at selected nodes of the distributed network is fundamental to the distributed database approach, we also noted that it introduces some significant problems. Let's take a closer look at them.

With files duplicated at several network sites, updating data becomes tricky. Look again at the distributed network in Figure 14.7. Let's say that a user at a particular site, for example Chicago, wants to update a particular piece of data in, for example file A. First of all the system must find a copy of the file involved. If the file is stored at the user's site (as it is in this example), fine, otherwise the system must find a copy of the file at another site. (In the more advanced distributed database thinking, the data locating operation is transparent to the user.) In either case, we might reasonably expect the system to update the data in that one copy of the file (file A at Chicago) and then update the same data in the other copies of that file around the network (at Denver and Los Angeles). But what if Denver or Los Angeles are down at the time; or what if the entire system goes down after some copies of the file have been updated, but before the rest are? The result will be an integrity problem, with different values for what should be the same data in different copies of the file at the different sites at which they are located.

A related problem can be described as follows. In Chapter 12 we discussed the concurrency problem involving two users attempting to update the same piece of data at the same time. As significant a problem as that is, its solution in Chapter 12 was at least containable by the fact that for each susceptible piece of data, that piece of data only existed in one file in the central database. In the distributed database case, with duplicated files at different sites, we can still have the situation of two users trying to update the same piece of data at the same time. But now one user might be accessing a copy of the data at one site to update it, while the other user might be accessing a different copy of the data at another site to update it. Clearly this compounds the problem significantly. For example, what if

the distributed database system is used for an airlines reservation application. Assume that there is one seat left on a particular flight on a particular
date and that the information is correctly indicated in each copy of the
appropriate file, say, file A at Chicago, Denver, and Los Angeles in Figure
14.7. It is entirely possible that salesagents in two different cities, say Chicago and Denver, may try to sell the seat to two different customers simultaneously. If the system processes the Chicago request against the Chicago copy of the file, and the Denver request against the Denver copy of
the file, then each salesagent will sell the same seat before the system has
had a chance to update all of the other copies of the file around the network.
The copy of file A at Denver will be unaware that the copy of file A at
Chicago has decremented its seat count from 1 to 0, and vice versa. By the
time each site informs the other of the update, it's too late, and the seat
has been sold twice.

Let's take a look at some of the proposed methods for overcoming these
potential integrity problems. One method is based on an extension of the
locking concept which we discussed in Chapter 12. To refresh the point,
the idea in locking is for one user to gain control over whatever data he
or she is updating so that no one else can access or modify it (depending
on the situation) until he or she is through with it. So in the distributed
update case, the system would attempt to lock all of the copies of a file at
all of the sites at which they are located before allowing the data to be
updated in any one copy of that file.

One way of performing that multisite update is with a sequence of operations that has been called "global locking". The sites must not only be
given orders on locking, they must acknowledge these orders as well. Note
the following sequence (continuing with the use of Figure 14.7 as an example):

1. One node, say Chicago, issues a command to the other nodes on
   the network to lock a file, say file A. It also locks its own copy of
   file A.
2. Denver and Los Angeles, which also have copies of that file, lock
   their copies of file A (as soon as they become free of any other locks)
   and so inform Chicago.
3. Once Chicago is told that the copies of file A at Denver and Los
   Angeles are locked (and notes that its own copy is locked) it issues
   the order to perform the update to all of the copies of file A.
4. Chicago updates its copy of file A and so do Denver and Los Angeles,
   which inform Chicago that they have performed the update.

5. Chicago then releases the lock on its copy of file A and informs Denver and Los Angeles to do the same with the locks on their copies.

Unfortunately, in addition to having large communication costs associated with it, this procedure can result in a massive deadlock, with transactions at different sites contending for files that each other has locked. This has led to procedures for detecting such deadlocks and then for forcing one of the transactions to give up its locks to allow the other transaction to finish its work, and then restarting the one that was forced to retreat.

A variation on this theme involves declaring one node as the "dominant" node for each of the files. All updates for data in a particular file must be sent to the node at which the dominant copy of that file resides. With this kind of limitation, the node with the dominant copy can exercise a much stronger degree of control on updates to the particular file. Unfortunately the dominant node might become a bottleneck for a volatile file. Also if the dominant node goes down all update activity on that file would have to stop, unless the system goes to another level of complexity with the ability to transfer "dominance" for a file from one node to another.

Yet another method for controlling updates in the distributed database environment involves not locks but *timestamps*. The idea is to record the time that every database transaction starts, as well as to record the time that every piece of data or record was last updated and last read. Then the integrity problem can be controlled by forcing everything in the system to stay in sequence. For example, let's say that two transactions, X and Y, both attempt to update a record in file A in Chicago. The following time sequence and actions show how one of the several variations of the timestamping concept proceeds:

10:00 AM	Transaction X accesses the record to update it.
10:01	Transaction Y accesses the record to update it.
10:02	Transaction Y updates the record.
10:03	Transaction X attempts to update the record, but the timestamping protection prevents it. Transaction X is cancelled and restarted with a new timestamp. Why?

As part of its initial processing, transaction X read the old (10:00 AM) values in the record. But by the time it is ready to update the data at 10:03, these values have been rendered obsolete by transaction Y, which updated the record at 10:02.

MultiSite Joins

In a truly distributed relational database environment, a transaction that involves a join, may require files that are located at two or more different sites on the network. There are a variety of ways in which such a join can be performed, and the proper choice for a particular join can make a huge difference in the amount of communication time required on the network.

Perhaps the simplest choice is to ship all of the files to one site and perform the join there. This would probably take a fair amount of time, particularly for large files. Clearly the choice of the target site is critical, as it would take a lot less time to ship a small file to a site where a large required file is already found, rather than vice versa.

The other major approach is to ship only parts of files to other nodes for further processing. If based on the query it can be determined that only certain records, and perhaps only certain fields in these records, are involved in the query, then that is the only data that needs to be shipped to the other node to complete the join. If three files are involved and two of them are at one site, then those two might be joined at their homesite and only the appropriate records of the result shipped for further processing.

Finally a variation on this last approach would be to send the appropriate data from records in the file at one node to the other node, one at a time in a look-up kind of a mode, rather than to ship many records at once for a more formal join.

Directory Management

Earlier in this book we referred to control blocks as the vehicles for describing the data to the database system. Recall that there were control blocks, or more generally system directories or catalogs to describe the physical data, the logical views of the data, security constraints, and so forth. Naturally, such information is also needed in the distributed database environment, with one addition: information on the location in the network of each of the data files. After all, in the discussion on distributed database up to this point we've been tacitly assuming that when a node needs data at another node to satisfy some kind of transaction, it "knows" where to find it. But that knowledge has to come from somewhere, and that somewhere is the directory.

Which brings up an interesting question. Where should the directory itself be stored? As with the matter of how to distribute the data files themselves, there are a number of possibilities, some relatively simple and others more complex, with many of the same kinds of advantages and disadvantages that we've already discussed. For example, the entire directory could be stored at only one site. This makes updating it easy, and each node knows exactly where to go to get directory information. But the amount of communications costs involved with all transactions going to that single node for directory information is clearly prohibitive. If the directory node goes down, the entire system grinds to a halt. And even if the directory node stays up, it becomes a bottleneck with transactions from all over the network needing to access it for directory information.

The other extreme is for the entire directory to be duplicated at every site. Actually this is not as bad as trying to store the entire database at every node because there is much less data involved. Nevertheless the amount of time and energy needed to update the directory at every site for every change to the directory can make this approach unappealing.

Another approach is to start with the premise that every node will have a directory that describes all of the data located at that same node. But then what happens when a transaction at a particular node needs data at another node? Not only aren't the directory entries for the data at the transaction's node, there isn't even a guide to which node the needed directory entries are at (much less the data itself). Presumably the transaction will have to search every node for the needed directory information. However, we could go a step farther by additionally placing a copy of the entire directory at one of the sites. Every transaction would know where to go to get information about nonlocal data, but the arguments about the directory node being a bottleneck and the system stopping if the directory node goes down become factors again. And so the next logical extension would be to allow copies of the directories of each node to be placed at several arbitrary sites on the network. The advantages and disadvantages of this arrangement should be rather clear by now. One improvement for any of these local/ nonlocal reference cases would be for a node to record the directory information that it just found in a nonlocal reference and hold the information temporarily. In many application situations it's likely that the node might need that same directory information again soon and finding it locally will speed things up.

As a final note, realize that the choice of these approaches to directory management should depend largely on the applications themselves and the data processing environment as a whole. Transactions that require mostly local data need the directory for the local data stored at the local site. If there is not much reference to nonlocal data, then storing many copies of each node's directory around the network is counterproductive.

On the other hand, a high proportion of nonlocal data references would encourage duplication of the directory information. And a large amount of directory update activity would discourage duplication of the directory information. All of the factors must be carefully weighed.

Database on Personal Computers

It wasn't long after the advent of personal computers that the need for database management on them was perceived. Of course, while the fundamental concepts of database are the same regardless of the size of the computer involved, the nature of personal computer hardware does give us cause to make some specific comments here about database in the personal computer environment. The essential points about personal computers are that at this point in time they are comparatively slow in processing speed, very limited in data storage capacity, and have limited or no capability for data sharing or multiprogramming. Also as we shall see, the fact that they can communicate with larger computers with much larger storage capacities is significant.

There is a very large number of personal computer data management software products on the market today. They vary greatly in capability and form. Most, but not all, are based on a simple linear file structure. That's not surprising both because of the limited computing power and, in many cases, the relatively nontechnical users of the machines. Among the features found in them are indexes, data range checking on input, report generators, and multiple data views. Some follow the definition of database developed in this book and include a join capability, while others do not; the term database is used a bit more freely with personal computers than with larger computers.

Many personal computers are capable of communicating with large, "mainframe" computers. The nature of the relationship between the two, as relates to data and database, varies. Perhaps the simplest is the use of the personal computer as a dumb terminal. In this mode the personal computer can access data in the mainframe's database, just as any appropriate terminal can, but it cannot record the data in any form.

The use of the personal computer as a dumb terminal contrasts with its use as an independent, albeit small, data processing system, communicating with another, albeit much larger, data processing system, that is, the mainframe. The simplest form in this mode is one in which the personal computer can download (get data from) and upload (send data to) the mainframe, with no particular commonality existing between the database/data

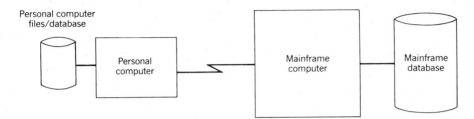

Figure 14.8. Mainframe to personal computer link.

management systems of the two. For example, the personal computer can bring data into its main memory from the mainframe's database and process it or store it, in some form, on its own diskettes, as shown in Figure 14.8. In a more advanced form, the same database software might be running in both the personal computer and the mainframe. These two database systems might or might not "know about each other" and be set-up to work closely together, but in either case the data formats will be in common.

References

Bray, O. H., *Distributed Database Management Systems*, D. C. Heath, Lexington, MA, 1982.

Bray, O. H. and Freeman, H. A., *Data Base Computers*, D. C. Heath, Lexington, MA, 1979.

Champine, G. A., "Six Approaches to Distributed Databases," *Datamation*, vol. 23, no. 5, May, 1977.

Champine, G. A., "Four Approaches to a Data Base Computer," *Datamation, vol. 24, no. 13, December, 1978, pp. 101–106.*

Date, C. J., *An Introduction to Database Systems*, vol. 2, Addison-Wesley, Reading, MA, 1983.

Epstein, R., "Why Database Machines?," *Datamation*, vol. 29, no. 7, July, 1983, pp. 139–144.

IBM Corporation, *CICS/VS Version 1 Release 5 System/Application Design Guide*, IBM Form No. SC33-0068, 1980.

IBM Corporation, *IMS/VS Version 1 System Administration Guide*, IBM Form No. SH20-9178, 1984.

Maryanski, F. J., "Backend Database Systems," *ACM Computing Surveys*, vol. 12, no. 1, March, 1980, pp. 3–26.

Mohan, C., "Recent and Future Trends in Distributed Data Base Management," Research Report RJ 4240, IBM Research Lab, San Jose, CA, May, 1984.

Rauzino, V. C., "The Present and Possible Future Data Base Machines," *Computerworld*, vol. 17, no. 23, June 6, 1983, pp. In Depth 1–20.

Rothnie, J. B., and Goodman, N., "A Survey of Research and Development in Distributed Database Management," *Proceedings of the Third International Conference on Very Large Databases*, October 6–8, 1977, pp. 48–62.

Questions and Exercises

14.1.   What is a database machine? Discuss the motivations for the database machine concept. Do you think they are convincing?

14.2.   What is a backend conventional processor? How might such a device aid the database environment.

14.3.   What is associative memory? How might such a technology aid the database environment.

14.4.   Describe the advantages and disadvantages of the database machine approach. Which do you think are the more compelling arguments? Why?

14.5.   What is a distributed database? What is a distributed database management system?

14.6.   Outline the major issues in distributed database.

14.7.   Describe the different ways of distributing data on a network.

14.8.   Outline the advantages and disadvantages of the different ways of distributing data on a network.

14.9.   What is locality of reference? How important a role does it play in distributed database? Why?

14.10.   How do you feel about storing files redundantly in a distributed network? What are the tradeoffs involved?

14.11.   What are the integrity problems associated with duplicate data on a distributed network?

14.12.   Describe global locking for distributed database. What problem does it attempt to solve? How practical do you think it is to implement?

14.13.   Describe timestamping for distributed database. What problem does it attempt to solve? How practical do you think it is to implement?

14.14.   What are the advantages and disadvantages inherent in splitting files among different network nodes in terms of multisite joins? Is it worth the trouble? Why or why not?

14.15.   Discuss the problem of directory management for distributed database. Do you think that as an issue, it is more critical, less critical, or about the same as the distribution of the data itself? Explain.

14.16.   Outline the ways in which personal computers can be involved with database. What are the advantages and disadvantages of each?

15

The Future

The Growth of Database

So there you have them—all of the wide-ranging aspects of the burgeoning field of database. And database will not only continue to be an important aspect of data processing, it will in fact increase in importance as its benefits become more widely understood, and as several factors which have limited its use evolve to more supportive levels of development.

As to the benefits of database, they are indisputable:

- The establishment of an atmosphere in which data is truly considered a corporate resource.
- The reduction of data redundancy for a manageable collection of data of high integrity. A well integrated collection of data for the optimum benefit in combining different kinds of data to satisfy complex queries.
- The ability to easily handle multiple relationships between different entities in the real world environment.
- The establishment of the collection of data as a resource independent of the programs that use it (data independence).
- The freedom of having such chores as security, concurrency, backup and recovery, and auditability managed by a well established and trusted set of procedures.

And then there are the factors that will improve to enhance these database benefits through more responsive implementations and more hospitable environments:

- Processor and data storage device speeds will increase, gradually reducing the performance limitations that have sometimes limited DBMS usage.
- Hardware costs will decrease, bringing the benefits of database to more and more potential users. (Of course, in a certain respect in the last few years, this has already happened with the advent of the microcomputer and of DBMSs designed for them.)
- Database management system software will continue to increase in sophistication.
- Corporate executives will increasingly become database advocates as they come to appreciate the ways that database can enhance their decision making capabilities.

- The costs of keeping redundant data and the consequences of data integrity problems will increase as more and more of the organization's data is kept in the automated data processing system.
- The costs of program maintenance will increase, and this is a problem that can be reduced by the data independence and standardization afforded by the the database environment.
- Standardized programs and packages, which can reduce application development costs will increase in popularity, and they benefit from the same kind of standardized data processing environment that results from the use of DBMSs.
- Increasingly user-friendly interfaces to databases will be developed, permitting a wider range of technically unsophisticated users to take advantage of the data stored in them.

Several of these factors will give some of the more speculative technologies that we discussed in this book a chance to become commercial realities. Improved hardware and software techniques, particularly in the concurrency and recovery areas, along with new and cheaper communications channels, will aid the advancement of the distributed database concept. Further hardware miniaturization, together with decreasing costs and increasing speeds, may make the associative memory database machine an exciting reality.

Future Application Areas

We've talked about the factors to watch for in the increasing prominence of database in our mainstay, "bread and butter" data processing applications. But perhaps even more exciting will be the emergence of database as the foundation for the expansion of some existing application areas, and the development of an array of new and fascinating applications.

Computer graphics is a truly thrilling application area that has received a great deal of attention lately. The promise of computer animation, computer aided design, and the pictorial display of business data, is great and has only begun to be realized. One of the major challenges of database will be the development of the ability to store pictorial data in databases. The data must be stored in such a way that it can manage complex pictorial images in meaningful ways, can be quickly displayed on graphics screens, and can accept rapid updates to reflect changes being made by users to the displayed pictures.

Figure 15.1. The factory of the future. (Courtesy IBM Corp.)

Database must be able to support the "factory of the future" concept, which entails the large scale integration of computer control mechanisms into the manufacturing process, Figure 15.1. In this regard the database must be able to store graphic data that involves the design of the items to be manufactured, test data for testing the finished products, data to control robot manufacturing devices, data that tracks the status of the various manufacturing processes and tools, and traditional data processing data to manage the parts inventory in the manufacturing process, ordering details, shipping details, and so on. Furthermore it must handle all of this data in a highly integrated way, as it will be either shared, highly interrelated, or both.

Turning our attention from the blue collar to the white collar environment, the database must form the basis for the "office of the future." Here again, the database must be able to accommodate and integrate a range of data including text for word processing, pictures for business presentations, and the usual alphanumeric data for all of the expected record keeping functions found in everything from personnel to accounting chores in the

Figure 15.2.   The office of the future. (Courtesy IBM Corp.)

typical office, Figure 15.2. One example of such a system is "Office-by-Example," a follow on to Query-by-Example (see Chapter 8), which treats files, reports, "desktops," and so on, all as "objects," effectively providing a very high level of sharing and integration in the data that supports all of them.

Another exciting new area is known as "knowledge base" or "expert" systems. Such systems are fed information about some real world problem, and are then expected, through heuristic and inference techniques, to respond to questions about specific sets of circumstances concerning that problem and its subject area. For example, such a system might contain "knowledge" about a particular area of medicine, and upon being given a set of symptoms, the system would be expected to produce a diagnosis. Clearly the underlying knowledge base is a database issue.

Natural language processing involves the computer being able to interpret, convert, and use, instructions and information given to it in human language form. The lexicon necessary for such a task, as well as elements of syntactic and semantic interpretation rules, must be stored for highly efficient retrieval, and that is a form of a database problem.

Another area for database is the storage and retrieval of digitized images. Whether used in a simple storage and retrieval mode, or operated on to discern features in them (a field known as "pattern recognition"), such images require a substantial amount of storage and present their own kind of database problem.

But beyond the specific areas that we've just mentioned the extraordinary challenge lies in the sharing of the same data for different kinds of applications and in the integration of separately (and perhaps differently) stored data for yet other applications (as we alluded to in a couple of earlier comments). Imagine automated product design, linked to production in an automated factory, linked to office accounting operations, linked to an executive ad hoc query system. Further imagine these operations using a combination of traditional, textual, and pictorial data. And finally imagine all of these operations working smoothly from a single integrated database. This is the challenge for the future.

We have come a long way in database in the last 20 years, but we have only begun to scratch the surface. Database will become the central focus of data processing as we come to recognize more and more that the term "data processing" means that we are concerned with a resource, *data*, which can serve us by the judicious processing of it. There is tremendous growth potential. The road ahead in database will be a very exciting one to travel.

References

Dertouzos, M. L., and Moses, J., eds., *The Computer Age: A Twenty-Year View*, MIT Press, Cambridge, MA, 1979.

Hayes-Roth, F., Waterman, D. A., and Lenat, D. B., eds., *Building Expert Systems*, Addison-Wesley, Reading, MA, 1983.

Sowa, J. F., *Conceptual Structures*, Addison-Wesley, Reading, MA, 1984.

Wegner, P., ed., *Research Directions in Software Technology*, MIT Press, Cambridge, MA, 1979.

Zloof, M. M., "Office-by-Example: A Business Language that Unifies Data and Word Processing and Electronic Mail," *IBM Systems Journal*, vol. 21, no. 3, 1982, pp. 272–304.

Questions and Exercises

15.1.   Use your imagination and describe the different kinds of data that will be needed in the "office of the future" environment. How will this data be shared among the different applications to be found there?

15.2.   Use your imagination and describe the different kinds of data that will be needed in the "factory of the future" environment. How will this data be shared among the different applications to be found there?

15.3.   In your own words, describe the technological and political changes that will take place in the computing field in the future that will encourage the use of database.

15.4.   Think of an application based on pictures and computer graphics and describe how the data used to describe these pictures can be shared with other nonpictorial applications.

15.5.   Do you think that in the foreseeable future a company will be able to have a single corporate database that contains all of its data? Why or why not?

15.6.   Do you think that the data administration manager of the future will report to the data processing manager, that the reverse will be true, or that the two will be equals? Defend your position.

Index